# Political issues
# in the world today

Published in our
centenary year
≈ **2004** ≈
MANCHESTER
UNIVERSITY
PRESS

**Politics Today**

*Series editor*: Bill Jones

# Political issues
# in the world today

## Edited by Don MacIver

Manchester University Press
Manchester and New York

distributed exclusively in the USA by Palgrave

*Published by* Manchester University Press
Oxford Road, Manchester M13 9NR, UK
*and* Room 400, 175 Fifth Avenue, New York, NY 10010, USA
www.manchesteruniversitypress.co.uk

*Distributed exclusively in the USA by*
Palgrave, 175 Fifth Avenue, New York,
NY 10010, USA

*Distributed exclusively in Canada by*
UBC Press, University of British Columbia, 2029 West Mall,
Vancouver, BC, Canada V6T 1Z2

*British Library Cataloguing-in-Publication Data*
A catalogue record for this book is available from the British Library

*Library of Congress Cataloging-in-Publication Data applied for*

ISBN    0 7190 6704 9 *hardback*
EAN    978 0 7190 6704 4
ISBN    0 7190 6705 7 *paperback*
EAN    978 0 7190 6705 1

First published 2004

13 12 11 10 09 08 07 06 05 04    10 9 8 7 6 5 4 3 2 1

Typeset by Freelance Publishing Services, Brinscall, Lancs
www.freelancepublishingservices.co.uk
Printed in Great Britain
by Biddles Limited, King's Lynn

# Contents

# Tables, boxes and figure

## Tables

## Boxes

## Figure

# Contributors

**Sita Bali** is a lecturer in International Relations at Staffordshire University. She took her first degree from the University of Bombay and was awarded her PhD at Kent. She has a well established interest in South Asian politics and the politics of migration and has published a number of articles and chapters in these areas.

**Emma Clarence** is a lecturer in Politics at Aberdeen University. She studied at Macquarrie University, Australia and then at Manchester Metropolitan University. Her main interest is public policy and she was recently guest editor of *Public Policy and Administration*. Her publications include 'Social Policy: Women and Asylum in the United Kingdom' in J. Freedman (ed.), *Gender and Insecurity: Migrant Women in Europe*, Aldershot: Ashgate, 2003; 'Railways: A Policy Derailed', *Parliamentary Affairs*, Vol. 56, No. 3, 2003; 'Ministerial Responsibility and the Scottish Qualifications Agency', *Public Administration*, Vol. 80, No. 4, 2002.

**Daniele Conversi** is a lecturer in Politics at the University of Lincoln. He took his first degree at the University of Rome and his PhD at the London School of Economics. His publications include *The Basques, the Catalans, and Spain: Alternative Routes to Nationalist Mobilization*, London: Hurst, 1997 and *Ethnonationalism in the Contemporary World: Walker Connor and the Study of Nationalism* (edited), London: Routledge, 2004. He has written widely on ethnicity and ethnic conflict, with many articles in European and American journals.

**Barbara Emadi-Coffin** is a lecturer in International Relations at, Staffordshire University. She took her first degree at Harvard and her PhD at Sussex. Her publications include *Rethinking International Organisation: Deregulation and Global Governance*, London: Routledge, 2002 and a number of articles on the transition in Eastern Europe.

**Chris Farrands** is a lecturer in International Studies at Nottingham Trent University. His publications include (jointly edited with M. Talalay and R. Tooze) *Technology, Culture and Competitiveness: Change and the World Political Economy*, London: Routledge, 1997.

**Dr. Jonathan Gorry** is a lecturer in Politics at Northampton University College. He was awarded his first degree at Staffordshire University and his PhD at the University of Warwick. His research interests are political violence and the ethics of war and peace.

**Graham Harrison** is a lecturer in Politics at Sheffield University and was awarded his PhD at Staffordshire University. He is currently editor of *Review of African Political Economy* and *New Political Economy*. His publications include *The Politics of Democratization in Rural Mozambique*, Lampeter: Edwin Mellen Press, 2000; *Issues in the Contemporary Politics of Sub-Saharan Africa. The Dynamics of Struggle and Resistance*, Basingstoke: Palgrave Press, 2002 and *The World Bank and Africa: the Construction of Governance States*, London: Routledge, 2004.

**Jeff Haynes** is professor at the Department of Politics, London Metropolitan University. He received his first degree and his PhD from Staffordshire University and his principal research interest is third world politics. His publications include *Third World Politics: a Concise Introduction*, London: Blackwell, 1996; *Democracy and Civil Society in the Third World*, Cambridge: Polity, 1997; *Religion in Global Politics*, Harlow: Longman, 1998.

**Graeme Herd** is professor of Civil-Military Relations at the School of International Security Studies, George C. Marshall European Center for Security Studies, Garmisch-Partenkirchen, Germany. His main research interests are new security problems and the political development of former communist countries since the Cold War and he has published extensively on these subjects.

**Barrie Houlihan** is professor at the Department of Sport Policy, Loughborough University. He graduated from Liverpool University and was awarded his PhD at Salford University. His publications include *Sport and international politics*, London: Harvester-Wheatsheaf, 1994; *Sport, policy and politics: a comparative analysis*, London: Routledge, 1997; *The politics of sport development* (with Anita White), London: Routledge, 2002; *Sport and Society*, London: Sage, 2003.

**David Morrice** was awarded his PhD at the University of Aberdeen and is recently retired from the position of lecturer in Political Theory and head of department of Politics at Staffordshire University. His publications include *Philosophy, Science and Ideology in Political Thought*, Basingstoke: Macmillan, 1996; "On the Justification of Political Violence", *Cogito*, vol. 10, no. 2, 1996; 'The Liberal-Communitarian Debate in Contemporary Political Philosophy and its Significance for International Relations', *Review of International Studies*,

2000, Vol. 26, No. 2, and several other articles on aspects of ethical political theory.

**Calum Paton** was awarded his DPhil at Oxford and is now head of the Centre for Health Planning and Management at Keele University. He is author of *World, Class, Britain: Political Economy, Political Theory and Public Policy*, London: Macmillan, 2000; *Competition and Planning in the NHS: The Consequences of the Reforms*, Cheltenham: Stanley Thornes, 1998; *Health Policy and Management*, London: Chapman and Hall, 1996; he is Editor of the *International Journal of Health Planning and Management* and a regular contributor to journals and advisor to governments and international agencies on health policy on health reform.

**Lloyd Pettiford** graduated from Staffordshire University and received his PhD at the University of Southampton and is currently acting head of department of International Studies at Nottingham Trent University. His publications include *Changing Security Agendas and the Third World*, Pinter, London, 1999; *Terrorism: The New World War* (with David Harding), London: Arcturus, 2003; *International Relations: Themes and Perspectives* (with Jill Steans), Harlow: Pearson, 2001; 'Simply a Matter of Luck? Why Costa Rica Remains a Democracy', *Democratization*, Vol. 6, No. 1, 1999 and a number of other articles and papers.

**James Radcliffe** is lecturer in Health Policy at the School of Health, Staffordshire University. He graduated from and was awarded his PhD at Staffordshire. He is author of *Green Politics: Dictatorship or Democracy*, London: Macmillan, 2000; *The Reorganisation of British Central Government*, Dartmouth Press, USA, 1991 and several articles and papers on various aspects of public policy.

**Alan Russell** is lecturer in International Relations at Staffordshire University. He graduated at Staffordshire and was awarded his PhD at the University of Kent. He is author of *The Biotechnology Revolution*, Brighton: Wheatsheaf, 1988 and co-editor (with John Vogler) of *The International Politics of Biotechnology: Investigating Global Futures*, Manchester: Manchester University Press, 2000 and has written a number of articles and chapters on aspects of technology within the global political economy, with special reference to biotechnology.

# Preface

Political issues provide an insight into politics at a particular time, not only of the issues themselves and their protagonists, but also of the structures and processes in which they are located. After the end of the Cold War there were extensive changes in both the structure and the agenda of world politics. Some of the old issues of the Cold War era disappeared; others changed or became more salient, while a number of new issues emerged. Many of these issues are active and significant in several locations and at different levels of governance and can be approached from a number of different perspectives. They impact on political systems in a variety of ways, affect the policies of many states and cannot be fully understood with reference to only one political system. This is a symptom of the polycentric, interactive and increasingly complex structure of contemporary world politics, a full understanding of which demands a multinational approach to issues, together with an awareness of their global context and the role of transnational actors. This book examines a selection of the more salient political issues, traces their development and explains their significance in the politics of the world today.

The book includes fifteen studies by a group of political scientists who have specialist knowledge of their specific subject. Each chapter provides a background of basic scholarship on its subject and gives an account of its development which is comprehensive and accessible to students in a range of disciplines as well as to the general reader. Their approach emphasises the transnational and global context of political issues today and the global approach necessary to understand them. The contributors have generally worked diligently to produce what was asked of them and they have each presented their own analysis and conclusions. The credit for whatever merits the work may have thus belongs to them, although responsibility for any shortcomings in the completeness of the work as a whole remains with the editor.

The completion of this work has involved the cooperation and support of many to whom I am indebted. First I am indebted to the contributors for carrying out the tasks I asked them to undertake and especially those who completed their contributions on time and returned their corrected proofs promptly. Then I wish to thank colleagues who read parts of the manuscript including the introduction and offered their comments, particularly Ian Armour, Graeme Herd, Mehrad Emadi-Moghadam, James Radcliffe and Alan Russell. Others helped in other ways for which I am also grateful. Last, but not least, I wish to thank Tony Mason and colleagues at Manchester University Press for their indispensable support in the production of the book.

# Introduction

*Don MacIver*

This book addresses some of the salient issues in the politics of the world today, provides some background to their development and discusses their current significance. These issues dominate the news media and demand the constant attention of political leaders and various global organisations. Some have emerged into the limelight of public debate only relatively recently while others have been on the world political agenda as matters of concern for several decades, varying in their salience from one time to another. The nature of the issues, their significance and the political context in which they appear may also change over time. Even a brief glimpse at the historical perspective of any of these issues reveals how they and the world itself have changed. Thus anyone interested in the events, processes and trends of politics in the world today must be interested in change, how it influences and interacts with the issues that shape our lives. To gain a full understanding of these issues, however, it is important to recognise that they emerge not from singular events, however decisive they seem at the time, but from long-term trends and cumulative change perhaps over several generations.

Change is a constant and integral feature of human society and social development. While people in all ages have lived through change, some periods of change are more noteworthy, times when change seemed to be more fundamental and far-reaching and some moments have seemed to be particularly significant. In this sense for example, when discussing the terrorist attacks on New York in September 2001, it became commonplace especially for journalists to declare that '9/11' had changed the world for ever. Closer examination however, suggested that, while 9/11 was undoubtedly an event of major significance, not least its impact on the American outlook, the idea that it had changed the world was more of a media cliché than a sober and realistic assessment.

A more significant defining moment, marking the most important political change in our time, is the fall of the Berlin wall in 1989 which came to symbolise the end of the Cold War and the collapse of communist regimes in

Eastern Europe. Francis Fukuyama, the Japanese-American historian, famously rushed into print to celebrate 1989 as 'the end of history', by which he meant the triumph of Western liberal capitalism in face of the prolonged challenge of authoritarian ideologies during most of the twentieth century. While Fukuyama was undoubtedly correct to recognise the special character of 1989, it was probably not the end of history but more of a resumption or even a new beginning. The events of 1989 marked the end of a long period of change and transition, which began with another defining moment of the twentieth century, the outbreak of the First World War on 1 August 1914, a date on which the world really did change.

The political and economic structure of the world of 1914 was largely shaped over the previous four hundred years by the major European powers especially the maritime empires and then dominated by them. The First World War began a process of change and transition, which lasted until 1989. This transition, which was a period of unprecedented destruction, stress and conflict, occurred in two phases, from 1914 to 1945 and then from 1945 to 1989. When the First World War was over the pre-war international structure, including much of the international financial and mercantile system which had developed in the nineteenth century, was smashed. The continental land empires were swept away and the great maritime empires undermined. Two new powers, the United States and Japan, emerged from the conflict both able to challenge European, especially British hegemony outside Europe. The two decades after the war were characterised by a severe worldwide economic depression and the rise of an axis of fascist powers, whose direct challenge to the dominant liberal powers of the West, especially Britain, culminated in the Second World War.

The second phase of transition began after the Second World War. This war eventually engaged all the great powers of the world including the United States, the Soviet Union and China. After the war Japan was devastated as were most of the European powers except Britain, which, however, was exhausted, nearly bankrupt and its power much reduced. Other features of this post-war period were the construction and development of the United Nations system, the growth of significant regional institutions in Europe, the Americas, the Middle East, Asia and Africa, the revival of the world economy, the final European retreat from Empire, the process of decolonisation and the emergence of the Third World. The most significant outcome of the war, however, was the emergence of two superpowers whose rivalry dominated world politics through the prolonged international confrontation known as the Cold War. The end of the Cold War in 1989 marked the beginning of a new phase in world politics.

### The world after 1989

Compared to the period between 1914 and 1989 or the period before 1914, the world after 1989 was very different. Both the structure of the international order and distribution of power within it were different to anything that the world had experienced in recent history. So also were the issues and problems which emerged in this new order. The principal features of the new order were the rapidly changing nature of the state system, the instability created by weak and failed states, the disturbing number of civil conflicts around the world and the new position of the US as the only superpower.

One of the questions that emerged after 1989 was the changing nature and role of the nation state and of the international state system within which it functioned. The idea of the modern state was expressed in its political independence, which had always rested on the principles of sovereignty and territoriality, as conceived in the Westphalia model of 1648. The argument about the changing nature of the state centred on its supposed loss of sovereignty, which was a matter of debate even before the end of the Cold War. Indeed the Cold War, with its political blocs, tightly structured alliances and cross-national command structures meant a considerable loss of sovereignty to many states and, at the end of it, very few were capable of truly independent action, even in limited and specific circumstances. However, states had always jealously defended the principle of sovereignty and their own sovereignty in particular, even though the sovereignty of weak states was in practice indefensible and could be easily breached. Thus the panoply of national interest, inviolability of borders, non-intervention in internal affairs and other corollaries of sovereignty were flourished by old and new states as expressions of their independence. On the other hand, from the beginning of the state system, the principle of sovereignty was accompanied by principles of international law, rules of international morality and a conception of international public opinion, all of which were at first intended to protect and reinforce the sovereign independence of states but which eventually tended to compromise it.

During the twentieth century and especially after the Second World War, the recognition and increasing acceptance of principles of law, morality, collective security, economic cooperation and the growing role of institutions like the United Nations, the International Monetary Fund, the World Trade Organisation, an expanding number and variety of international regulatory institutions and finally, the internalisation by states of standards of behaviour generated from these sources increased the importance of international decision making in many areas and eroded the reality of sovereignty. Thus the state appeared to operate within a multilateral framework of international organisations, institutions, regimes and global networks, which had taken over many of the responsibilities and activities of states and that, in some respects at least, appeared to be the real locus of sovereignty. Sovereigntists of course could claim that these international institutions were themselves an expression of the sovereign will of states and practitioners could maintain that state sovereignty remained intact as a working principle. Nevertheless, in exercising their sovereign will, states faced a number of challenges, both from

within and without. Faced with the new challenges of international terrorism, organised crime, illegal migration, growing threats to the environment,
the penetration of global communication technologies and the world-wide
movement of investment and finance, states usually have little alternative but
to turn to international agencies or forums and cede their power to act independently. Even for the developed states of the West, including the more powerful among them, sovereignty is more likely to be exercised in cooperation
than alone and, for the least powerful, even maintaining the state has become
a challenge.

Maintaining a nation state, or establishing and developing a new state, is a
major undertaking which demands vision and conviction, commitment and
determination, considerable resources and expertise, political skills and organisation. It also requires a coherent and self-directed society and a cohesive
population with a shared identity, which can support the state and give it
legitimacy and continuity. Unfortunately these conditions are more rare than
the citizens of the well-ordered and effective states of the West are usually
aware, but in their absence states are very much more likely to fail. A significant feature of the contemporary international system is the large number of
weak and failed states and the threats to stability and security produced by
them. Two to three decades after decolonisation many recently independent
states were in serious difficulty. In the first place this may have been due to
the immense and possibly unforeseen problems of nation building, namely of
integrating diverse communal, regional and tribal identities into a unified
national consciousness that could provide a cohesive and legitimate foundation for a modern state. Many post-colonial states contained deep communal
divisions and unresolved conflicts, which inhibited national unity and even
resulted in civil war. Secondly it may have been partly due to a failure of state
building, that is, the failure to maintain and develop effective government
institutions or any basis of coherent authority. In some states the authority of
the national government does not operate effectively very far beyond the capital city. Finally, it may have been due to mismanagement of economic development including inappropriate investment and expenditure programmes,
misdirection of international aid, fraudulent dealings with foreign companies
and appropriation of national resources to the benefit of a particular section
or elite. In several cases the new rulers regarded independence as an opportunity to favour or advance 'their own' people or simply to enrich themselves. In
some cases the state became more like a criminal enterprise run by a personal
dictator, a mafia rather than a state. In these ways states became corrupt,
ineffective and unable to serve their citizens, control the development of their
resources or maintain order in their territories. This had important consequences as such states frequently fell into disorder, poverty and debt to foreign governments, banks and international financial institutions.

Shortly after the end of the Cold War there were some signs of a new
approach to the problem of failing states. A scheme, which became known as

Jubilee 2000, supported by a number of Western governments and a wide range of other organisations, sought to write off the debts of the poorest developing countries provided they adopted viable and sustainable development programmes. In the good governance initiative the British government, and others including international agencies like the World Bank, attempted to link the supply of aid funds and assistance programmes to evidence of good governance particularly respect for human rights and the maintenance of democratic government institutions. During the Cold War the major Western powers, embroiled in their ideological and strategic conflict with the Communist Bloc, were more concerned to find and keep allies than to criticise their politics. After the Cold War, however, non-democratic forms of government were quickly discredited and soon came to be widely regarded as unacceptable. Even the single party state, which had been proclaimed as a democratic form and widely emulated, especially in Africa, was denounced by Julius Nyerere, once its leading advocate. Democratisation, which had begun in some countries like Brazil in the 1980s, gained momentum in the 1990s and there were campaigns and demonstrations for greater democratisation in several countries such as South Korea, Burma, Nigeria and Peru. While this process was no doubt boosted by the collapse of communism, it was mainly inspired and sustained by the Helsinki Agreements and the subsequent process of consultation and exchange. Democracy and democratic government may hang by a thread in many countries, but it has a foothold where it once had none. Moreover, democratisation has been accompanied by a greater attention and concern for human rights and gender issues, which also stemmed from Helsinki, and an enhanced interest in questions of international morality, which had often been ignored during the years of the Cold War.

With the end of the Cold War and the collapse of communism the effectiveness of communism as a doctrine and a political system that could provide a challenge to Western capitalism and an alternative path to development was questioned. In third world countries, Marxist and radical leftist critiques of society and analysis of social problems, such as poverty, inequality and dominance of the West, were discounted and movements based on them lost support. Opposition movements which challenged not only the West, but also their own national leaderships as privileged, authoritarian and corrupt, if not actually pro-Western, now looked to their own societies and into their own cultures for inspiration and ideas and often found it in the texts and customs of traditional religion. This produced a mixture of religious dogma and radical politics in which political movements were driven by allegedly religious principles and hatred of Western ideas, which then frequently developed into a kind of religious nationalism, directed against foreigners and the West in particular. Out of this a number of movements emerged in the 1990s, which came to be known as fundamentalist, among which Islamic fundamentalism was the most militant. Of the various groups that came to be associated with Islamic fundamentalism, the most aggressive and the most challenging to

Western interests was Al-Quaeda, which organised a number of attacks on Western targets including the attack in New York in September 2001. In this respect, then, '9/11' was itself another product of the end of the Cold War.

During the Cold War the bipolar alignment of the major blocs overshadowed the political scene and to some extent concealed other confrontations and conflicts around the world. In Europe and the North Atlantic area the years since 1945 are regarded as a period of peace broken only by the conflicts associated with the dissolution of former Yugoslavia. In the rest of the world, however, it has been otherwise. In Asia, the Pacific, Africa and South America there were well over one hundred major armed conflicts, many of which continued after 1989. Since 1989 there have been about forty armed conflicts either new or continuing from the Cold War era. Armed conflict in the sense of declared war between states has been uncommon since 1945 and even more so since 1989. Most wars have been civil wars or proxy wars fought by client groups supported by rival states. In some cases states or factional groups within states were sponsored by one of the Cold War blocs who supplied them with arms and technical assistance, drawing them into the remote peripheries of the Cold War alignment. While the Cold War was not usually a determining factor in the origin of most of these conflicts, this involvement probably did structure their development and prolonged and intensified the armed struggle. When the Cold War was over supplies of arms remained plentiful and several conflicts persisted at least for some time. Even when sophisticated weapons were not available extensive damage and terrible casualties could still be inflicted as they were in Rwanda. Many of these wars have been immensely ferocious, destructive and extremely costly in terms of life, resources and development prospects. Not only government institutions and political systems but whole societies and economies in countries like Nicaragua, Colombia, Angola, Congo, Ethiopia, Rwanda, Somalia, Yemen, Lebanon, former Yugoslavia, Chechnya, Tajikistan, Afghanistan, Sri Lanka, East Timor and Cambodia were ravaged and ruined by civil wars or cross-border conflicts which were often sustained by external powers.

Failing states, weak and corrupt governments and civil conflict are not only bad for the countries directly affected, they are also bad for the rest of the world. Weak and failing states, because of their economic instability and lack of public order, tend to threaten the security of other states, especially their neighbours. Weak states may become a haven for international criminals, including pirates, drug dealers and money launderers, whose activities can create serious damage to the economies of other states. Failing states and rogue states may sponsor or collude with international terrorists and may provide them with bases and safe havens from which they can then pose a serious and unquantifiable threat to other countries far and wide. Some countries, of course, have been exposed to the threats of particular kinds of terrorism for many decades. Difficult as this threat was for the governments concerned to deal with, contemporary international terrorism poses an altogether more complex and challenging security problem. Other problems associated with failing states, such as political instability, repression, rebellion, the breakdown of societies, civil and ethnic conflict pose another problem by creating tens of thousands of refugees as frightened and displaced people migrate in search of safety, usually to neighbouring countries where their presence puts pressure on local resources and may lead to conflict with the settled population.

Perhaps the most significant effect of the collapse of the Soviet Union and the end of communism in Eastern Europe was to leave the United States alone and unrivalled as the only economic and military superpower. Although the European Union and Japan are able to challenge American economic dominance in certain sectors and China is emerging as a potential new superpower, none has the effective economic and military capability to match the worldwide reach of the United States. Because of this uniquely powerful position the United States is sometimes regarded as the protector of the new world order, frequently under pressure to give leadership, take responsibility or provide economic or military support when problems and crises arise. On the other hand the attitudes and behaviour of the United States are often regarded by other countries and organisations with suspicion, subject to relatively hostile scrutiny and sometimes reviled for arrogant behaviour, clumsy diplomacy and botched interventions. This has created a new and ambiguous situation in the relationship between the United States and the international community and has led to serious tensions and clashes with some countries.

The reaction of the United States to this new situation has also been ambivalent. On the one hand, it reaches out to the international community for support for the 'war on terror' and for its promotion of its own vision of democracy, for acceptance of its new food technologies and its idiosyncratic position on issues like religion and international morality. On the other hand, it has sometimes adopted a more unilateralist and occasionally isolationist posture, reluctant to intervene as in Bosnia or Palestine, for example, while also cold-shouldering or simply rejecting a number of international agreements including the Kyoto Accord, the International Criminal Court, the Protocol on Land Mines and the Nuclear Test Ban Treaty. Factors contributing to this ambivalence are the number of different sources of policy in the American political system and the think tanks and special interest groups associated with them as well as the sharp competitive clashes that sometimes occur between Congress, the State Department, the armed forces and the White House on matters of foreign policy. Part of the explanation may also be that the United States is very large country and a democracy in which most people have travelled little beyond their home state, much less abroad (less than ten per cent of Americans have ever applied for a passport) and for whom international political issues do not feature prominently in their concerns. On the other hand, American foreign policy is managed and serviced on a day-to-day basis by a skilled, accomplished and experienced professional elite who have a well informed view of the international scene and expertise as good as any, even though they are, from time to time, politically over-ruled. Perhaps the tension between these factors in United States foreign policy is something that its allies and the rest of the world will have to continue to live with in the twenty-first century.

## The resumption of globalisation

Although the world of pre-1914 ended with the First World War, certain trends, which began and indeed were well advanced in that period, persisted into the period after 1989 to re-emerge with a renewed intensity and velocity. These trends, particularly the increasing connections and interactions between regions of the world, can be summarised as globalisation, a process which probably began with the development of contacts between Western Europe and the so-called New World of the Americas, Africa, Australia and the Pacific. The key feature of globalisation has been the transformation of communication, especially over the last one hundred and fifty or so years, in which a series of technical innovations has produced an apparent shrinking of distances and a reduction of the time in which information can be communicated and people and goods transported between regions of the world.

The first breakthrough was probably the invention of the telegraph in the mid-nineteenth century which created a quantum leap in the speed of communication and brought centres that were previously remote from each other into close and continuous contact. Thus European capitals, beginning with London and Paris, were connected and far-flung parts of the British Empire were brought into a few minutes reach of London and sometimes of each other, while in Europe and North America the telegraph followed the railway and the steamship, dramatically reducing communication times across continents and oceans. Before the telegraph it could take several weeks to get messages between Britain and India, Singapore or Western Canada. After the telegraph this time was reduced to minutes. When Krakatoa erupted in 1883, it took over three hours for the news to reach Singapore but only minutes to get it by telegraph from Singapore to London and then on to New York and Paris. By contrast, when Abraham Lincoln was assassinated in 1865, it took twelve days for the message to reach London by sail. Within a few decades there was an emerging global market for telegraph equipment, with the American group ITT competing in almost every country in Western Europe and some of the colonial territories. The telegraph was quickly followed by other technologies, notably the telephone and radio. Two-way radio communication soon became relatively reliable and the first major international broadcast network, the BBC Empire Service (now the World Service), began in the 1930s. The introduction of this service accelerated the development of communications and its success considerably enhanced the position of English as the leading international language. As radio prospered in the inter-war years, however, another new technology called television was just being born. Television, linked to other technologies not yet invented, would again revolutionise communications in the second half of the twentieth century.

Within two decades of the Second World War, however, these remarkable developments could be seen as the very early steps in a process that now seems to have no foreseeable limit. During the post-war years there was a new wave of innovation, bringing a host of revolutionary technologies including digitalisation, fibre optics, satellites, fax, cell phones, the Internet and the World Wide Web which further increased the speed, but also the volume, clarity and reliability of communications around the world. Some of these innovations, particularly satellites and the Internet, which really came into its own in the 1990s, were spin-offs from Cold War military research and in their peaceful application in post-Cold War conditions immensely accelerated the development of communications. Moreover, the fact that American interests, supported by the economic and political dominance of the United States, led the development of most of these technologies has further consolidated the position of English as a world language. Today the globe is swathed in a massive and constant flow of personal, commercial and diplomatic communications and it is technically possible for any person to communicate with any other at any point on the earth's surface, however remote from a major centre. It is these advances in communication technology that inspired the idea of the 'global village', which has been the principal metaphor of globalisation since the 1960s.

Another major trend, which originated in the nineteenth century, if not actually before then, is the globalisation of economic activity. Economic globalisation is an extension of the transformation and growth of capitalism, but it has to be contextualised in the globalisation of communications. Capitalism, as a socio-economic system based on the private ownership of the means of production and directed mainly by private interests, was transformed by the industrial revolution. Its growth and international expansion were driven by its constant need to create surplus value and the consequent search for markets, raw materials, cheap labour and deregulated operating environments. This was made possible by the growth and globalisation of communications but, once the breakthrough was made, the expansion of international business activity became the main driver of economic globalisation. In the late nineteenth century and the early twentieth century, in the decades before the First World War, the globalisation of trade, commerce and finance, principally centred on the city of London and sheltered by a British international hegemony, reached a level which was probably not matched again until the 1980s. One of the effects of the First World War was to disrupt the relationships and structures on which this emerging global system was based, even though there were factors in the system, already a complex one, that might have temporarily slowed down its development. Compounded by the two world wars and the great depression of the inter-war years, this disruption set back the development of globalisation in the following decades. After the Second World War and the massive and widespread destruction that entailed, the world economy had contracted and in most regions and sectors was derelict. The need for revitalisation and reconstruction was recognised but, because of the withdrawal of the Soviet Union and its allies and the prostrate condition of continental Europe and Japan, the task was effectively left to Britain and the United States, who were in any case the two leading economic and financial powers of the time.

Reconstruction began at the Bretton Woods conference in 1944 when a new political and institutional framework for international economic relations was devised under the guidance of the British economist, John Maynard Keynes. This was intended to provide a stable regime within which international economic transactions and policies could be conducted with confidence. Within the new system the United States, now indisputably the greatest economic power, assumed economic dominance and political leadership. This American leadership, linked to the rapid recovery and massive growth of American industry during the war and the newly established supremacy of the dollar as a world currency, produced the conditions and the initial impetus for expansion of the world economy and the resumption of globalisation. For about forty years after 1950 or so the world economy grew at a rate unprecedented in both pace and continuity, led mainly by re-industrialisation and investment in Western Europe, the United States and Japan. The principal motor of this expansion was the private sector, namely capitalist free enterprise and private investment, although public sector investment also made an important contribution, especially in Europe and in post-colonial developing countries. Indeed many developing and newly industrialising countries achieved high growth rates during this period and some, such as India, Malaysia, Brazil and China became significant players in the world economy before the end of the century. This course of generally successful economic development did not proceed without a few problems, such as the dollar crisis of 1971, the universal slow-down induced by the oil price crisis of 1973, perennial trade disputes and a number of debt scares, especially in Latin American economies. On balance, however, sustained growth and expansion transformed the world economy in the second half of the twentieth century and, by bringing new players into the system, opened new opportunities for many millions of people and created the conditions for increasing the spread and intensity of globalisation.

Since the end of the Cold War in 1989 the pace of globalisation has accelerated, producing further transnational economic integration, but this has been accompanied by the emergence of new uncertainties in the world economy. The entry of Russia and East European countries to full participation in the international economic system raised expectations of new development opportunities and new markets that have not been fully realised. A series of unexpected banking and finance crises in the Far East and the subsequent collapse of the currencies of the Asian 'tiger' economies in the 1990s caused concern about their effects on growth and economic development in other parts of the world. The stagnation of the economies of Japan and much of continental Europe through the late 1990s also produced adverse effects including a slowdown in world trade at the beginning of the new century. The ever-present temptation for some politicians, especially in the United States, to raise tariffs in adverse economic circumstances raised the spectre of trade wars between major trade blocs and the possibility of growing conflict between developed and third world countries over the unfavourable trading conditions experienced by developing economies. Finally, while media and economic globalisation gave an immense boost to the international development of activities like sport, increasing the numbers of both participants and spectators, and of course the economic value of major events, it also raised new concerns in other areas such as health, where there was increased anxiety about the spread of new diseases and the difficulties faced by health care services, especially in the West, beset by pressures on their costs and resources from an increasingly open and mobile world economy.

These difficulties were compounded by another range of problems arising from the growing resistance to certain new technologies, notably genetic engineering of food products, which threatened a confrontation between the United States and the European Union and possibly some developing countries. New doubts about the capacity of global oil supplies to meet future demand and continued forebodings of environmental deterioration again raised questions about the sustainability of current low-cost energy strategies and the conventional industrialisation route to economic growth. Before the late 1980s these matters would have been considered principally the domain of states and governments. After 1989, however, the world economy was more open, the movement of capital and finance and to some extent of people and labour less restricted. These developments were driven mainly by the private sector and private enterprise; decisions and outcomes were governed by tens of thousands of multinational companies and transnational businesses, which were difficult for most governments to control. Indeed governments became competitors and even supplicants for the favours of international business especially in matters relating to inward investment and research and development. This vision of the increasing mobility and power of transnational capital and multinational corporations created unease and disquiet in many countries around the world and led to the emergence of a counter movement which demanded more accountability from both governments and business.

### Global civil society

For at least two centuries people have generally welcomed the process of global modernisation and the personal comforts, lifestyle improvements and social benefits that it brought. They welcomed the social improvements, medical advances and better health care systems that enabled people to live longer and better lives. They also welcomed the technological and economic developments that enabled people to travel, goods to be transported and information to be communicated faster and more reliably and activities like sport and tourism to be practised more easily and widely. By the late twentieth century, however, some were beginning to notice the cost of globalisation. During the 1970s and 1980s people at first in the advanced societies of the West and then all around the world became concerned about the environmental and social costs of technological development and economic growth.

First, there was a sense that the increased population, together with the vastly increased levels and intensity of human activity, were placing ever increasing and possibly unsustainable pressure on the environment. This included concern about population growth, the future of non-renewable resources, the survival of many species of wildlife and eco-systems, but the attention of most observers has tended to concentrate on the issue of global warming which became an allegory of the general environment question and the key to a solution, if there was one. As the global warming issue was more closely examined and defined, however, clear and strongly opposed positions began to emerge. The most widely canvassed view is that global warming caused by human industrial activity is producing climate change which could seriously damage the environmental conditions for human life. Supporters of this view cited evidence from corals, tree rings, ice cores and human records to argue that the earth in the late twentieth century had become warmer than it had been for one thousand years. Directly opposed to this is the view adopted by certain American business interests, especially the energy industry, which repudiates global warming and maintains that it is not happening or that its effects are exaggerated. An alternative view is that while global warming probably is happening, it is not due to human activity but to cyclical solar activity and that the environment will survive as it has through such cycles in the past. The argument between these groups has become highly politicised and impassioned, with interests and reputations on the line, especially in the United States. As long as this argument continues the environment question itself is unlikely to be resolved.

Secondly, there was awareness that the benefits of modernisation and globalisation were not equal and that this inequality was a threat to the vision of perpetual growth and prosperity. It became clear to some that globalisation had not only created one world; it had also created a divided one world. Everyone was not included in the global village. Many millions were left outside its boundaries, excluded from the benefits of economic development, the knowledge economy and global networking, thus condemned to ignorance and deprivation from which they were powerless to escape. Across the world people fell into two increasingly differentiated and estranged classes. There were the rich who had educational and vocational qualifications, jobs, houses, consumer goods and a comfortable standard of living; and then there were the poor who had little or none of these things and were in most countries getting poorer. Most but not all of the rich lived in rich countries, while most but not all of the poor lived in poor countries. In some of the poor countries, such as India and Brazil, there was a substantial middle class and pockets of immense wealth. In some of the rich countries such as the United States and even in Europe there was an underclass living in dire poverty. Whatever the distribution of wealth and poverty, however, the focus of international attention (when there was one) was mainly on the poor in the poorer and less developed countries. International charitable organisations, aid agencies, informed public opinion and even some governments and business leaders realised the urgency of redressing this balance, not simply for the sake of the poor but to ensure the long-term stability and security of the global economic system. This has always been a minority position, however, opposed by many powerful interests and, as long as this remains the case, the deeply and perhaps dangerously divided condition of global society is unlikely to change.

Since 1989 the balance of rhetoric and articulate participation on these issues has begun to change. This has been mainly due to the flowering of a global civil society which had been developing and consolidating gradually over the previous thirty or forty years. Global civil society is a term used to describe the collective existence of a wide range of institutions and organisations operating in the international community outside the state system but in partnership with it. These groups bring together the interests and energies, the aspiration and commitment of various communities of people, which have a transnational identity and presence, but do not usually figure prominently or frequently on the political agendas of inter-state forums, conferences and summits. They mostly originate in the liberal and economically advanced societies of the West, but they have gained an increasingly important presence in developing countries and more recently in former communist societies. The oldest of them, which tend to be politically traditional if not actually conservative, are rooted in socio-economic structures such as trade unions, chambers of commerce, professional associations and academic connections. They tend to be conservative in their approach and to confine their activities to consultation and traditional lobbying.

In recent years, however, there has been increasingly high profile and, on some occasions, very significant participation by new social movements, including voluntary and humanitarian organisations and citizen's action groups. These groups are part of a long tradition of protest and dissent in Western countries. They have recent antecedents in groups like CND, Anti-apartheid and the civil rights campaigns. They have also drawn on the example and experience of sustained anti-communist opposition in Eastern Europe as these ideas were disseminated in the West by contacts made through the Helsinki process during the years of détente. From this they constructed an intellectually driven, persistently questioning, confrontational but non-violent kind of challenge to global power structures and the elites who inhabit them. In the 1990s and the early years of the twenty-first century the new social movements fused these various sources and traditions into a new approach and organisational strategy. They launched a series of well-organised and well-supported protests on issues like environment, poverty, trade and technology at major international conferences, notably at Seattle and Genoa, for which they gained wide international publicity. Thus the new social movements tend to be more visible, ostentatiously active and sometimes disruptive than the older and more established groups in the global civil society. Their tactics include staged and highly publicised demonstrations, public sloganising and confrontations with authority, which are not generally in the repertoire of the older groups. They also tend to be more volatile and unpredictable and more dependent on the active involvement of their members for the success of their activities.

The mobilisation of these groups has meant that the policy makers in governments and the major international corporations who in the past might have dealt only with government leaders, politicians, civil servants and businessmen, now have to consider a wider range of ideas, interests and demands. Moreover, these demands tend to be articulated in a style that pays little respect to the conventions of multilateral diplomacy and reflects the urgency with which the protesters and their publics regard the issues. Whether this has a significant effect on the making of policy is uncertain, but the emergence of a forum for global protest and debate has undoubtedly brought a new element into the process. The best prospect is that it will have a democratising effect on the process and, by acknowledging the validity of an emerging global public opinion, add to the legitimacy of global decision making. What is certain is that, if globalisation continues to become more extensive and intensive, as it has in recent years, major political issues will be increasingly global, rather than simply national or international, in their significance and effects. These issues will affect everyone and it will become important for everyone to understand them.

**Part I**

Challenges to the state

# 1

# Security

*Graeme Herd*

## What is security?

If it can be said that most concepts in the Social Sciences are contested, then none more so than the scope and nature of 'security'. What are the causes of insecurity and what policies are best able to lessen the impact of these threats to societies, states, regions and the global international system? These key questions are currently analysed and debated by policy makers in government ministries, parliaments, academic analysts, non-governmental organizations, transnational corporations and international organizations; the answers to these questions and the policies and strategies that are then formulated by states and societies to manage insecurities will determine the quality of peace and stability in the twenty-first century. Despite its contested nature, most analysts agree that it is 'the threat to use, or the actual use of, force that essentially demarcates the study and practice of security as a discipline distinct from the broader study and practice of international relations' (Terrif, 1997: 253).

In the seventeenth century the international state system took shape, as conceptions of sovereignty and territorial integrity were codified in the Treaty of Westphalia (1648). The rise of nationalism and nation states in the eighteenth and nineteenth centuries was accompanied by attempts by the Great Powers to orchestrate stability in the international system by balance of power/ through application of balance of power theory. The First World War – with its immense socio-economic, political and military disruption – broke the balance of power system and saw the rise of a system based on collective security principles, institutionalised in the League of Nations. However, the failure of the League of Nations with the outbreak of the Second World War, consigned this attempt at containing state aggression and promoting international peace and stability to the 'dustbin of history'.

In the second half of the twentieth century, during the Cold War (1947–90), superpower rivalry dominated the international system and had a profound impact on what analysts and policy makers understood as the fundamental nature of security. Deterrence ('balance of terror') and containment strategies were enacted by the Soviet Union and the USA and their respective allies in an effort to prevent the hegemony of either side over the course and content of international politics. In this period perspectives of security were diverse, ranging from countering threats to state sovereignty and territorial integrity, to invoking directly or indirectly, the notion of threat.

By the late 1970s and 1980s, with the rise of new social movements such as environmentalism and feminism and a growing realisation of the transformational impact of globalisation on state sovereignty and territorial integrity, debates about the boundaries of the subject took place as perceptions of security began to be re-evaluated. The oil crisis of 1973 focused attention on energy resources and economic security, while the Bhopal chemical plant disaster in India – 2000 killed, 200,000 injured – in 1984 and the Chernobyl nuclear disaster in the Soviet Union in 1986 helped promote an awareness of non-military sources of instability and the transnational impacts of such catastrophes underpinned the need for cooperative management of these security threats. The 1987 World Commission on Environment and Development (the 'Bruntland Report') and the UN Conference on the Environment and Development in Rio in 1992 were evidence that the relationship between poverty, injustice, environmental scarcity and conflict had become accepted and that this issue was now of greater strategic interest and importance to states.

With the end of the Cold War in 1989–91, the traditional or classical politico-military definition that had been reinforced by the Cold War era of state defence against the threat of military (nuclear) aggression was broadened to include the recognition that states might be threatened by non-military sources of insecurity that could entail non-military response from official state structures and institutions. In this re-defined and 'extended' concept the military security sector was understood as one – albeit the most important – of five, the other four being the political, economic, societal and environmental security sectors.

At the close of the twentieth century, as competing conceptual frameworks (paradigms) struggled to assert their primacy, no one dominant paradigm had arisen in international relations to rival and replace the explanatory power of the Cold War – though Francis Fukuyama, Thomas Kaplan and Samuel Huntington among others had attempted to promote their own views as definitive. Each of these post-Cold War paradigms did have one common feature; each focused on the dynamic of security and the stability of the international system, though each proposed different explanations to clarify the nature and scope of security in the post-Cold War era.

## Security and the Cold War

The Great War of 1914–18 was the midwife for the birth of International Relations as a discipline, with the Royal Institute of International Relations (Chatham House) in London providing a forum for academic and policy debates and research and the University of Aberystwyth in Wales founding the world's first academic Department of International Relations. In the interwar years a debate over the core characteristics of international relations took place between two schools of thought – between those that deemed themselves 'Realists' and 'Idealist'. Each side argued that they knew best how to avoid war and its attendant chaos and insecurity.

The debate was encapsulated from one point of view by E.H. Carr whose seminal work, 'The Twenty Years Crisis' remains the classic study of this issue. For Realists, like Carr, power is the critical ingredient of international politics: self-interested states compete constantly for power or security. International politics concerns the survival of states in a hostile environment through economic and especially military power. By contrast, the Idealist tradition emphasised that state concern for power was overridden by economic and political considerations, not least the desire for prosperity and a commitment to liberal values. The role of international institutions, international law, economic exchange and the promotion of democracy were the main instruments underpinning this perspective (Walt, 1998). The debate between these Realist and Idealist schools became entangled in the events of the 1930s when the Idealist view was discredited by the failure of appeasement policy. Then the effective deployment of military power during the Second World War and subsequently in the Cold War allowed the Realist perspective to gain predominance – a dominance consolidated by the start of the Cold War between East and West.

At the height of the Cold War, Western policy makers perceived a divided Europe straddled by a hegemonic Soviet Union at the head of an 'anti-imperialist' camp, controlling a bloc of satellite states in Central and Eastern Europe (CEE) whose foreign and security policies it dominated. Joseph Stalin, the leader of the Soviet Union commanded the Soviet ('Red') Army and, as a key ally of Great Britain and the United States from 1941–45, captured Berlin in April 1945 and proceeded to ensure that Stalinist-type regimes were installed throughout CEE.

Following the Stalinisation of CEE, Europe was divided between great power blocs, East and West, each with its own sphere of influence within a bi-polar international environment. In the West the North Atlantic Treaty Organization (NATO) 'marshalled' Western democracies into a military alliance. In 1950 the European Coal and Steel Community – which evolved into the European Union – was founded on the belief that Western Europe was developing into what Karl Deutsch described as a 'security community' – that is a group of states that projected cooperative foreign policies and stable domestic environments, a community within which war between these states was 'unthinkable'. A concomitant of the development of this 'security community' was the development of a set of institutions and practices strong enough to assure that dependable expectations of peaceful change became a defining characteristic of international community.

In CEE although Soviet control was never as uniform, homogenised or consistent as the myth of a 'monolithic bloc' might suggest, the creation of the Warsaw Treaty Organization (WTO or 'Warsaw Pact') alliance in May 1955 and Comecon bound CEE militarily and economically to the Soviet Union. This provided the Soviet Union with a secure platform from which to project power globally and promote communist victories in China, North Korea and North Vietnam. The Soviet Union was the core of the 'Soviet bloc' – if not the Communist bloc after the split from Belgrade and Beijing. It became, to paraphrase Article 6 of the Soviet Constitution, the 'guiding hand' and played the 'leading role' in the formation and implementation of foreign and security policy in CEE. Communist Party elites and key constituencies and interest groups within the Soviet Union held and exercised power, but as more recent Cold War reassessments have emphasised, although ideological stereotypes and established doctrines predominated, Soviet foreign and security policy decision-making process did allow for debate and differences of emphasis over the means to agreed ends.

Despite Yugoslavia's determination to remain free from direct Soviet political-ideological, military and economic control and that Albania developed an isolationist foreign and security policy, the Communist bloc was strengthened by the Stalinisation of CEE. Admittedly there were attempts by some CEE states to break free from Soviet control – most notably the 1956 'Budapest Uprising' in Hungary, and 1968 'Prague Spring' in Czechoslovakia – but these events did not seriously threaten Soviet hegemony at a fundamental level. Arguably, these 'counter-revolutions' in CEE only served to make more explicit the Brezhnev doctrine of limited sovereignty as Warsaw Pact armies suppressed by force the uprisings in Budapest and Prague. The exercise of the Brezhnev doctrine in CEE upheld Soviet strategic parity with the West and also reinforced Soviet control, power and legitimacy within the borders of the Soviet Union. Indeed, in the historiography of the Cold War the 'New Left' revisionists argue that Western containment policy was a key factor in underpinning rather than undermining Soviet totalitarianism.

Superpower nuclear rivalry gave rise to a 'security dilemma' (referred to as the 'zero-sum game' of Cold War politics) in which the security of any one state could only be gained at the expense of another's – if one state were to achieve greater security (win) then it followed that another state would become more insecure (lose). In this period the Soviet Union and the United States were key international actors, and shaped the nature and scope of security in the international system. As members of the UN's Security Council, global nuclear powers and key sources of ideological and political competition and economic power, they gave meaning to our understanding of the international system. The Cold War paradigm became the predominant framework through which we conceived the distribution and practice of power on the international stage. The Soviet 'second world' (the 'East') challenged the ethos of capitalist economies and democracies in the 'first world' (the 'West') and offered an alternative model of development for 'third world' states (the 'South'). The Soviet and market-democratic blocs constituted a fundamental governing dynamic in global security politics for the second half of the twentieth century, a role that has been totally and universally undermined by the collapse of the Soviet Union and the simultaneous end of the Cold War.

### Post-Cold War security debates: extending the concept

The collapse of Soviet power in CEE in 1989 and then of the Soviet Union itself in 1991 took scholars, analysts and policy-practitioner elites by surprise. The ending of the Cold War refocused debates on the meaning of security. Just as with the ending of the Great War, some drew 'lessons' from the Cold War, arguing that Soviet collapse vindicated the Realist understanding of international security – military power as demonstrated by the arms race of the 1980s which was believed to have bankrupted the Soviet system, causing the collapse of the state. For others, the arms race and military competition with the USA was of secondary importance when explaining the collapse of the Soviet Union and end of the Cold War. Internal systemic weakness was promoted by the failing legitimisation of the communist ideology, while environmental and societal pressures generated national political assertiveness within many of the soviet socialist republics within the Union.

These interpretations were highly contested and heralded what was to become a central characteristic of the post-Cold War era: unpredictability, ambiguity and ambivalence. A wider range of unpredictable risks that states and their inhabitants now faced replaced military threats to security. As the dangers of large-scale conventional or nuclear war receded a myriad of low intensity, high casualty intra-state wars and regional conflicts erupted, switching the focus of security studies from the USA, Europe and the former Soviet Union to the developing world. Here in 1994 the 'panga' (large chopping knife) was in Rwanda and Burundi turned into a weapon of mass destruction, as up to one million civilians were killed, while two million died in Sudan in the 1990s, with intensive ethnic cleansing reported in Darfur province in 2004, and a staggering three million have been murdered in the Democratic Republic of the Congo (DRC) since 1998. Clearly, the unknown soldiers of the post-Cold War era are civilians, as unconventional warfare, insurgency movements and terrorism began to replace 'traditional warfare' based on structured violence, orders of battle, rules of engagement and laws of war.

Although many of these wars and conflicts in the developing world had been ongoing throughout the Cold War and could partially be understood as 'proxy wars' between the superpowers, some wars were largely independent of the international security environment. Conflicts in Eritrea, Sudan and Somalia, between India and Pakistan, and in Nicaragua and El Salvador fall into this 'proxy war' category. By contrast, other conflicts were generated and then driven by internal factors that reflected intra-state weaknesses and failures – and although in some cases they were kick-started by external interference – conflicts within them continued into the post-Cold War era, helping to create 'virtual' or failed states.

These states were considered 'failed' because they were 'incapable of projecting power and asserting authority within their own borders' (Rotberg, 2002: 128). Haiti in the Caribbean, Sudan in Africa, and Afghanistan in Central Asia serve as examples from three continents of failed states. They were characterised by the prevalence of famines, ethnic, tribal, religious and other sectional or communal conflicts and dislocations, which undermine, destabilise or otherwise challenge the political authority and stability of the state. Conflict can be exacerbated by the presence of oppressive rulers or dictators who despoil and weaken their own states and threaten others – President Idi Amin in Uganda in the 1970s, or President Saddam Hussein of Iraq until April 2003 provide such examples. State recovery is challenged by a weakened state capacity, deeply divided societies, devastated economies, squandered resources and traumatised populations.

As a result of the consequences of the changes in the global balance of power after the end of the Cold War two predominant views of security became apparent and this had an influence on policy makers. One argued for a 'narrow' definition of security while the other favoured a 'wider' agenda. As the 1990s progressed the 'wide' or 'extended' definition was generally accepted as providing the most useful framework through which to understand insecurity in the transformed international system.

'Narrowers' focus on the military aspects of security and have argued that the key element of strategic analysis is the possible use of force. They concede that non-military elements of security may occupy more of the strategist's attention than previously, but ultimately military security should remain the primary focus of analysis as this security sector continued to pose the greatest and most profound and far-reaching threats to states. Security was still to be fundamentally understood as based upon the state, and particularly on the necessity of states to fulfil their raison d'etre – survival. Security then concerned the study of the threat, use and control of military force. National security was no longer to be construed in simple Cold War terms – 'defence' in which the concepts of deterrence and containment would prevent an invasion by the West or the East, depending on one's perspective in Washington DC or Moscow.

The 'wideners' questioned the primacy of the military element of the security debate (Buzan, de Wilde and Waever, 1998). They argued that the focus on territorial integrity of the state and traditional conceptions of sovereignty in which security encompassed the stability of the core institutions of the state and the integrity of state decision-making structures, ought to be widened to include societal (and human), economic and environmental security. Now security was perceived to mean more than simple military might and publics and elites alike understood and measured it increasingly in terms of the impact and scope of non-military threats on the daily lives of peoples and the integrity of states. These threats include corruption, criminal groups, private militias, insecure borders, smuggling (weapons, drugs, contraband and people), illegal migration, proliferation of nuclear, chemical and biological weapons of mass destruction (WMD), environmental scarcity (for example, access to fresh water or cropland) and, of course, terrorism.

'Economic security', for example, became a particular focus of interest following the collapse of the Russian, South American and South East Asian economies in July to August 1998, as the social, political and economic fabric and even government stability of these states was threatened by currency speculation and the structural inflexibility of their economies. For some states the rapid growth of criminal influence upon governance has undermined the moral authority and legitimacy of the state, as national and local power structures are 'colonised' by criminal groups.

The very nature of criminal activities – tax exemption, money laundering and embezzlement of state funds – all weaken the resources of the state, thereby limiting its ability to fulfil its federal functions and administrative capacity within the regions. Criminal activities also distort the transition to market economy and the international standing of the state, so threatening its political and economic integration with the rest of the world. Political elites that act in criminal ways subvert democratic norms, corrupt legislatures and undermine civil society.

As these political elites tend to have access to military force, and so hold a monopoly of power within a contested territory, they present complex challenges and 'credibility traps' for foreign intervention. In these states or quasi-states combatant and non-combatant roles are difficult to distinguish; army, paramilitary and armed group status cannot easily be separated out and it is in the interest of local power elites – criminal warlords – to maintain the instability and institutionalise the status quo. The tri-border area between Argentina, Brazil and Paraguay constitutes one such lawless region in South America; Eritrea, Somalia and Sudan in East Africa another.

The break-up of large multinational states in the early 1990s (in particular Yugoslavia and the Soviet Union) raised the prospect that such states are unsustainable in the contemporary international global system. It suggested that the twenty-first century might be characterised by the collapse of others (India, China, Indonesia, Nigeria and Brazil are possible contenders). In some cases state break-up is associated with 'ethnic cleansing' and ethno-nationalist state-building projects. These tendencies have increased interest in 'societal security'. Societal security focused on the integrity of societal identity and the various factors that can undermine that integrity, destabilise a state or communities and precipitate a series of violence outcomes (including inter-communal violence, civil war and inter-state conflict) became the object of attention for analysts and security policy-makers and practitioners. This is reflected in the growing sophistication of conflict prevention tools, crisis management policies and post-conflict reconstruction programmes, applied to Bosnia-Herzegovina (Europe) in 1995 and onwards, East Timor (SE Asia) after 1999, Afghanistan (Central Asia) after 2001 and Iraq (Middle East) in 2003.

While some analysts accepted that the traditional military-security definition should be expanded to include economic and societal security concerns, environmental security was for many a bridge too far. Those that argued for a causal relationship between the environment and conflict demonstrated the linkage in a variety of ways. They noted that 'environmental scarcity' could be characterised by the lack of land, water or timber, for example. This scarcity contributed to societal stress, political instability and economic hardship. The migration of rural communities to urban slums – where high unemployment, widespread poverty and poor education were prevalent – provided the social base for charismatic leaders, with 'liberation' ideologies and dynamic organisations to capitalise on community disintegration, group radicalisation and social explosions. These groups were particularly powerful when one exclusive ethnic or social group controlled access to key resources to the disadvantage of another group, as in the southernmost state of Chiapas in Mexico – the majority Spanish-Mexican population controlled access to key resources (particularly land) to the disadvantage of the excluded and poor indigenous local communities. In January 1994 this resulted in the Zapatistas, a revolutionary group in the state of Chiapas, initiating a violent uprising against the government and the declaration of a state of emergency in this province. A ceasefire was agreed after 12 days of fighting, but sporadic clashes have continued, fuelled by disputed land rights claims.

Environmental resources themselves might become a cause of conflict as opposing factions might fight to obtain or retain control over them. The wars in Central (the DRC), West (Sierra Leone) and South West (Angola) Africa have been fought for the control of mineral resources (in particular 'blood diamonds' and other precious minerals) and timber. These commodities have funded the conflict and it is the promise of great wealth that has sustained these forgotten wars in Africa. The devastation of the environment itself or environmental infrastructure might also become a war aim – a means of inflicting unacceptable pain upon an enemy state or people in order to prevail in conflict. It may also constitute inflicting a Parthian blow in defeat, as was the case with Saddam Hussein setting fire to the oil fields in Kuwait in 1991 when his invasion was repulsed.

Although the environment-conflict nexus is of rising strategic importance for states and international organisations, it should be noted that in many cases the effects of conflict upon the environment are unintentional and the impact usually international rather than national, demanding non-military responses to manage the disaster or catastrophe. While it can be argued that environmental factors are much more likely to act as an increased incentive for international and regional cooperation, the evidence for such a contention is questionable. Although the proposals for inter-state environmental cooperation are plentiful – for example, the international Jordan Valley Water Authority (linking Israel, Jordan, Syria and Palestine) has discussed the potential for managing water sharing for the last forty years, while similar projects are proposed in Central Asia to halt the shrinkage and pollution of the Aral Sea – little practical cooperation is forthcoming.

Moreover, as two-thirds of the world's population live in areas with a quarter of the world's fresh rainfall, fresh water supplies, particularly ground water, are under increasing strain. If changes in rainfall patterns and rising sea levels due to global warming continue then the Gangetic plain off North India and Bangladesh would become threatened – and with it 500 million people and their communities. The January 2004 outbreak of Avian flu and the SARS outbreak of March 2003, spreading rapidly from Beijing to Hong Kong, Singapore, Tokyo and Toronto, and before it the spread of HIV/AIDS in the 1990s, also highlights the difficulties of international and national actors coordinating effective responses to diseases with a global reach.

### Understanding international security paradigms

With the fall of the Berlin Wall in 1989 and the euphoria that accompanied the end of the Cold War, the expectation among most scholars, analysts and practitioners was two-fold. Firstly that the newly emergent – in some cases re-emergent – independent states would in the post-Cold War era move from authoritarian state-building towards democratising their political systems, economies and foreign and security policies. As a result the international system would be characterised by the gradual proliferation of a zone of peace and stability as the threat of armed conflict, use of force, military power and nuclear devastation declined and, ultimately, disappeared.

Francis Fukuyama was the first to suggest that 1989 represented the triumph of market capitalism and liberal democratic ideology over all possible alternatives. The ideological dialectic that had shaped the international system – the struggle before 1945 between communism, capitalism and fascism – had been reduced after 1945 to competition between capitalism and communism. In the post-Cold War world, 'market-democracy' was set to become the modernisation project of choice for all states. The future of the international system was to be characterised by the gradual democratisation and consolidation of market-democratic institutions, policies, values and culture. Liberal institutionalism – internationally generated norms, procedures and institutions for the enforcement of mutually agreed legal frameworks – would, ultimately, lead to the replacement of international anarchy with the international rule of law (Fukuyama, 1992).

The adherents of democratisation predicted that as a result tensions and cleavages within and between the states would gradually diminish, as all undertook a gradual strategic reorientation westwards and reintegrated into a globalised economy. Democratic states shared the same norms and values and as a result enjoyed the efficiency of inter-democratic bargaining and conflict resolution. It was also argued that democratic states choose their wars more wisely than non-democratic states, have larger economies, form stronger alliances, and make better and more consensual decisions. When they do go to war they have higher levels of public support and can count on greater support from their militaries. The accountability and transparency within democratic states and in their oversight of the military reduces corruption in the defence sector and increases public legitimacy.

By 1996 Samuel Huntington, analysing the same events as Fukuyama, agreed that 1989–91 represented the demise of the Cold War international system, but offered a radically divergent interpretation of its implications. Huntington argued that as a consequence of the breakdown of the Cold War order, the future was not one of 'democratic peace' and cooperation within a single global system in which the triumph of Western-style modernity was set to create one universal world civilisation, but rather continual and protracted wars between 'civilisational blocs'.

Seven civilisations spanned the globe, each at its heart characterised by alternative belief systems and the values they encapsulated. Western Christianity, Slavic Orthodoxy, Islam, Buddhism, Hinduism, Confucianism and 'possibly African' civilisations were now unconstrained by rigid bi-polar stability. Although the Soviet Union had been a superpower with foreign and security policy objectives that were global in reach, with the collapse of the Soviet bloc Russia had been downgraded to a major power. It had regional security interests – particularly in the former Soviet Central Asia and the South Caucasus – and a civilisational resonance as the core state of Slavic Orthodoxy (Huntington, 1996). Where civilisations brushed up against each other, Huntington argued, cultural fault-lines could be identified and it was along these fault-lines that future conflicts were most likely to occur. This left hanging the question of where the cultural faultiness were to fall in the Caucasus and Central Asia – was Ukraine to be divided? These quibbles aside, a 'Clash of Civilisations' paradigm emerged to challenge that of the 'End of History'.

Both of these mutually exclusive paradigms have been subjected to powerful attack, although they are not entirely discounted. Neither of them was considered a sufficient explanation to account for the myriad of changes and new security threats that dominate the international system. In particular, some that focused on the impact of globalisation argue that Huntington and Fukuyama fail to appreciate the extent to which a fast changing globalisation challenges the ability of a state to drive forward the process of state modernisation. Improvements in technology, communications and transport increased interconnectedness between peoples, societies, states and regions – underpinning the idea of a 'global village'. By the mid- to late 1990s globalisation was increasingly promoted as a process that offered to account for integratory pressures and fragmentation processes ('fragmegration') unleashed by ever-closer global interconnectedness. It was noted that there appeared greater disparities in per capita income, the share of world trade and foreign direct investment between North America, the EU and the Asian Tiger economies (the triad states) with their open economies and the rest of the world. Is the globalisation process a constructive force for peace and stability or an unintentional dynamic for destruction and conflict? (Hoffman, 2002).

Increasingly critiques of international capitalism – which was perceived by many as the cutting-edge of the globalisation process – argued that it was a force for oppression, exploitation and injustice, undermining traditional cultures and communities, increasing income inequalities within and between states, leading to political disintegration, the growth of failed states and, ultimately, the promotion of stateless, decentralised criminal and terrorist networks. 'Exclusive globalisation', it was argued, was the reality, rather than an 'inclusive globalisation' process. The 'exclusive' nature of globalisation supported the closely interdependent triad states, exacerbating divisions between 'winners' and non-industrialising 'losers' in the globalisation process. This outcome – the creation of '20/80' societies in which elites benefited at the expense of the majority of the world's population, was a source of conflict. In short, the markets, multinationals, the IMF, World Bank and World Trade Organisation – the institutional embodiment of globalisation – undermined the role and function of the state (sovereignty and territorial integrity) and, indeed, democracy. The violent anti-globalist movements from Seattle (2000) through to Genoa (2001) appeared as the radical forefront of a transnational undercurrent of unease at the perceived destructiveness of globalisation.

However, others who have studied the impact of globalisation upon security and stability have understood globalisation as a dual process, with some states benefiting from 'thick globalisation' and its attendant sources of stability, others from 'thin globalisation' and the insecurities that follow. Here it is argued that the 'functioning core' of the globalised world embodies rule sets, norms and ties that bind it in mutually assured dependence. This 'thick globalisation' is characterised by network connectivity, financial transactions, liberal media flows and collective security systems that underpin stable governments and populations enjoying rising living standards. Open economies lead to interdependence, greater prosperity and decrease the likelihood of insecurity. These states perform well according to the standard indicators: per capita GDP, UN 'Human Development Index', Transparency International's 'Corruption Perception Index' and Freedom House's 'Freedom in the World' report.

By contrast, 'thin globalisation' allows for politically repressive regimes to consolidate, which can be characterised in extreme cases by the prevalence of widespread poverty, corruption, high infant mortality, disease, disenfranchisement, marginalisation and massacres. These regions have been called the 'non-integrating gap' – they cannot control their borders, they suffer from ethnic and religious conflict and export insecurity – and they constitute a strategic threat environment for the functioning core. Indeed, as four-fifths of the world's oil reserves lie within this 'non-integrating gap', the potential for resource wars is high. Seam states, such as Greece, Mexico, Brazil, Indonesia and Pakistan, lie between the non-integrating gap and the functioning core.

Tadjikistan in Central Asia and Lebanon in the Eastern Mediterranean demonstrate the ability of some states to gradually recover from near collapse, while East Timor in SE Asia, Bosnia-Herzegovina and Kosovo in the Balkans also illustrate the ability of the international community to effectively organise protectorates and trusteeships to stabilise troubled and turbulent regions. The extent to which both the international community and these seam states are able to play a major role in containing the spill over of insecurity into the functioning core and then roll back the non-integrating gap will largely shape security politics in the twenty-first century. However, such efforts are complicated by the events of 9/11.

## Security post-9/11: new challenges and responses

In the early twenty-first century and hard on the heels of the events of September 11 2001, many analysts argued that international politics had been irrevocably transformed. One view was that a new paradigm had replaced those of the 1990s – a US-led 'global war on terror' (GWOT) – in which, as President George Bush argued, democratic and other 'freedom-loving' states struggle against an 'axis of evil' (Iran, Iraq and North Korea) and global terror networks and transnational terrorist groups, such as Al-Quaeda. This war was to target terrorist groups that were global in scope and was projected to last decades rather than the lifetime of one administration. Terrorists had blurred the dividing line between internal and external security and state responses included the integration of diplomatic, economic, military and intelligence capabilities to prevent terrorist attacks, reduce states' and societies' vulnerabilities to such attacks, minimise the impact of such attacks when they do occur and recover quickly from such attacks.

In the Cold War the USA had built coalitions to contain communism and protect the 'free world', making it safe for democracy and capitalism. In the new century, it appears that the USA and its allies are rebuilding 'coalitions of the willing' to protect market-democratic states and contain global terror. The shocking impact of 9/11 determined that the Bush Administration 'would seek to dominate the international system to such an extent that no strategic challenge would ever again be posed' (Lyndley-French, 2002: 802). US primacy in the international system allows the USA to have huge weapons and technology advantage over nearest rivals, but does this power allow the USA to set the international security agenda, or, indeed, provide security in the new century?

We can note the impact of GWOT on transatlantic unity and on the likely global security agendas in the future. Although many pre-emptive wars have occurred in history, the US-led invasion of Iraq on 20 March 2003 represented the first pre-emptive war in accordance with the US September 2002 National Security Strategy. 'Operation Iraqi Freedom' brought fully into the open differences within NATO, between the USA and in particular France, Germany, Belgium and Luxembourg; between the USA and Turkey (where the US strategic partnership with Turkey was deemed to be 'in tatters'); between European NATO member states – Britain, Italy, Spain, Denmark and Portugal and the new NATO member states in Central and Eastern Europe (the 'Vilnius 10') – between 'Old' Europe and 'New' Europe. In the eyes of many analysts these splits were now fundamental in nature and constituted a crisis for NATO, only comparable in NATO history to the Suez Crisis of 1956, when the USA opposed an Anglo-French led 'coalition of willing' occupation of the Suez Canal to the point of forcing a humiliating retreat on its erstwhile allies.

There are two constant threads that run through the Euro-Atlantic security tapestry. Firstly, at the fundamental level the USA and European states are based on liberal political cultures, have common interests and goals (global justice, democratisation, stability) and a shared security community if not strategic culture. However, there was a growing divergence within and between members of the Euro-Atlantic security community over the means by which these shared ends are achieved. For example, one key disagreement has emerged over when, how and where to use force and what justifies coercive intervention. NATO allies – particularly the USA and France or Germany – tended to agree on what the threats were, but disagree as to their priority, characteristics and the most appropriate methods and instruments of responding. Such divergence in the means (not ends) to achieve security and stability has shaped debates concerning the likely future transformation of NATO: containing communism brought unity of purpose; containing terrorism has not.

Secondly, US hard military power will remain an Olympian constant – with the military emulating the self-same ethos (longer, faster, higher) – as 'military transformation' takes root. US 'military transformation' is a deliberate policy choice to undertake major changes in war fighting capability to address emerging strategic challenges. It has facilitated fundamental changes in equipment, doctrine, operational concepts, organisation, training and military culture. At its heart is a focus upon C4ISRT (Command, Control, Computers, Communication, Intelligence, Surveillance, Reconnaissance and Targeting) and S2PL (Speed, Stealth, Precision and Lethality). But is the USA now at the apex of its power – unable to resist the temptation to climb even higher? Some might argue that the logic of the US strategy is to create a de facto global, albeit liberal, democratic empire through the creation of trusteeships and neo-colonial protectorates that were formally failed states (where local tyrants and terrorists flourished), and that such an ambitious programme will necessitate the acceptance of the need to act in alliance with other states, so the USA will become more dependent on informal multilateral institutions and groupings to assure the global security it seeks.

Thus it appears that 9/11 and the 'battle for Afghanistan' and 'battle for Iraq' have highlighted structural, technological and institutional weaknesses and tensions within the transatlantic security community – the birthplace of the modern Westphalian state system. It has also caused a reaction around the globe as many states struggle to respond to the new security environment at the start of a century which appears will be dominated by a paradoxical force – a US-led liberal democratic imperial project which will impose democratic values in place of terrorists and tyrants (Cooper, 2003).

This project faces several serious challenges – not least through the proliferation of WMD. The dominance of US conventional arms, especially in the electronics, database management technology and remote battlefield systems spheres, reduces the likelihood that any one state can oppose US military power using conventional arms. In the face of overwhelming power, most terrorist groups or rogue states are likely to either decide not to fight the US military or, at best, to adopt an insurgency campaign and rely on non-technology driven WMD variants such as home laboratory engineered chemical and biological WMD, dirty bombs (radiological materials strapped to conventional explosives) and cell phone activated bombs – the 'donkeys and rockets' approach to insurgency. In late 2003 the US and Italian accidental electricity blackouts underscored the extent to which power generation production and power supplies infrastructure is vulnerable and the effectiveness of the 'My.Doom' global computer virus in early 2004 points to an increasing likelihood that terrorists will adopt cyber attacks as a weapon of choice.

For rogue states an alternative security strategy exists: build nuclear weapons to deter external threats. This strategy was adopted by India and Pakistan in 1999 and North Korea in June 2003 (and could tempt Iran over the next few years). Secondly, as nuclear technology is expensive to acquire and hard to keep secret, many states – particularly dictatorships – will most likely opt to gain chemical (e.g. nerve agents such as Sarin) and biological (e.g. anthrax, Ebola virus and botulins) WMD and have the willingness and ability to use them. WMD proliferation is more likely when no conventional parity is possible.

Rather than representing a terrible new future – atrocious as the events in New York and Washington DC were – 9/11 rather can best be understood as highlighting and bringing into sharper focus the nature and pace of security and conflict-related developments since the end of the Cold War. These changes are numerous and interlinked, but three processes are particularly notable, and pose difficult challenges to the stability of states – even the most wealthy, well organised and powerful – and the international system (Carothers, 2003).

Firstly, changes in the global balance of power brought about by the end of the Soviet Union and the growing gap between rich and poor countries still have to be properly understood by policy-makers. Secondly, the technological revolution and its uncontrolled proliferation pose threats to all states – the weak and the powerful. Thirdly, the changing public attitude – particularly in Western societies – to the role, mission and duties of the military is occurring at a time when new sources of insecurity are becoming more numerous and profound. Collectively while these processes have made the study of security extremely interesting they have also rendered the security challenges, obstacles and dilemmas for states and regions alike much harder to overcome. Thus, whilst the post-Westphalia model remains a primary guide to states – sovereignty, boundaries, armed forces, national interest – in the world today, many states lack the capacity to live up to the model (Krauthammer, 2002/2003).

The concept of security, then, can be seen to reflect the concerns of particular states in specific periods as much as it corresponds to any existing reality. Security is a particularly malleable and flexible concept and a study of security politics reveals as much about the objective nature of stability and instability as about the subjective perceptions of the societies and states that use it.

Looking to the future, how might demographic change, natural resources and the environment, science and technology, the global economy and globalisation, national and international governance and future conflict affect the security of individuals, societies, states, regions and the global international system? Although the evolution and impact of these key global trends and dynamics are difficult for the student of international relations to discern, the questions themselves are of importance. Our study of these issues will allow us to anticipate and hopefully better manage future sources of insecurity and conflict and so gradually manage the proliferation of sustainable peace globally.

## Bibliography

Allinh, Dana (2002), 'Debating Intervention', *NATO Review*, Winter, www.nato.int/docu/review/2002/issue4/english/art1.html.

Buzan, B., de Wilde, J. and Waever, O. (1998): *Security: A New Framework of Analysis*, Boulder, CO: Lynne Rienner.

Carothers, Thomas (2003), 'Promoting Democracy and Fighting Terror', *Foreign Affairs*, Vol. 82, No. 1, Jan/Feb, pp. 84–97.

Cooper, Robert (2003), *The Breaking of Nations: Order and Chaos in the Twenty-first Century*, London: Atlantic.

Fukuyama, Francis (1989), 'The End of History?', *The National Interest*, Summer, pp. 3–18.

Fukuyama, Francis (1992), *The End of History and the Last Man*, New York: Free Press.

Hoffman, Stanley (2002), 'Clash of Globalisations', *Foreign Affairs*, Vol. 81, No. 4, July/August, pp. 104–15.

Huntington, Samuel (1996), *The Clash of Civilizations and the Remaking of the World Order*, Norman, OK: University of Oklahoma Press.

Krauthammer, Charles (2002/2003), 'The Unipolar Moment Revisited', *The National Interest*, No. 70, Winter, pp. 5–20.

Lyndley-French, Julian (2002), 'In the Shade of Locarno? Why European Defence is Failing', *International Affairs*, Vol. 78, No. 4, pp. 789–811.

Rotberg, Robert I. (2002), 'Failed States in a World of Terror', *Foreign Affairs*, Vol. 81, Issue 4, pp. 127–40.

Terrif, Terry (1997), 'Environmental Degradation and Security', in Richard H. Shultz, Jr., Roy Godson and George H. Quester, *Security Studies for the 21st Century*, Washington and London: Brassey's, pp. 253–80.

Walt, Stephen M. (1998), 'International Relations: One World, Many Theories', *Foreign Policy*, No. 110, Spring, pp. 29–44.

# 2

# Democratisation

*Lloyd Pettiford*

Apparently simple political ideas and concepts often turn out to be complex and difficult to explain. So it is with power, with security, with democracy and with the related idea of democratisation. Given this complexity, this chapter aims to offer a framework for analysis; it asks key questions, illustrates key points and concludes with ideas for further exploration. The chapter is structured as follows. First, the idea of democracy is discussed. If we accept that democratisation must involve a process in which there is a move towards democracy, then it is important to establish an understanding of the idea of democracy. Since democracy is a contested idea, we should also expect democratisation to be a fiercely debated topic. The next section outlines the history of democratisation. The current historical phase of democratisation has been described as a 'third wave'. This section considers what that means. The third section provides case material and examines democratisation in terms of similarities and differences both within and between regions. Finally the chapter draws conclusions about the political significance of democratisation. The idea of democratisation is considered as part of an assessment of the prospects for democracy. Has contemporary democratisation been shallow or does it have deeper roots and significance?

## What is democracy?

If democratisation is the move towards democracy, then we must start with the idea of democracy itself. It is a word which is very familiar to most people and is certainly used by politicians as if their audience were fully aware of its meaning and content. However, although its meaning is so often taken to be 'obvious', you might write a sentence now expressing your own view of the meaning of democracy, and in the context of your studies your definition might change over time. Furthermore it is important to remember from the outset that the changing context of international relations itself is likely to have an effect in thinking about the meaning of democracy.

Any intuitive sense of what democracy is, or ought to be, hides a rather more complicated situation. The former East Germany, condemned in the West as a communist regime, styled itself the German Democratic Republic. Similarly the countries of the former Soviet bloc dismissed Western governments as examples of bourgeois democracy; controlled by elites rather than offering genuine power to the people. The fact is that democracy is, and has been, such a powerful idea that very few regimes have felt able to dismiss it altogether. As a term democracy can be said to have been frequently used, and, at least as often, abused. As C.B. MacPherson pointed out clearly, though dismissed in the West, there was serious substance behind the arguments for democratic credentials made by the former Soviet bloc, even if their practice may be considered to have deviated from the ideal. Such societies claimed to have taken a detour from liberal-bourgeois democracy on the road to a higher ideal of human equality; the West on the other hand had entered a cul-de-sac which would never allow humankind to reach its potential (see MacPherson, 1966).

At the level of democratic practice we also run into complications. Consider the following questions: is a country as democratic if less than half of eligible voters exercise their right to do so? Is a country democratic if sizeable minority groups are disadvantaged and discriminated against? Is a country democratic if only very rich people have access to the corridors of power? Can a country be democratic if a large percentage of the population are illiterate? These and other politically loaded questions can be used to interrogate the strength or vitality of any democracy/society. Subject to these types of question, there are certainly weaknesses in the practices of some existing and long-standing democracies. When people ask such questions they are very often implicitly stressing the importance of either civil and political *or* socio-economic rights in determining what constitutes democracy.

In the face of such controversy it is tempting to seek a simple yardstick for democracy against which to measure democratisation. One well known writer who makes this mistake is Samuel Huntington. He suggests that, since a 'not-democracy' is where leaders have become so by means of 'birth, lot, wealth, violence, corruption, learning, appointment or examination', then the 'central procedure of democracy is the selection of leaders through competitive elections by the people they govern' (Huntington, 1991: 6).

Huntington's simple formula is certainly one accepted by many Western politicians and the one they will have had in mind when discussing 'democratisation' in say Chile, El Salvador, Bulgaria or South Africa since the 1980s. These countries could hardly have met the wider criteria of democracy offered and rejected by Huntington of 'effective citizen control over policy, responsible government, honesty and openness in politics, informed and rational deliberation, equal participation and power and various other civic virtues'

(1991: 9). Huntington argues that widening the debate simply complicates the matter and that popular election is the key to democracy; democratisation therefore, is about how a government which was not elected by this manner gets replaced by one that is. But it is a highly *political* act to insist upon the narrowing of democracy's definition in this way. Implicit in Huntington's work is a rather obvious political bias; the challengeable claim that 'the United States is the premier democratic country of the modern world' (1991: 29–30) lurks below the surface of his thinking. Democracy becomes what Huntington believes the USA to be, and what the USA lacks becomes irrelevant to democracy.

Huntington's version of democracy overlooks too much, in other words. We cannot afford to forget the context in which popular elections take place. If they offer little real choice or hope of change then they may merely rubber-stamp privilege and injustice respectively. To analyse effectively the idea of democratisation we must start with a more complicated and subtle sense of democracy than the 'mere' act of voting.

A more helpful way to look at democracy, and hence democratisation, is in terms of a kind of continuum or spectrum in which democracy can be regarded as a range – something which can be stronger or weaker – rather than defined by a single criterion. An excellent summary of this approach is provided by Potter who argues that 'it is important not to equate liberal democracy with democracy as such' (Potter *et al.*, 1997: 5). To an extent the labels attached to any spectrum are arbitrary; the current literature on democratisation includes a number of terms such as 'façade democracy'or 'low-intensity democracy' which give an idea of the type of phenomenon we are discussing but may be too imprecise to be of much descriptive value. The important thing about a spectrum is that it goes beyond Huntington's single-factor dichotomy of democracy/non-democracy. Clearly there is an authoritarian direction but also a direction which includes theoretical models of more participatory forms of democracy. Extending our range beyond the single criterion of voting, we can begin to discuss the quality of democracy and debate whether democracy is actually meaningful to people or merely useful to elites.

For the present it is enough to point out the idea of the 'quality of democracy'. This depends on the extent of civil and political *and* socio-economic rights. Put at its simplest the citizen must be free from repression *and* free from hunger to actively take part in democracy; and a democracy is only strong if citizens are able to (and mostly do) actively take part. Taking part includes the ability and the opportunity to express oneself which is why the question of whether educational attainment is an essential requirement for exercising full democratic citizenship has a long history (Mill, 1859). David Held offers interesting observation and analysis around such points in his *Models of Democracy* ([1987] 1996) and usefully quotes Robert Dahl (1989); 'in order to express preferences adequately, each citizen must have adequate and equal opportunities ... for discovering and validating his or her preferences on the matter to be decided' (Held, 1987: 278).

A crucial element in this discussion is the level of socio-economic development, not least because health and education are *correlated* with it. As Diamond, following Lipset, argues, 'the more well-to-do the people of a country, on average, the more likely they will favour, achieve and maintain a democratic system for their country' (Diamond, 1992b: 13). Although this is a narrow statistical, rather than explicitly causal, argument, national wealth does seem to be important in stimulating belief in the power of democracy as well as encouraging people to be involved. If people are materially comfortable, along with those around them, they are likely to endorse the system. It should however be pointed out that relatively poor countries, such as Costa Rica, have maintained democracy through a particular model of social democracy and political culture which has sought to emphasise the education, health and inclusion of all. Part of Costa Rica's political culture includes lively national debate (through media, tradition and propagation of national mythology) on the meaning of democracy, which brings us to a second crucial factor in thinking about the quality of democracy, and that is the idea of 'civil society'.

Although it is a much debated term, a useful starting definition of civil society is 'the space of un-coerced human association and also the set of associational networks – formed for the sake of ideology, family, faith and interests – that fills this space' (Walzer, 1995: 7). Put at its simplest, a democracy where people meet and talk is more vibrant than one where people trudge, sometimes coerced, to vote. Robert Putnam's key idea of 'social capital' is usefully employed here. Social capital is about trust, voluntary cooperation and norms of reciprocity. To an extent, the contemporary neo-liberal project, while tying its colours firmly to the mast of 'liberal democracy defined as voting', has weakened the bonds of civil society in many countries, reducing the potential for social capital and weakening democracy in the process (see, for example, Putnam, 1993).

To sum up and conclude this section there are key points to bear in mind:

1 This discussion is a simplified version of a very lively debate.
2 For reasons ostensibly related to clarity of analysis, but often implicitly or explicitly motivated politically, some people choose to define democracy very narrowly as 'voting'.
3 A broader definition of democracy allows us to talk about the quality and meaningfulness of democracy; this in turn may allow more satisfactory conclusions on democratisation regarding the idea of 'democratic consolidation' as opposed to an initial democratising phase of 'democratic inauguration' related to voting.
4 The quality of a democracy may particularly be judged against the ability of people to take part in society as active citizens; their ability to do so may be connected to levels of socio-economic development but is also a func-

tion of political culture, social organisation and the strength of civil society including its stock of social capital.

## A history of democratisation

It is now apparent that the claim that 'the word "democratisation" refers to political changes moving in a democratic direction' (Potter *et al.*, 1997: 3) requires some qualification. Such a definition, combined with the idea of a 'spectrum' or range of democratic criteria, suggests that democratisation is an ongoing process. It is not simply a journey from A to B, a transition from one condition to another, but an ongoing journey in which some will make more progress than others and where setbacks may occur. To think about democratisation in this way allows us to apply it to states which are already widely acknowledged as democratic. For instance, in the current era there has been much talk of a 'democratic deficit' whereby people feel increasingly remote from power and decision making; the changing context of international relations has provided challenges to the state which, it could be argued, have led to the opposite of political changes 'moving in a democratic direction' in many countries accepted as democracies by Huntington's criterion.

Despite the possible application of democratisation in the manner described above, there is also a history of democratisation which does suggest that it is a process of moving from A to B. This history provides a framework for many of those currently investigating democratisation's 'third wave'. Though criticism can easily be levelled at this approach to democratisation, the historical processes of democratisation are briefly outlined here as background for the contemporary regional case-studies that follow.

Huntington encapsulates the idea of an A to B journey when he suggests that 'a wave of democratisation is a group of transitions from non-democratic to democratic regimes that occur within a specified period of time and that significantly outnumber transitions in the opposite direction during that period of time' (Huntington, 1991: 15). The 'first long wave' of democratisation is said to last from 1828 to 1926 including particularly European countries. The second wave of democratisation covers the period 1943 to 1962 including post-war settlements and decolonisation. Huntington argues that we are currently in a third wave beginning with a Portuguese coup d'état in 1974. Significantly, both previous waves are said to have had something akin to a 'backwash' when the tide moved in the opposite direction of de-democratisation or authoritarianism.

It ought to be recognized that Huntington's argument is both shallow and political. It fits evidence to what Huntington wants to happen and it supports a particular political notion of what Huntington thinks democratisation ought to be. However, as above, he is useful to us here in offering us a way into this political debate.

Of the 'third wave' Huntington enthuses that 'the movement towards democracy seemed to take on the character of an almost irresistible global tide moving from one triumph to the next' (1991: 21). Leaving aside for now the question of whether the irresistible tide was actually at times a rather less welcome wave of neo-liberalism, there certainly does seem to be an impressive list of democratic transitions which have taken place and which have been largely welcomed. Robert Schaeffer enthusiastically entitles his book on this 'third wave' *Power to the People* and in the triumphal atmosphere of the post-Cold War period, it is embraced by Western politicians as unquestionably positive.

Despite the many reasons for optimism surrounding democratisation it is worth interjecting a note of caution. Burnell and Calvert (1999) note, for instance, that if they were forced to sum up progress to democracy in one word they would use 'tortuous'. Similarly, in emphasising the strength of rules and norms backing some European democracy, Bideleux points out that they have emerged 'as the outcome of *endless* mutual adjustment of human behaviour without the intervention of an ultimate arbiter' (Bideleux, 1999: 50, emphasis added). In other words we must be very careful when interpreting the meaning of a rather recent and brief period of history in which different countries actually have rather different experiences of the politics of democratisation. Democracy did not emerge, for the most part, from a popular outpouring or groundswell of opinion and in many cases new voting rights could not disguise the continuing fear, intimidation or apathy felt by some populations.

Even so, the reasons for Huntington's and Schaeffer's enthusiasm – beyond support for their own political preferences – is not difficult to fathom. Around the world, dictatorships have fallen, civilian administrations have emerged after periods of civil war and the military have withdrawn from politics. From southern Europe in the 1970s democratisation swept through Latin America and parts of Asia in the 1980s before continuing into Eastern Europe and Africa in the 1990s. With all the caveats about the idea of 'quality of democracy' firmly at the back of our minds, the next section offers brief case-studies of what has been happening in the 'real world'.

## Case studies of democratisation

### *Africa*

According to some theories of democracy (particularly those which emphasise modernisation and levels of socio-economic development alluded to above, such as Diamond, 1992b and Lipset, 1983) Africa does not appear to offer the best conditions for the establishment of democracy. Despite widespread belief in its suitability as a model (among theorists such as Huntington and among Western politicians) its fortunes have ebbed and flowed 'even when operating within the framework of the limited model of liberal democracy'. Some continue to believe that the African experience offers the possibility of undergoing a process of democratisation even where conditions appear far from favourable and, indeed, 'the movement away from authoritarianism and towards democracy in so many African states in the period since 1989' has been described as 'particularly striking' (Potter *et al.*, 1997: 272).

The characteristics of the African state which could hinder democratisation are quite familiar: cultural heterogeneity, poverty, gender inequality and artificial colonial boundaries. Indeed, in assessing the role of artificially created states and the parliamentary legacies of colonial powers, Naomi Chazan suggests that 'Africa's potential for democracy is more convincingly revealed by the creation of small collectivities established and controlled by rural and urban groups than by parliaments or parties' (in Diamond, 1992b: 92).

Despite this, and from the late 1980s, many African nations moved to construct a more (Western) democratic form of politics, and by 1995 'the classic single-party system, which had for so long been the most common form of civilian rule, could be observed nowhere in Africa' (Potter *et al.*, 1997: 285). Unfortunately, democratic practice has failed to live up to its promises for social, economic and political freedoms and fell short of acceptable on many occasions. Vague labels of the type referred to above became attached to the region's countries: terms like partial-, façade- or quasi-democracy and liberalised authoritarianism attempted to capture a rough picture of what was going on.

Explanations may be sought in various contexts but the end of the Cold War may have much to do with what happened. During the Cold War, Africa had a geo-political significance such that superpowers vied for influence there. In the case of the United States, loyalty had always been a more important commodity than democracy and they were happy to buy support from whoever offered it or from whoever they could acquire it. In some senses, the support of authoritarian regimes was preferred since it provided greater stability; democratic choice, of course, could bring unpredictability.

However the end of the Cold War saw Africa marginalised in both global geo-political and global economic terms. Dictators could no longer expect to sell their allegiance and 'by the end of the 1980s Africa's single party and military-ruled states looked increasingly anachronistic' (Potter *et al.*, 1997: 288). In the continent's ebb and flow of democracy, authoritarian rule had often emerged in the first place because democratic development appeared to be failing, but by the late 1980s it was clear that less freedom had not produced significant economic development either.

In this situation, loans and aid increasingly became tied to 'conditionalities'. Seeking guarantees for their investment, global (backed by private) financial institutions demanded 'democratisation' as a condition for funding, or the somewhat fuzzier idea of 'good governance' which ultimately amounted to the same thing. Africa is now free from most of the unambiguously authoritarian regimes which have characterised it in the past. Whether this has happened for reasons of short-term expediency or because of genuine democratic pressures is something you may want to consider.

Waves of democratisation have crashed over Africa before and then receded. The current period of re-democratisation has, as yet, tended to be a process of inaugurating democracy; whether or not Africa can consolidate democracy is debatable, but there have already been enough set-backs to make anyone seeking predictions about the future very cautious. One particular problem is that the conditionalities that have been used to encourage democracy (such as voting) have also encouraged economic policies which have cut back on health and education and encouraged a more individualistic mindset, all of which limit effective participation and depreciate social capital.

### Eastern Europe

Although President Omar Bongo of Gabon is reputed to have said that 'the winds from the East are shaking the coconut trees' there is every reason to believe that those winds, ultimately, may have had a more beneficial and long-lasting effect in Eastern Europe than in Africa. The initial process of democratisation in Eastern Europe seemed on the one hand to be extremely swift. In April 1989 the Solidarity Union after many years of tense resistance reached agreement with the Polish authorities about its legalisation. In December of the same year the tyrannical Ceauçescu regime was overthrown in Romania. In no time at all seemingly strong and dominant communist regimes throughout the region had begun to fall apart and then collapsed.

In longer term perspective, declining Soviet control had gradually laid the foundations for rapid collapse. The Soviet Union had withdrawn from Afghanistan, de-emphasised military power and redefined its notion of security via Gorbachev's 'new thinking', thus allowing degrees of political liberalisation in its satellite states and in its relations with them. Though the peoples of Eastern Europe may have long wished for democracy in order to reap its perceived material benefits, economic performance was not a crucial factor in democratisation. At least until the 1970s the East had not fared badly in terms of economic growth and it only became a real factor in promoting democratisation once the Soviet Union had allowed it to.

Part of the reason for optimism in the case of Eastern Europe lay with its existing wealth (relative certainly to Africa) and its proximity to the democratic club of the European Union, membership of which is a short-term or long-term aspiration of many in the region. However, the allure of the EU and the demands of membership also create some interesting ambiguities for these democratising states. Though democratisation has already taken place in the sense of holding competitive elections – in Poland, Czech Republic, Slovakia, Romania, Bulgaria and Hungary – there are a number of issues with which Eastern Europe must grapple.

First, only real, national democracies can join the European Union. This is not always easy to promote where minority ethnic tensions have emerged in the post-Soviet era. More to the point, the European project itself is about moving away from the nationally contained model of democracy. The EU moves towards a model of cosmopolitan law (which might actually be more appropriate to the Eastern European situation) even as being a 'national democracy' is a condition of joining. In the EU, rule-making and legal frameworks have been taken out of the hands of national parliaments just as these same national parliaments are becoming – and are expected to be – the focus of democracy in prospective East European members.

Second, in seeking public allegiance to democracy, governments have slender means but at the same time, high post-Soviet expectations. The context for this is a global economy which exerts rather than succumbs to influence. Maintaining people's faith in democracy is quite difficult if part of their expectation is an increased material standard of living which it is a struggle to provide. Increased inequity can exacerbate this problem and add further tensions.

Third, and related to the second point, the new democratic regimes have had relatively low satisfaction ratings compared to previous communist regimes. Moreover, by 1998 corruption was regarded as worse (in surveys of voters) than under communism. In Hungary 77 per cent thought corruption worse compared to only 3 per cent who thought the situation had improved. In Bulgaria the figures were 71 per cent and 3 per cent and in Poland 58 per cent and 12 per cent. In fact in both Poland and Hungary former communists won elections, though the fact that they subsequently returned to opposition benches does suggest that democracy may have taken deep roots (Bideleux, 1999: 33).

Thus Eastern Europe faces a challenging set of circumstances. Can it forge democracy at a national level while being a member of an organisation (EU) where national democracy is ever weaker in what is essentially a supranational liberal legal order? Put less 'euro-sceptically', can it forge democracy in a world where politics in so-called democracies seems to have become more about economic management than debate about appropriate political choices for society? In an era of declining social capital and 'democratic deficit' can democracy win hearts and minds still? Can it do so in party systems which have incorporated the politicians of the previous totalitarian system to a large degree? Although the prospects seem reasonable, nonetheless, of achieving some kind of consolidated democracy, the context will remain a challenging one where 'the experience of Communist Party states has bequeathed popular legacies of deep suspicion and sullen mistrust towards political parties and towards the state as an institution' (Bideleux, 1999: 31).

## Latin America

Striking though the differences between African and Eastern European democratisation are, Latin America presents us with another different set of

general circumstances, and within that general context interesting and different examples. Stability has certainly not characterised the region, with democracy often appearing and disappearing with great rapidity. Some countries,
such as Chile and Uruguay, have suffered dictatorial/military interludes despite appearing to foster relatively strong democracies, whereas others, such
as Costa Rica, have maintained democracy seemingly against all odds (see
Pettiford, 1999).

Particularly in the Cold War years (a factor connecting all the regions, but
in different ways) the United States was most concerned with preventing communism establishing a foothold in Latin America. Especially once communism became established, as in Cuba, the USA was quite prepared to take
what action was necessary to ensure its interests were protected. Brutal
militaries were trained, advised and funded. Covert action was taken. Justification for supporting authoritarian regimes as a bulwark against communism was provided by Reaganite Jeane Kirkpatrick (Kirkpatrick, 1979). But
more recently the geo-political experience *has* allowed re-democratisation and
liberalisation to characterise the Latin American experience.

Latin America's particular brand of democratisation has been elite-led and
seems to stem from a recognition that authoritarian economic policies were
no more successful than democratic ones and that those in power might better protect their interests through concession and control rather than repression and rebellion (e.g. Chile). As Mark Thompson has put it, democratisation
took place because the powerful 'became convinced that their ... interests
could be better protected by relinquishing power voluntarily rather than risk-
ing forced eviction' (Thompson, 1995: 329).

One thing, then, which is quite noticeable is that 'pressure from below ...
was only rarely a factor in the democratization process' (Little in Potter *et al.*,
1997: 181). According to Schaeffer's analysis 'when democratization finally
occurred, they [grassroots, revolutionary groups] generally played only a minor role' (Schaeffer, 1997: 127). However, after decades of effective repression we might turn this on its head to suggest that democratisation finally
occurred – in the 'shallow' guise it did – precisely because such groups were
only *able* to play a minor role. The upshot was that 'throughout much of
Latin America, democratization resulted in the status quo ante, in which governments were led by the same people [and] the same parties', in essence, the
'same social elite' (Schaeffer, 1997: 125).

Behind democratisation (in Huntington's terms) as people electing their
leaders through popular ballot, what has actually happened in Latin America?
In a very real sense the answer is not very much, with social structures from
Brazil and Argentina to Honduras and Guatemala little affected. Walter Little
says as much when he says of Latin American democratisation 'if a single
cause *had* to be identified it would be that the [previous] authoritarian inter-
lude had broadly served its purpose and hence was no longer needed.' (in
Potter *et al.*, 1997: 182). The democracy espoused by dominant parties is

clearly elitist (with Presidential 'beauty contests' which may equally likely be won by film stars and writers as by professional politicians). Apathy and exhaustion of the populace mean that power can be maintained more easily through democracy than overt repression. Political parties are weak rather than mass based. The military still lurk in the background.

Thus the latest wave of democratisation as applied to Latin America does not have deep roots, which makes consolidation difficult though not impossible. Events in the early 2000s in Argentina (economic collapse) and Colombia (increased violence) only serve to emphasise this point. Though the influence of privatisations in the former and narcotics in the latter should not be underestimated, each has only intensified existing patterns of corruption. The political culture of Latin America, heavily influenced by deep rooted traditions of nepotism, familism and clientilism remain both untouched by democratisation and a threat to the quality of future democracy

## Conclusion

Democracy is not, of itself, a simple idea. This in turn means that democratisation may be a complicated idea too. Despite this potential, the so-called 'third wave' of democratisation has largely been understood in terms of countries in Africa, Eastern Europe and Latin America (especially) which until fairly recently did not elect their leaders by competitive electoral process but are now doing so. Even with this simple understanding, an overview of events in each of these three regions already suggests different things going on, although all, in some way, seemingly related to the end of the Cold War and ensuing political space. Each region also seems to face different types of challenges for the future; having ushered in periods of democratic rule, how are these to be maintained? Will or can they be? This issue involves an assessment of democratic consolidation, the significance of democratisation and the quality of democracy. In the triumphal atmosphere which surrounded the end of the Cold War examining this issue of how really important democratisation is will be significant. The previous waves of democratisation have accompanied the struggles of workers, women and former colonial peoples for a share of power. Can the 'third wave' truly be said to be of the same magnitude? Is it a mere ripple in comparison? Or perhaps its political imposition makes it significant for rather different reasons?

In terms of consolidation, as with the inauguration, of democracy we must always be aware of 'the importance of *historical uniqueness* and contingency (chance events) and hence the timing and context of democratization in individual societies' (Leftwich in Potter *et al.*, 1997: 522). With this important caveat inserted, we can say that there appear to be general factors which make democratisation look less like a solid and irresistible tide than a wave which has rolled in and lost its momentum in some cases and elsewhere looks in danger of rolling back out again.

In the most general terms, Africa has a history of democratising and de-democratising waves. The continent faces serious social, economic, cultural and political challenges. In this context the (perhaps instrumental) adherence to democracy in the short term does not have deep roots and shows signs of weakness already in terms of 'reverses' perhaps most depressingly illustrated by events in Sierra Leone and Zambia. In Eastern Europe the course to democratisation is not easy but for the richer countries bordering the European Union the imitation of neighbours suggests a more comfortable consolidation of democracy than in Africa. Some countries like the Czech Republic, Poland and Hungary look in a better position to make the journey sooner rather than later. In Latin America meanwhile, a whole generation from Chile and Argentina through to El Salvador and Guatemala are scared and scarred from brutal military repression. A radical position is still a dangerous one in polarised countries whatever formal freedoms now exist. Acquiescence in elitist democracy for the poor majority seems to be a pragmatic move motivated by fear and exhaustion but in a continent with strong military and revolutionary traditions consolidation feels far from secure.

What emerges from the above is that the current wave of democratisation is not the result of a noble struggle from which emerges hope. To an extent, the Eastern European experience of Stalinism, including the presence of Soviet troops and invasions, means that here there is some proximity to the idea of democracy being the culmination of a long battle. But elsewhere the motivation behind democracy seems to be various styles of pragmatism. In Africa, the pragmatism stems from the latest phase of vulnerability in terms of global politics and economics. In Latin America, revolutionary attempts to overthrow some of the most unequal social systems in the world finally appear to have been quietened. Democratisation has emerged as a consequence of this defeat of people demanding many of the rights associated with broader or more radical conceptions of democracy. People have 'domesticated' their concerns; politics is an elite business which does not threaten traditional elites and social structures. Democracy needs some level and types of equality to work; the social apartheid of societies such as Brazil is unlikely to provide even the bare minimum.

If we think about the quality of democracy, therefore, we can see that what has really happened is liberalisation rather than democratisation. Eastern Europe rushes to join the economic liberal club. In Africa and Latin America too the choices offered through elections seem to be contests between groups with remarkably similar economic platforms and therefore about which group will continue to promote 'development' primarily through the export of raw materials and the attraction of foreign investment through tax-breaks and cheap labour. The 'third wave' of democratisation may thus be considered as a part of globalisation, the latest phase of neo-liberal expansion.

In those regions we have looked at here, like elsewhere in the world, a narrow elite control democracy and they control the media. In general terms, civil society has diminished, social capital is in decline and a 'democratic deficit' is the right way to describe the lack of genuine political options in the face of ever more powerful global capital and financial markets. Democracy never easy to accomplish, and the lesser of evils even perhaps today, is still, nonetheless, difficult to present (in its 'third wave' form) in an entirely positive light. That is because 'democracy' is hardly about 'choice' in any sense at all. Democracy is the only game in town and everyone is being forced to play, but according to a particular set of rules and an acceptance of Huntington's rather bland and unsatisfactory assertion that if the people vote in competitive elections to elect their leaders then that is democracy.

In the above context *all* countries can afford to reflect on their democratic practice. Voter turnouts in US and UK elections in 2000 and 2001 were low. In another established democracy, Costa Rica, abstentionism has increased despite the fact that voting is compulsory. If a country has declining voting rates, a concentration of the media in a few hands, political parties little distinguishable from one another and doubts about the honesty and integrity of public officials they ought to be seeking democratisation as much as any other. But some broader points need to be made. All states face a particular challenge not in the context of waves of democratisation but in the face of a different global political tide.

Influenced by the ideas of Hayek, justified by those of Fukuyama and driven by the forces of technological innovation the tide is of a globalising political economy where many of the previous assumptions about democracy have been difficult to hold on to. The big challenge for democracy in this context is 'how to reconcile the principle of rule by the people with a world in which power is exercised increasingly on a trans-national or even global scale' (McGrew in Held and McGrew (eds), 2000: 405). The major point here is that, while this discussion has not even questioned the assumption that our analysis ought to be at the level of the state, there are, in fact, an increasing number of reasons to suppose that state-based models of democracy grow ever more unsatisfactory. Our discussion of Eastern Europe and its possible disappearance within an EU supranational legal order hinted at this earlier.

Things change sometimes imperceptibly but they do change. While democratisation has brought important benefits – most notably peace – to some people, and while analysis has tended to concentrate on the level of the state, democratic theory is increasingly engaging with the changed global context and the liberalising economic tide. Normative theorists have tried to look at the potentialities of democracy in the new context, suggesting reform, reconstruction or replacement of state-based democracy and the need for vision; about democratisation and the reinvigoration of democracy, for instance in the form of cosmopolitan democracy and based upon a global civil society (see Held, 1996 and Patomaki, 2000). Such ideas give pause for thought. The German Green theorist Rudolf Bahro once talked about his move from the communist East Germany to the federal West and suggested that in a certain respect 'the more indirect control of the West was more effectively repressive than the direct control of the East' (see Bahro, 1984). If democracy is not to become meaningless – except as just another form of social control – democratisation must mean more than state-based competitive elections. Otherwise we face a reality of 'inescapable "democratic deficits" at all levels as [the world] gradually falls to the hammer of global capitalism' (Bideleux, 1999: 58).

## Bibliography

Bahro, R. (1984), *From Red to Green: Interviews with the* New Left Review, London: Verso.

Bideleux, R. (1999), ' "Europeanization" versus "Democratization" in East-Central Europe, 10 Years On', *Society and Economy in Central and Eastern Europe*, Vol. 3, pp. 24–61.

Burnell, P. and Calvert, P. (eds) (1999), *The Resilience of Democracy: Persistent Practice, Durable Idea*, London: Frank Cass.

Chazan, N. (1992), 'Between Liberalism and Statism: African Political Cultures and Democracy', in L. Diamond, *Political Culture and Democracy in Developing Countries*, Boulder, CO: Lynne Rienner.

Dahl, R. (1989), *Democracy and its Critics*, New Haven, CT: Yale University Press.

Diamond, L. (1992a), 'Economic Development and Democracy Reconsidered', *American Behavioral Scientist*, Vol. 35, No. 4/5, pp. 450–99.

Diamond, L. (1992b), *Political Culture and Democracy in Developing Countries*, Boulder, CO: Lynne Rienner.

Held, D. (1987 first edition and 1996 second edition), *Models of Democracy*, Cambridge: Polity Press.

Held, D. and McGrew, A. (eds) (2000), *The Global Transformations Reader*, Cambridge: Polity Press.

Huntington, S.P. (1991), *The Third Wave: Democratisation in the Late 20th Century*, Norman, OK: University of Oklahoma Press.

Kirkpatrick, J. (1979), 'Dictatorships and Double Standards', *Commentary*, Vol. 68, No. 5 (November), pp. 35–45.

Lipset, S.M. (1983), *Political Man* (second edition), London: Heinemann.

MacPherson, C.B. (1966), *The Real World of Democracy*, Oxford: Clarenden Press.

Mill, J.S. (1974) [1859], *On Liberty*, ed. Gertrude Himmelfarb, London: Penguin.

Patomaki, H. (ed.), (2000), *Politics of Global Society: A Global Perspective on Democratisation*, Nottingham: NIGD Working Paper 2.

Pettiford, L.K. (1999), 'Simply a Matter of Luck? Why Costa Rica Remains a Democracy', in Burnell and Calvert (eds), *The Resilience of Democracy*.

Potter, D., Goldblatt, D., Kiloh, M. and Lewis, P. (eds) (1997), *Democratization*, Cambridge: Open University Press/Polity Press.

Pridham, G. and Vanharen, T. (eds) (1994), *Democratisation in Eastern Europe: Domestic and International Perspectives*, London: Routledge.

Putnam, R. (1993), *Making Democracy Work: Civic Traditions in Modern Italy*, Princeton, NJ: Princeton University Press.

Schaeffer, R.K. (1997), *Power to the People: Democratization Around the World*, Boulder,

CO: Westview Press.
Thompson, M.R. (1995), 'Democracy After Sultanism: The Troubled Transition in the Philippines', in H. Chebai and A. Stepan (eds), *Politics, Society and Democracy: Comparative Studies*, Boulder, CO: Westview Press.
Walzer, M. (ed.), (1995), *Towards a Global Civil Society*, Oxford: Berghan Books.

# 3

# Ethnic conflict

*Daniele Conversi*

Ethnic conflicts are conflicts whose protagonists are inspired by a heightened perception of their own and others' ethnicity. *Ethnicity* is a sense of belonging and collective identity based on a subjective belief in a common origin and descent from common ancestors. This belief may or may not reflect historical facts or a true chronology. Authors who conceive ethnicity in these terms are often inspired by Max Weber (1864–1920) whose approach has been adopted by several subsequent scholars, including Ernest Gellner, Anthony D. Smith, Walker Connor and John A. Armstrong. Weber believed that both ethnicity and nationalism are based on myths of common descent from distant ancestors.

Myths of descent have existed since antiquity, but with modernity and the expansion of literacy they have been supplemented by history as documented in written records. Both myths and history are built into nationalist propaganda, although the demarcation line is thin. The past provides a key inspiration for both historians and myth-makers, whose worlds meet in *ethno-history* or 'history from below', devised to legitimise traditions and aims of ethnic groups still without a state. Since ethnicity is a sense of belonging, sustained by a myth of common origin, what matters is its subjective and psychological quality, rather than its alleged objective substance (Connor, 2002). Attempts to reify this perception in terms of more evident 'tangibility' have remained elusive.

The term *ethnie* is increasingly used in lieu of 'ethnic group' to define a group's cultural-ancestral heritage and was only recently imported into English from the French (Smith, 1998). Some authors stress the continuity between ethnicity and nationhood, postulating pre-modern ethnic conflicts as primary forms of nationalism. In its original Greek connotation, *ethnos* was already associated with the idea of common descent and lineage. Classical authors used it to refer to contiguous peoples, and it is rendered by the *Oxford English Dictionary* as *nation*.

The word 'nation' derives from the Latin substantive *natio* ('to be born'), and was used in the sense of common descent since at least the Middle Ages.

It shares with *ethnie* and *ethnic group* a stress on common origins. The main difference between the two concepts lies in the fact that the shift from 'ethnic' to 'national' indicates an aspiration to control political power and possess a sovereign state destined to shelter and protect a group's identity. Nationalism manifests itself in the aspiration to a state on the part of an *ethnie* now redefined as a 'nation'. Alternatively nationalism refers to the opposite process: to the enforcement of ethnic supremacy within a state. Thus a 'stateless nation' is a nationalist movement which does not control a state, as opposed to a 'nation state' which claims to be a nation embodied in, and possessing its own state. However, the latter is probably a misnomer as there are virtually no 'pure' nation states in the world, insofar as all of them contain ethnic minorities (Connor, 2002).

Ethnic conflicts are the most common form of contemporary conflicts. They are the catalyst of both internal and international wars – a trend which has increased since September 11 and 7 October 2001 (date of the US attack on Afghanistan) (Gray, 2003). The Cold War created the illusion of a world forever freed from ethnonational conflicts, whereas they were simply frozen. That was particularly true in the satellite countries forming the Soviet bloc. The disintegration of multi-national states in the former Soviet Union and Yugoslavia permitted the resurgence of long-repressed ethnic identities, leading to civil conflict and even international war.

One of the characteristics of ethnic conflicts is to endure over time. Typically, they persist through generations, independently of their visibility; their obstinacy and recalcitrance distinguishing them from other conflicts. Another characteristic is their solipsism, their weak adhesion to universalist principles, except for the nationalist principle, which conceives people as naturally divided into distinctive nations, each endowed with a right to self-determination.

The belief, encouraged by political science since the mid-twentieth century, that 'primordial' attachments to roots and 'blood' would be superseded by modern nation-building, gave way in the 1990s to the opposite belief in the persistence of ethnic loyalties. A dominant view has emerged that democratisation inevitably leads to an increase in ethnic conflict, with a notable degree of consensus regarding the relationship between ethnonationalism and democracy. On the other hand, authoritarian rulers have used the alleged threat of social disintegration brought about by ethnic insurgencies as a pretext to limit democratic progress and clamp down on human rights. Advocates of the doctrine of universal human rights tend to search for more elaborate ways of accommodating or controlling such conflicts by democratic means.

Ethnic conflicts are often seen as forms of nationalism, but the difference is substantial. Nationalists seek statehood and the recognition of their own nation in a world of 'nation states'. Ethnic conflicts, on the other hand, typically develop as a defence against intrusion by the state in an attempt to limit its exercise of political power. They do not constitute an attempt to control the state directly or to modify its frontiers and the legitimacy of the state is not usually in question. Several ethnic conflicts in Africa (including those in Nigeria, Rwanda and Burundi) were not concerned with secession or autonomy. They originated in inter-ethnic rivalries, although they may be encouraged by the state, development agencies, terrorist groups, ethnic lobbies, international diasporas, opposition parties, and foreign powers. The Tutsi genocide (1994) was implemented by the Rwandan state and pro-state institutions facilitated by the activities of the media and international development agencies (Uvin, 1998). The anti-Muslim pogroms in Gujarat (2002) were promoted and financed by US-based diaspora groups. The sectarian conflict between the Christian and Muslim communities in the Moluccas Islands of Indonesia (1995–98) were caused by mass immigration resulting from the Indonesian government's policy of mass population transfers and forced migration.

A particular state's lack of legitimacy (Connor, 2002) can lead to ethnic conflict, because of its lack of ethnic representativeness. Conflicts can then turn into violent confrontations between ethnic groups, whether or not galvanised by a particular regime. Some authors argue that such conflicts are never spontaneous, but always manipulated by elites aiming to exploit ethnic symbols for personal or sectional goals, even if they often lead to open political demands. The main rationale of nationalist movements, on the other hand, is a lack of legitimacy on the part of the state, rather than of a given government or regime (Connor, 2002). In this way ethnic conflicts which develop in relation to the state tend to transform themselves into nationalist movements which are frequently described by the term 'ethnonationalism' (Conversi, 2002).

A variety of ethnonationalism has emerged among indigenous peoples residing in ancestral lands which were incorporated into a state following conquest and colonial settlement by imperial powers. The movement for indigenous peoples' rights has recently expanded among Native Americans, Maori, Australian Aborigines, Sami (Laps), Inuit (Eskimos) and Hawaiians. In April 1999 the first indigenous autonomous territory, Nunavut, was created in Northern Canada: its surface of around two million square kilometres is settled by only 20,000 inhabitants, whose two official languages, English and *inuktitut* have entirely distinct alphabets.

Ethnic conflicts must be distinguished from so-called 'cultural' conflicts. Indeed, conflicts are rarely 'cultural' at all, except perhaps in a very superficial sense. On the contrary, the most violent conflicts tend to occur between highly similar groups speaking the same language and sharing the same territory, as in the cases of Hutu and Tutsi, Serbs–Croats–Bosniaks, Irish Protestants and Catholics. Culture and language are factors only in a negative sense: the perception of loss, supposed or real, of one's own culture can inform the rationale of many radical nationalist confrontations. In other words, cultural elements come to the fore mostly when they are threatened by policies of assimilation and dislocation. Indeed, cultural assimilation can often result in the widespread diffusion of ethnic violence. Where assimilation has destroyed local culture, violence can even replace culture as a binding mechanism.

There are no universally accepted typologies of ethnic conflicts, but several dichotomies around particular variables may be recognised. For instance, violent and non-violent conflicts, intra-state (or local) and inter-state (or international) conflicts, language conflicts and religious or racial conflicts and so on.

The contrast between violent and non-violent conflicts is particularly enlightening as it sheds light on the very causes of violence and civil wars. The amplifying influence of mass media in a globalising age may mislead us into believing that ethnic conflicts are intrinsically violent. Donald Horowitz (1985: 13) noted that 'the spilling of ink awaits the spilling of blood'. In reality most ethnic conflicts are non-violent, but the violent ones are noticed more. Few studies have systematically compared violent and non-violent conflicts (Conversi, 1997). In general, the literature on peaceful conflicts is remarkably scarce, although they probably make up the majority of existing ethnic claims. Various studies have been produced on the peaceful struggles of the Tibetans, the Australian Aborigines and the Ogoni in Nigeria while many others have been studied little or not at all.[1] Non-violent movements tend to be led by moderate autonomists who are aware that a 'secessionist' agenda could harm their cause. For them, the search for a *modus vivendi* with the government is a priority, and coexistence the preferred outcome. Moreover, the international community has usually upheld the integrity and unity of the state wherever it has come under threat from ethnic secession, even in cases in which the central government was blamed for destroying inter-ethnic coexistence. Each country has had to confront the phenomenon in its own way with different outcomes: on the one side, a few bloody conflicts have been partially 'resolved' through peace agreements, such as the agreement reached between the Mon and the Burmese government in 1995 or, closer to home, between the Austrian and Italian governments over South Tyrol (1964–72). Yet, other initially peaceful movements have degenerated into armed confrontations such as the one pitting the Chinese government against the Uighurs of Sinkiang, re-christened by nationalists as 'East Turkestan'.

### Language and religion

Both linguistic and religious conflicts must in principle be distinguished from ethnic conflicts *tout court*. Language and religion can both work as 'bridges' to cross the ethnic divide, even though they may be chosen as vessels of national identity. While ethnicity locks peoples and individuals into foreordained categories, religion, and to a lesser extent language, can bridge this gap, bringing together peoples from different ethnic groups, while providing a way out of the 'ethnic prison'. The selection of supra-ethnic languages affiliated neither to tribal identities nor to the colonial past has been a hotly debated issue in post-colonial societies. In several countries the colonial language could only be replaced by arbitrarily selecting from ethnic languages, an act which many feared would lead to heightened inter-ethnic rivalry. This is what happened in the case of the 'Sinhala Only Act' adopted by the Sri Lanka government in 1956, allegedly one of the factors leading to the Tamil rebellion.

The situation is easier when there are languages which are not associated with a particular ethnic group. For instance, the selection of alternative non-ethnic languages like Swahili or Kiswahili in Tanzania, Kenya and Uganda, was designed to replace English without provoking ethnic rivalries. The African statesman Julius Nyerere was a prominent advocate of this alternative. The country he led, Tanzania, has indeed been remarkably peaceful and devoid of inter-tribal conflict in comparison to neighbouring countries. On the other hand, countries which kept the colonial language as an administrative tool such as Zaire (now Democratic Republic of Congo), Liberia, Sierra Leone and Ivory Coast, have experienced interethnic conflict and devastation by ferocious wars, although the colonial language may not have been even the primary cause of these problems. Nyerere deliberately chose language as a unifying tool, while rejecting religious and confessional divisions. Other cases of supra-ethnic languages include Bahasa Indonesian, invented from scratch by Indonesian anti-colonial intellectuals, and Malay, which despite being associated with ethnic Malays, tends to be seen as a unifying instrument by other ethnic groups. Each of these non-Western languages is spoken by a plurality of ethnic groups in their countries, providing an invaluable tool of nation-formation for anti-colonial elites.

The other side of the language problem is the persistent association between language and ethnicity. Some languages are exclusively associated with one single and exclusive ethnic group, so the latter's linguistic requirements are perceived as varieties of ethnic demands. The term *ethnolinguistic conflict* is therefore used to describe ethnic conflicts with a preponderant and pervasive linguistic element. In Belgium Flemish is the common language of the people of Flanders, while French is spoken by the Walloons, the inhabitants of Wallonia. Both these populations share a well defined sense of common origins and separate historical development. However, for about a century, French was the only language of public life to the great disadvantage of Flemish-speakers. Their political demands were framed in the idiom of language rights and the resulting strife became a classical instance of *ethno-linguistic* conflict. On the other hand, in Yugoslavia the creation of a single homogeneous language, Serbo-Croat, for three ethnic groups (Croats, Serbs and Bosnian Muslims) did not prevent the eruption of one of the most brutal ethnic wars in modern times.

Religious conflicts should also be distinguished from ethnic conflicts. In some conflicts, religion plays an ascriptive role merely denoting group belonging, while remaining circumstantial and detached from faith. *Ethno-religious* conflicts must be distinguished in principle from *religious* conflicts. In the former, religion plays an identifying function secondary to that of ethnicity. In the latter, religious beliefs are preponderant, while ethnicity tends to be seen as accessory: this is the case of cosmopolitan and apocalyptic sects, whose followers typically belong to a plurality of *ethnies* and races. In these cases, ethnicity may even be dismissed as distracting.

As for ethno-religious conflicts, religion is not in itself a cause of conflicts, but a subordinate element of ethnic identity or national demarcation (Coakley, 2002, Conversi, 1999). This confers a sacral aura to the ethnic cause, as the people carrying those religious symbols become *ipso facto* parts of an 'elected' nation by divine will, independently from their inner beliefs. Indeed, leaders manipulating religious symbols may be believers, agnostics or atheists. For this reason, ethno-religious conflicts can be particularly violent and difficult to resolve: religious symbolism featured in Bosnia, Lebanon and Nigeria and in the Armenian–Azeri war over Nagorno-Karabagh. Atheist leaders, such as Slobodan Milosevic and other ex-Communist *apparatchiki*, are known for their unscrupulous use of religious symbology to legitimise their extremist deeds. This gives us insight into the non-religious nature of many conflicts ordinarily portrayed in the media as ethno-religious conflicts.

Religion also plays a founding role in secular nationalism. According to Adrian Hastings (1997), nationalism has Judeo-Christian roots: the translation of the sacred scriptures into the local vernacular helped to conceive the latter as a Godly agency and divine medium. Therefore, the people speaking it were God-chosen. For Hastings, the first nation in history was Israel. But, with the translation of the Old Testament from Hebrew into other vernaculars, the mythical vicissitudes of the Jews became more and more associated with every people in whose language the Bible was in turn translated. The Bible was often the first book to be rendered into the indigenous languages of several populations, from the Basques of Spain to the Ibos in Nigeria and Native American tribes, setting the basis for a sense of mystic unity with the Divine that turned them into nascent communities and embryonic nations. This 'divine' and simultaneously 'language-centered' birthmark remained anchored to later forms of secular nationalism (Hastings, 1997; Smith, 1998). Secularisation does not imply 'de-sacralisation' and nationalism has indeed turned the profane unto the sacred. The object of the new idolatry is usually the 'people', i.e. the nation, but the beneficiary is always a thin elite who can claim a popular mandate.

The use of religious symbology as a mobilising tool has been appropriated by minorities and *ethnies* of disparate religious faiths.[2] Typically, this has occurred in periods of deepening secularisation. Despite the partnership between ethnicity and religious symbology, many of these wars, like the one in Bosnia, can rightly be defined as 'atheist wars', given the circumstantial use of religion in exclusive reference to ethnicity.

### The role of the state

The most widespread cause of ethnic conflicts is the state or, rather, the politics adopted by a particular state in dealing with ethnic dissent. Coercion and repression can momentarily silence ethnic claims, but rarely succeed in eliminating them. On the contrary, draconian measures breed negative reactions which tend to spread far and wide (Van den Berghe, 1990). Government repression discredits the most moderate ethnic elites, inasmuch as extremists can play on a sense of grievance and threat: if the group's survival is thought to be at stake, some members may respond with violence (Gurr, 1993: 70). However, if ethnic elites opt for a strategy of cultural revival, the perception of a threat to the group may be diminished, making more likely the survival of a moderate leadership concerned with cultural continuity rather than radical politics. Hence, cultural preservation and renewal can inspire a concern for the maintenance of core values which restrains a drift towards violence, a choice that has been made in Tibet (Ghai, 2000), Catalonia (Conversi, 1997), Quebec and the British Celtic fringe (Cormack, 2000).

State repression can also lead to *ethnogenesis*, or to the emergence of new collective identities. Eritrea is a nation made up of several ethnic groups affiliated by the common experience of a thirty-year war that cut across class, race, tribe, religion and language. This struggle led to the 'rediscovery' of a common history endowed with its own myths of descent. The problem of such violence-based identities, however, is that they are precarious and that violence tends to persist and become a necessity. This partly explains the recurring war between Eritrea and Ethiopia following Eritrean independence and may also explain the irreducible fringes of violence in several peace processes (Irvin, 1999).

Other peoples who rebelled against Ethiopian rule under the Derg Marxist dictatorship (1974–91), including the Oromo, Somalis, Tigreans, Afars and Anuaks, have also experienced a process of ethnogenesis. A pan-Maya 'ethnicity' in Guatemala grew out of the repressive action of the state and its paramilitary militias in the 1980s. Among the indigenous peoples of the Philippine Cordillera, an alliance between seven major ethno-linguistic groups has developed a pan-tribal 'ethnic' identity with a shared language, *Ilocano*, in the course of their peaceful struggle against the central government. A common identity was moulded among the eighteen linguistically-related groups and tribes of the Bougainville islands in Oceania during their conflict with Papua New Guinea.

Other 'ethnic' identities have been forged out of the struggle against colonial domination and power abuse by the state. In some cases, this has taken an overtly racial form as in the Pan-Africanism of the Afro-American diaspora and in the Pan-Indianism of Native Americans.

The centrality of the state as the catalyst of conflict emerges clearly in the circumstances of political change, such as a decline in regime legitimacy or a radical discontinuity in the system of political representation. There are at least two reasons for this. First, there is a close relationship between breaks in the continuity of a political system and the emergence of ethnic movements. During periods of drastic political change there are opportunities for the emergence of new elites. Emerging elites can take advantage of discontent among unrepresented ethnic groups whose mobilisation may provide them with effective support. Second, there is an awareness among ethnic elites that during periods of political transition crucial choices are made which shape the pattern of a political system for years to come and the opportunity to influence them may not come again for some time. These phenomena occurred during every major democratic transition in the last thirty years with varying outcomes. In most Latin American countries democratisation has propelled the issue of indigenous rights into the spotlight. In post-1975 Spain, ethnonational conflicts re-emerged after the end of the dictatorship and played a key role in transforming the old centralist state (Conversi, 1997). But in former Communist countries the triumph of nationalism led to the demise of multi-national and nominally federal states (Coakley, 2003), ushering intolerance vis-à-vis minorities and neighbouring populations. The nationalist upsurge has lent new legitimacy to irredentist projects (Greater Hungary, Greater Serbia, Greater Albania, Greater Russia and Greater Croatia) and a nationalist 'contagion' effect spread further afield among neighbouring countries, such as Turkey and Greece, who had not been Communist.

The dialectics between state repression and 'ethnic' retaliation lies at the core of most conflicts. In Turkey, the military has barred any rational solution to Kurdish aspirations, pushing ordinary Kurds into joining one of the most intransigent guerrilla groups, the PKK's (*Partiya Karkeren Kurdistan* or Kurdistan Workers' Party). Since the PKK's 'declaration of war' (15 August 1984), disaffection has deepened and separatism has acquired an unprecedented following among Turkish Kurds, an outcome cold-bloodedly anticipated by paramilitary leaders. (Rugman and Hutchings, 1996). The Tamil guerrillas applied an analogous principle in order to establish an independent Tamil Eelam in Sri Lanka's North-East. Government repression disseminated the myth of armed struggle among the Tamil youth, generating an intergenerational schism which marginalised the more moderate elements of Tamil autonomism. A similar development took place in Kashmir, with dire and baleful international repercussions. In Chechnya, the most extremist factions seized the initiative following the Russian army's fierce repression (Lieven, 1999). The state's slow drift towards radical confrontation and coercion does often legitimise counter-violence as the only possible avenue, but the brunt of repression is normally borne by unarmed local populations.

State repression is an universal catalyst of human misery, but it has not always led to guerrilla conflict. In many historical cases, the state's apparent successes have been ephemeral, coming often at the price of establishing authoritarian regimes. Wherever an illusory peace was reached by coercion alone, its impermanent nature invariably emerged at a later stage. In 1975 the Indonesian army invaded the former Portuguese colony of East Timor and, with the full support of the USA, conceived a 'final solution' leading to one of the worst genocides of the Cold War era. For over twenty years the region seemed to be silenced and 'pacified', only to openly explode at the first regime crisis, which finally led to East Timor's independence in 1999. The Indian army's suppression of the separatist insurgency in Punjab (where a movement for free Khalistan operated) alienated a considerable part of the Sikh population, largely among the younger generations, while ultra-nationalist groups grew stronger amongst the Sikh diaspora in Britain, Canada and the United States.

## Globalisation and ethnic conflict

Modernisation is the most common source and cause of ethnic conflict, a trend dramatically increased in recent years in the form of 'globalisation'. The sense of threat, instability and lack of security for traditional societies produced by modernisation and globalisation is particularly pronounced when accompanied by state interference.

A major anxiety today is that globalisation can lead not just to the destruction of the world's cultures, but also to a global spread of ethnic conflict. Until thirty years ago, a dogmatic faith in economic progress reigned supreme, identifying development as the panacea capable of extirpating ethnic loyalties once and for all. Even though the number of inter-cultural contacts and all sorts of 'transactions' (economic, commercial and cultural) has expanded exponentially, ethnic passions are actually strengthened by such transactions. In fact, homogenisation of consumer behaviour, material culture and even language, has not automatically led to a convergence in values; nor has it led to a sense of belonging which transcends the ethnic community. Ethnic identities tend to resist this homogenisation process and can assume increasingly more violent forms once the support and moderation provided by traditional culture has been lost. In nationalism studies, 'modernist' scholars argue that radical changes in lifestyle exert unbearable pressure on the ancient cultures, values and structures of traditional societies. This invariably leads to a re-awakening of nationalist feelings with an ever greater possibility of ethnonational conflicts and wars.

Given the strong correlation between modernization and ethnonationalism, a corporate-run global world would be the opposite of the idea of *cosmopolis* as envisaged by universalist philosophers, from the Stoics to Kant (Conversi (ed.), 2000). Moreover, cultural levelling and dispossession often lead to a vertical fall in societal values, with no suitable alternatives. The massive import of Western, and particularly American, cultural icons has dismantled the inter-connective texture between ethnic groups and even between bordering countries. Globalisation therefore irreparably corrodes the very basis of international communication, as the emerging global order assumes a culturally pyramidal structure, dominated at its apex by the US entertainment and communications industry. The intermediate strata of this pyramid (the non-American West including Western Europe) feels more and more besieged, while the rest of an increasingly homogenised world lies at the bottom of the pyramid (Sardar and Davies, 2002).

On the other hand, despite a dramatic increase in global transactions, individual mobility and mass media overreach, inter-cultural contacts have not actually expanded. To the detriment of human coexistence, even neighbouring cultures ignore each other in favour of a US-made culture of mass consumption, making mutual comprehension increasingly difficult. New barriers are raised across generations, so that the inter-generational transmission of culture and values is becoming impossible in large parts of the world (Sardar and Davies 2002). Both these phenomena contribute significantly to the global expansion of ethnic conflict and war.

Referring to the diffusion of 'made in the USA' consumer products and their devastating impact, Benjamin Barber anticipated in 1996 that the reaction against the assault of 'Mac World' had begun in the form of spontaneous rebellions, at once extreme and uncoordinated. Barber uses the Arab term '*Jihad*' to encompass patriots, fundamentalists, neo-fascists, ethnonationalists, hooligans, tribalists, anti-imperialists and the new right. He observes that Serbian snipers targeting Sarajevo's town-dwellers and peasants in the Bosnian countryside often listened to US rock tunes while massacring unarmed local folks. So-called 'fundamentalists' are often themselves 'captured' by the products of global consumerism, from 'fast food' to Hollywood movies. Terrorist leaders have frequently lived in Western and highly mobile metropolitan milieux, in close contact with international culture. Moreover, both ethnic cleansing and religious-political fundamentalism have received substantial support from dislocated émigré communities, who are often less in contact with the traditions and culture of the 'mother country'. Indeed a decisive role in the diffusion and radicalisation of ethnic conflicts is played by diasporas and émigré groups, the most Westernised sections of ethnic communities.

Historically, European nationalism also prospered among diaspora figures based in London and other Western capitals, including remarkable individuals like Mazzini, Garibaldi, Kossuth and Herzen. The Liberation Tigers of Tamil Eelam accessed strategic resources through the support of émigré networks in Europe and the USA. The role of international student groups advocating a 'free' Khalistan (corresponding approximately to the current state of Punjab in India) among the Sikh diaspora was pivotal in organising international terrorist attacks. Independentist groups have risen and declined among the 50,000-strong Moluccan community who have lived in the Netherlands for several generations. Kosovar, Irish, Kurdish, Chechen, Ibo and other separatists are championed by diaspora groups. Thus, although diasporas can spawn peaceful and pacifist organisations, such as those among Tibetan and Ogoni refugees, the most radical elements are often the most 'de-traditionalised' and assimilated into mainstream or foreign culture.

## War and genocide

Following the unforeseen explosion of ethnic conflict after the Cold War, Western elites were caught in an impasse. Their inability to identify adequate solutions pushed some leaders and 'analysts' to redefine these conflicts in atavistic terms as ancient, neo-tribal rivalries. In the 1990s this 'interpretive' approach was widely used to 'explain' conflicts such as those in Rwanda and Bosnia to an uneasy and outraged public opinion. It was used by Western elites whenever pressures for greater international involvement forced them to find alibis for non-intervention. In this way, they could deny the possibility of settling violent conflicts through any form of intervention. Naturally, critics have dismissed this approach as cynical or indifferent and many accused Western governments of complicity in genocide (Power, 2003).[3] Some countries, such as Britain, have been singled out as carrying out the most genocidal forms of foreign policy (Curtis, 2003; Simms, 2001).[4] Such a line was internationally followed until the demise of the Chateau Rambouillet Conference (24 March 1999). The ensuing NATO attack on Serbia was justified on the ground of liberating Kosovo to avert genocide, therefore heralding a new era of 'humanitarian intervention' (Power, 2003).

Since the genocide of Armenians by secular Turkish elites in 1915, centralising states have from time to time attempted to resolve ethnic conflicts by eliminating diversity. This has included assimilation strategies, population transfers and even the killing of millions, with the mass extermination of children. In all these cases, the goal was total state control by standardising and homogenising citizens on the Western model. Genocide is not limited to physical extermination and has even more sinister cultural-psychical components: state terror leads to the destruction of all forms of privacy, sentimental attachment and cultural values, beginning with '*domicide*', the devastation of home and habitat (Porteous and Smith, 2001). There is also a systematic link between war and genocide. Genocide can be redefined therefore as 'a form of war directed against civilian populations' (Shaw, 2003).

## Resolving ethnic conflict

Experience has shown that ethnic conflict can not only be 'resolved' but also 'prevented'. The issues at stake are primarily political, rather than economic. Ethnic conflicts can rarely be settled through economic palliatives or policies of redistribution, even though claims of economic exploitation may figure prominently in nationalist agendas. More central is the contractual dimension of political accommodation and compromise.

The possible 'positive' solutions (that is, excluding policies of 'elimination of diversity', such as assimilation, genocide and partition/separatism) range from federalism to consociationalism, from autonomy to confederalism, from multiculturalism to 'hegemonic control' (Coakley, 2003). Historically, federalism has manifested itself as a union of territorial units (regions, provinces, states, *länder*, cantons, autonomous communities) in which sovereignty is shared between the central authority and the authorities of the member unit. These units can be ethnically based, as in the case of Belgium, or territorially based, as in the case of the USA. Consociationalism applies a similar principle, but not on a territorial basis: autonomous representations of local communities and interests at the central level is founded on non-territorial autonomy.

In general, a fully multicultural state can eliminate the perception of lethal threat which characterises violent conflicts. A polity which officially recognises ethnic and cultural diversity by unequivocally securing plural coexistence can avert the very conditions which spark ethnic conflicts. The archetypal example is the Swiss Confederation: this was initially conceived as a defensive alliance by several ethnic communities, bestowing on Switzerland a unique civic identity which slowly consolidated through centuries of common history. Switzerland is one of the few remaining non-ethnic states whose existence dates back to before the French Revolution. However, a comparable type of civic identity can only be created during the span of several centuries, mostly as a defensive partnership against predatory and expansionist neighbours.

It is difficult to re-activate a 'civic identity' once violent inter-ethnic conflict has erupted. Therefore, a civic identity can hardly provide a solution once trouble has consolidated. Rather it is a precondition for the absence of ethnic conflict. Insofar as one may attempt to create a 'civic identity', it can only exist as a long-term project, rather than as the immediate response to a political crisis. The European Union embodies the prototypical long-term solution for inter-nation rivalry. Its undeniable civic identity is necessarily divorced from the hegemonic projects or expansionist goals of any of its component countries. On the contrary, it is based on the coexistence of different national histories, regional cultures, local pasts and peculiarities.

In general, the creation of supra-national institutions can alleviate existing conflicts, introducing an element of external arbitration, while retaining executive power. The creation of supra-ethnic structures (and eventually identities) can help to attenuate and eventually resolve long-lasting ethnonational conflicts: the Irish peace process could hardly have begun without the practical and psychological power exerted by the EU. Conflicts can be greatly de-radicalised once Irishmen, Corsicans, or Basques consider themselves as belonging to their own ethnic groups while simultaneously seeing themselves as European citizens, that is, as members of a larger community which includes English, French and Castilians.

Peace processes have been undertaken or initiated in several areas of persistent conflict. Among the major difficulties encountered in resolving conflicts, are the radicalism of their protagonists, the protean form and multi-faceted profile of their movements and the inexorable emergence of 'spoilers' in peace processes. The chief obstacle is usually 'outbidding' by extremist groups in the form of radical-moderate. The presence of 'irriducibles' has marred the peace processes in the Basque Country, Northern Ireland, Palestine and Sri Lanka. Progress was made in Northern Ireland after the 1992 Anglo-Irish agreement and among the Tamils, although final success remains unpredictable. Peace processes have been initiated in other countries with diverging results. In Burma the cease-fire negotiated in 1995 between the Rangoon government and the Mons guerrilla seems to have held, while a similar initiative invoving the Karenni was largely unsuccessful. In a better known case, the Palestinian peace process, begun with the 1993 Oslo agreement, has failed because of the uncompromising attitudes of its main protagonists and US support of the most intransigent of all Israeli regimes. In Spain, the aborted Basque peace process has experienced a long and tortured itinerary, without yielding the expected results, despite a short-lived cease-fire (September 1988 to December 1999) (Irvin, 1999). Probably the greatest success was achieved in South Africa by the African National Congress (ANC) under the leadership of Nelson Mandela (Stone 2002).

De-escalation of violent conflicts rarely follows a linear path. The activity of groups and individuals who have turned violence into their *raison d'être* may persevere. Those who believe that national survival is at risk without military self-defence feel bound to carry on armed struggle even when the conditions for peace are mature. A typical problem encountered in peace processes is the endurance of a grassroots 'culture' predicated on antagonism and opposition. Violence and counter-violence notoriously fortify ethnic identities in areas where local forces have clashed with the central state and its repressive apparatus. It is important to remember that nationalism provides an ideological tool for boundary construction. When violence is conceived as a 'necessary evil' for the maintenance of ethnic boundaries, its renunciation becomes exceptionally difficult (Conversi, 1999).

Moreover, once a conflict degenerates by producing widespread intolerance and mass hatred, it tends to become nearly irreversible as its victims are less inclined to accept rational solutions. In this case, incentives for peace become extremely limited, since conflicts tend to be protracted through generations. Examples of such inter-generational persistence include the Armenian–Turkish conflict, the Greek-Turkish rivalry, and, more recently, the war between the Turkish government and Kurdish guerrilla. A 'threshold' (or point of non-return) may be reached when the deterioration of human relations, as well as environmental catastrophe, reaches a pinnacle from which there is no return, or at least the return to the *status quo ante* is unlikely.

## Conclusion

Most ethnic conflicts arise from a sense of collective threat and develop in conditions of political and cultural instability. They tend to be driven by two key variables, the state, whose assimilatory politics antagonises local interests and folk cultures, and modernisation, which dislocates, uproots, de-tradizionalises and assimilates, but also creates social isolation.

The ultimate consequence of ethnic conflict can be the incapacity of the central government to exert full control over specific areas by democratic and peaceful means, which in extreme cases may lead to the emergence of 'quasi-states'. Although not recognised by the international community, the latter act as *de facto* sovereign entities. The Transdniestrian Republic in Moldova, Abkhazia and Southern Ossetia in Georgia, Nagorno-Karabakh in Azerbaidjan, Kosovo and Montenegro in the former Yugoslav federation, Iraqi Kurdistan, the Bougainville islands in Papua Niugini, Northern Cyprus, Somaliland and Puntland in ex-Somalia, and several regions of Burma, are all instances of states not recognised by the international community and therefore situated in a position of political limbo.

Globalisation has led to an expansion of ethnic conflict in areas which until recently were free from it. In 1993 and 1994 alone, tensions between states and ethnonational groups left around four million dead. Of the twenty-three wars fought in 1994, only five were not caused by ethnonational factors (Gurr 1994). Most of the world's refugees escape from areas beleaguered by confrontations between the state and ethnic resistance movements. Eight of the thirteen peace operations led by the United Nations in 1993 concerned ethnic conflicts (Gurr, 1994). Yet, such conflicts are not insoluble (Coakley, 2003; Kriesberg, 1998), and their outcome can be a new constitutional order, short of the establishment of new states.

## Notes

1 Other relatively under-investigated non-violent movements, whose demands are sometimes limited to 'cultural autonomy', have emerged among Iraq's Assyrians, the Batwa of Rwanda, the Buddhists tribes in Bangladesh's Chittagong Hills Tracts, the Hawaiians, the Taiwanese (vis-à-vis mainland China), the Mapuche of Chile, the Lahu and the Palaung of Burma, the Rusyn (or Ruthenians) of Slovakia and Ukraine, Moldova 's Gagauzs, Crimean Tatars (in Ukraine), and many stateless nations within the Russian Federation: Bashkortostan, Buryatia, Chuvashia, Ingushetia, Ingria (or Ingermanland), Komia, Mariy-El (among the Mari), Sakha (or Yakutia), Tatarstan, Tuva, and Udmurtia.

2    Religious has been associated with ethnic conflict among all major religions: Catholics (Northern Ireland, East Timor, Bougainville, Croatia), Protestants (Moluccas, Nagaland, Karenni), Eastern Christians (Armenia, Georgia, Serbia), Muslims (Mindanao, Ache, Kashmir), Sikhs (Punjab), Buddhists (Tibet, Sri Lanka, Maghi, Mru, Tangchangya and Tipera in Bangladesh' s Chittagong Hill Tract), Hindu (Tamil in Sri Lanka, Tripuri and Manipuri in Bangladesh) or even pagans and semi-pagans (Southern Sudan, Oromo, Jharkhand).

3    Power, Samantha, *A Problem from Hell: America and the Age of Genocide*. Flamingo, 2003. Reviewed by both Niall Ferguson, 'Never say never again', *The Times*, 6 July 2003; and Anthony Holden, 'A Blind Eye to Genocide', *The Observer*, Sunday 29 June 2003.

4    Curtis, Mark, *Web of Deceit: Britain's Real Role in the World*, New York: Vintage, 2003; reviewed by: Caroline Lucas, 'Perfidious Albion', *The Guardian*, Saturday 5 July 2003.

## Bibliography

Barber, Benjamin R. (1996), *Jihad vs. McWorld*, New York: Ballantine Books.

Coakley, John (2002), 'Religion and Nationalism in the First World', in Daniele Conversi (ed.), *Ethnonationalism in the Contemporary World: Walker Connor and the Theory of Nationalism*, London: Routledge.

Coakley, John (2003), 'Towards a Solution?', in John Coakley (ed.), *The Territorial Management of Ethnic Conflicts*, London: Frank Cass.

Connor, Walker (2002) 'Nationalism and Political Illegitimacy', in Daniele Conversi, Daniele (1997) *The Basques, the Catalans, and Spain: Alternative Routes to Nationalist Mobilization*, London: Hurst.

Conversi, Daniele (1999), 'Nationalism, Boundaries and Violence', *Millennium. Journal of International Studies*, Vol. 28, No. 3.

Conversi, Daniele (ed.) (2002), *Ethnonationalism in the Contemporary World*, London: Routledge.

Cormack, Mike (2000), 'Minority Languages, Nationalism and Broadcasting: The British and Irish Examples', *Nations and Nationalism*, Vol. 6, No. 3, pp. 383–98.

Curtis, Mark (2003), *Web of Deceit: Britain's Real Role in the World*, Vintage.

Edwards, John (2002), 'Sovereignty or Separation? Contemporary Political Discourse in Canada', in Daniele Conversi (ed.), *Ethnonationalism in the Contemporary World*, London: Routledge.

Ghai, Yash (ed.) (2000), *Autonomy and Ethnicity: Negotiating Competing Claims in Multi-Ethnic States*, Cambridge: Cambridge University Press.

Gray, John (2003), *Al Qaeda and What It Means to Be Modern*, New York: Faber and Faber.

Gurr, Ted Robert (1994), *Minorities at Risk: A Global View of Ethnopolitical Conflicts*, Washington, DC: United States Institute of Peace Press.

Hastings, Adrian (1997), *The Construction Of Nationhood: Ethnicity, Religion, and Nationalism*, Cambridge and New York: Cambridge University Press.

Horowitz, Donald L. (1985), *Ethnic Groups in Conflict*, Berkeley, CA: University of California Press.

Irvin, Cynthia L. (1999), *Militant Nationalism: Between Movement and Party in Ireland and the Basque Country*, Minneapolis, MN: University of Minnesota Press.

Kriesberg, Louis (1998), *Constructive Conflicts: From Escalation to Resolution*, Lanham, MD: Rowman & Littlefield Publishers.

Lieven, Anatol (1999) *Chechnya: Tombstone of a Russian Power*, Newhaven and London: Yale University Press.

Porteous, J. Douglas and Smith, Sandra E. (2001), *Domicide: The Global Destruction of Home*, Montreal: McGill-Queen's University Press.

Power, Samantha (2003), A *Problem from Hell: America and the Age of Genocide*, Flamingo.

Rugman, Jonathan and Hutchings, Roger (1996), *Ataturk's Children: Turkey and the Kurds*, London: Cassell.

Sardar, Ziauddin and Davies, Merryl Wyn (2002), *Why Do People Hate America?*, London: Icon Books.

Shaw, Martin (2003), *War and Genocide: Organized Killing in Modern Society*, Cambridge: Polity Press.

Simms, Brendan (2001), *Unfinest Hour: How Britain Helped to Destroy Bosnia*. London: Allen Lane/Penguin Press.

Smith, Anthony D. (1998), *Nationalism and Modernism: A Critical Survey of Recent Theories of Nations and Nationalism*, London: Routledge.

Smith, Anthony D. (2002), 'Dating the Nation', in Daniele Conversi (ed.), *Ethnonationalism in the Contemporary World*, London and New York: Routledge.

Stone, John (2002), 'When Prophecy Fails: Social Science and the South African Revolution', in Daniele Conversi (ed.), *Ethnonationalism in the Contemporary World*, London and New York: Routledge.

Uvin, Peter (1998), *Aiding Violence: The Development Enterprise in Rwanda*, West Hartford, CT: Kumarian Press.

Van den Berghe, Pierre (ed.) (1990), *State, Violence and Ethnicity*, Niwot, CO: University Press of Colorado.

Weber, Max (1994), 'The Nation', in John Hutchinson and Anthony D. Smith (eds), *Nationalism*, Oxford: Oxford University Press.

# 4

# Refugees and asylum

*Sita Bali*

One of the pre-eminent political issues in the world today is the problem of refugees and political asylum. It reflects the divided, unequal and volatile nature of our world, and brings the conflicts and instability of the poor third world into the streets and ultimately the policy forums of the comfortable and comparatively secure developed world. It also adds to the deprivation, instability and violence of the third world. It affects all areas of the globe, and impacts on states' domestic and foreign policies. It raises questions of human rights, international law and state sovereignty. And it is a hotly debated, live and difficult issue in the contemporary politics of many states, both rich and poor.

The 1970s saw the largest increase in numbers of displaced people since the end of the Second World War. This refugee crisis included the migrations of hundreds of thousands fleeing Vietnam, Cambodia and Laos to escape repression and civil war. Conflict in Lebanon created yet another aspect to the already existing Palestinian refugee problem in the Middle East. The Soviet invasion of Afghanistan in December 1979 produced a refugee flow in the millions from that country to Pakistan and Iran. Conditions in Sudan, Uganda, Zaire and South Africa also created refugee movements, as did repression by military dictatorships in Chile and Argentina. This crisis continued into the last decade of the twentieth century. In the 1990s the end of the Cold War and the collapse of communist states across Eastern Europe and the former Soviet Union and the consequent relaxation of emigration restrictions again enhanced refugee numbers. The continuing civil wars in Afghanistan and Sri Lanka, the Balkan wars which created European refugees for the first time since the Second World War, and the Gulf War of the early 1990s all led to an increased movement of refugees. Greater instability in parts of Africa including Rwanda, Burundi, Ethiopia, Eritrea, Sudan and the collapse of states like Somalia, also contributed to the outflow of people. Continued repression by tyrannical regimes in Iraq and Iran, to name but two, have ensured a steady exodus as well.

The United Nations High Commissioner for Refugees (UNHCR) records that there were just over twelve million refugees and one million asylum seekers worldwide at the end of 2001.[1] Through the last decade, the European Union has received an average of nearly 375,000 asylum seekers a year, while the United States alone has received over 125,000 a year.[2] The countries that have borne the largest burden of refugees throughout the decade and continue to do so are Pakistan with 2.2 million, Iran with 1.9 million and Germany with nearly one million refugees in 2001.[3] This seemingly permanent refugee crisis, involving millions of people and affecting every continent and country, has ensured that the issue has established an important place on the twenty-first century international agenda.

Table 4.1 *Estimated number of refugees and total persons of concern to UNHCR worldwide (all figures as at 31 December of each given year)*

| Year | Refugee estimate | Persons of concern |
|------|-----------------|--------------------|
| 1980 | 8,439,000 | — |
| 1981 | 9,696,000 | — |
| 1982 | 10,300,000 | — |
| 1983 | 10,602,000 | — |
| 1984 | 10,710,000 | — |
| 1985 | 11,844,000 | — |
| 1986 | 12,614,000 | — |
| 1987 | 13,103,000 | — |
| 1988 | 14,319,000 | — |
| 1989 | 14,706,000 | — |
| 1990 | 17,370,000 | — |
| 1991 | 16,829,000 | — |
| 1992 | 17,802,000 | — |
| 1993 | 16,242,000 | 23,033,000 |
| 1994 | 15,637,000 | 27,419,000 |
| 1995 | 14,855,000 | 26,103,000 |
| 1996 | 13,312,000 | 22,729,000 |
| 1997 | 11,966,000 | 22,376,000 |
| 1998 | 11,430,000 | 21,460,000 |
| 1999 | 11,626,000 | 22,257,000 |
| 2000 | 12,062,000 | 21,814,000 |
| 2001 | 12,051,000 | 19,783,000 |

*Source: UNHCR website.*

Table 4.2 *Major refugee arrivals during 2001 (ten largest movements)*

| Origin | Main countries of asylum | Arrival numbers |
|---|---|---|
| Afghanistan | Pakistan | 199,900 |
| FYR Macedonia | Yugoslavia | 93,200 |
| Angola | Zambia/DRC | 44,800 |
| Sudan | Kenya/Ethiopia/Uganda/DRC | 35,000 |
| DRC | Tanzania/Zambia/Rwanda/Burundi | 32,700 |
| Central African Republic | DRC | 26,500 |
| Burundi | Tanzania/Zambia | 15,700 |
| Liberia | Cote d'Ivoire/Sierra Leone/Guinea | 11,700 |
| Rwanda | Uganda/Tanzania | 6,500 |
| Senegal | Gambia | 2,000 |

*Source: UNHCR website.*

Table 4.3 *Origin of major refugee populations in 2001(ten largest groups)*

| Country of origin | Main countries of asylum | Refugee numbers |
|---|---|---|
| Afghanistan | Pakistan/Iran | 3,809,600 |
| Burundi | Tanzania | 554,000 |
| Iraq | Iran | 530,100 |
| Sudan | Uganda/Ethiopia/DRC/Kenya/CAR | 489,500 |
| Angola | Zambia/DRC/Namibia | 470,600 |
| Somalia | Kenya/Yemen/Ethiopia/USA/UK | 439,900 |
| Bosnia-Herzegovina | Yugoslavia/USA/Sweden/Denmark/Netherlands | 426,000 |
| DRC | Tanzania/Congo/Zambia/Rwanda/Burundi/ | 392,100 |
| Vietnam | China/USA | 353,200 |
| Eritrea | Sudan | 333,100 |

*Source: UNHCR website.*

This chapter will explore the definition of 'refugee', distinguish between refugees and asylum seekers and examine the difficulties in so doing. It will then consider the causes and nature of movements of refugees/asylum seekers. It will analyse the international regime for dealing with refugees, and demonstrate that it is individual sovereign states that decide whether or not someone is a 'genuine' refugee. The majority of the world's refugees are hosted by third world countries, with Asia hosting 48.3 per cent, followed by Africa 27.5 per cent, Europe hosts 18.3 per cent and North America 5 per cent, at the end of 2001.[4] Third World countries usually deal with refugees with the assistance of the UNHCR, other governments, charitable and non-governmental organisations. But wealthy industrialised countries have found it difficult to deal with the comparatively smaller numbers who reach their shores. The reasons for the tensions created by the increasing numbers of refugees seeking recognition by and entry into industrialised countries, and the strategies adopted by these countries to cope with these demands will also be explored.

## Who is a refugee and who is an asylum seeker?

A refugee, according to Gordenker, is someone who has been the victim of human rights abuse. They have been denied some basic human rights, and have therefore taken the extraordinary step of leaving their homeland (Gordenker, 1987: 7). A refugee has fled from some intolerable conditions or personal circumstances, and 'implicit in the meaning of refugee lies an assumption that the person concerned is worthy of being and ought to be assisted, and if necessary protected from the cause of flight' (Goodwin-Gill, 1983: 1). A fugitive from justice trying to escape a criminal prosecution, for example, does not fall into this category.

The 1951 Convention Relating to the Status of Refugees defines a refugee as:

> any person who is outside the country of his nationality, or if he does not have a nationality, the country of his former habitual residence because he has a well-founded fear of persecution by reason of his race, religion, nationality or political opinion and is unable or because of such fear unwilling to avail himself of the protection of the government of the country of his nationality, or if he has no nationality to return to the country of his former habitual residence.[5]

This definition focuses on the individual refugee as the victim of political persecution. It has been widened through the work of the UNHCR to include refugee groups and not just individuals, as well as those fleeing various kinds of upheaval, such as civil conflict or war, not just persecution. For instance, UNHCR was involved in assisting Chinese refugees fleeing to Hong Kong in 1957, Greek-Cypriots in the 1960s and the Indo-Chinese in 1975 after the wars in Vietnam and Cambodia, none of whom, strictly speaking, came under the definition set out above.

There is further provision in the 1951 Convention and its attendant 1967 Protocol for temporary protection for people fleeing war or persecution in large numbers. This is to enable people to receive protection and assistance without having to go through the long process of recognition as a refugee by any state, and is usually used to provide temporary help in a crisis situation, as was done for Albanian refugees from Kosovo in 1999.

An asylum seeker is someone who claims to be a refugee, i.e. to have fled from his or her home in fear of their life. Asylum seekers want to be accepted as refugees and allowed to live in the country to which they have come, but their claim has yet to be accepted by that or any other country. Increasingly, industrialised countries are adopting ever-tighter interpretations of the definition of a refugee, and thus denying recognition to those fleeing wars and other conflicts, as well as disasters and dire poverty. Today in most European countries, an asylum seeker has to prove that he or she personally was being persecuted in his or her country to stand any chance of gaining refugee status. But it must be pointed out that persecution is not the only reason that makes people fearful enough to flee their homelands; they may also do so due to famine, civil conflict and war. Persecuting people is not the only way to make them flee, as starving them or letting them starve is probably a more efficient way to get them to do so. And can human rights mean anything to a poor, ill and malnourished person other than health care and security of access to food supplies? Thus many people move because of extreme deprivation and poverty, disease, malnutrition and the absence of opportunities to better themselves in their home countries. These latter, however are seen as 'economic migrants' or 'bogus asylum seekers' not refugees. Exactly where, on this scale of human deprivation, misery and fear, an economic migrant becomes a refugee is at least arguable. A more detailed examination of the causes of refugee movements should help explain this further.

## What causes people to flee their homes?

A wide variety of reasons force people to flee their homes and seek refuge in a foreign country. Most of these are usually caused by the actions of their own governments, trying to achieve various domestic and foreign policy objectives. Alternatively, a government's inability or incompetence in dealing with a range of crises may also produce refugee flows.

Governments often follow policies or take actions that will create refugee flows, to achieve certain domestic policy objectives or goals. Many refugee flows are linked to the rise of nationalist movements, and the desire to create a homogeneous state, by ejecting those from minority religious or ethnic communities within the state. This process is not new to the twentieth century, but was used by the Spanish Crown in the fifteenth century to rid Spain of the Jews, as well as by the French in the sixteenth century to expel the Huguenots. In the period of decolonisation directly after the Second World War, there were several large refugee flows caused by similar factors. The partition of India and the creation of Pakistan led to eight million Sikhs and Hindus fleeing Pakistan to come to India, and about six million Moslems moving from India to Pakistan. The creation of the state of Israel in 1948 led to a large movement of Arabs from that territory. The movement of people in the Balkan wars in the 1990s was inspired by the desire of the governments of the new states to create such homogeneity through 'ethnic cleansing' policies.

Minority communities have been expelled from several third world countries. It is a politically popular action for governments faced with a rising tide of economic and social problems, to make scapegoats of a prosperous or well-placed minority. This sort of treatment has been meted out to the Bahais in Iran, the Ahmediyas in Pakistan and Indians in East Africa, causing members of these communities to seek refuge elsewhere. In these cases governments used refugee movements to fulfil their domestic ambitions.

Governments use refugee emigration to deal with political opposition, and dissidents may be expelled or compelled to leave because of their political opinions. Authoritarian governments find this a particularly useful way of getting rid of internal opposition as the Soviet Union did, for instance, in the case of Alexander Solzhenitsyn. The numbers involved in such emigration are not always limited to a small perhaps high-profile group of individuals, but can include whole sections of the population. The departure of more than half a million members of the Cuban middle classes was seen by the Castro regime as a way of getting rid of a class of people that would never accept the socialist revolution. Sometimes it is not easy to distinguish between the effects of a deliberate policy intended to make dissidents leave, and the situation in which conflict, uncertainty and harassment have this as the unintended, yet convenient consequence. Clearly government policy and action towards dissident individuals and groups can play a large role in forcing people to leave, or in creating conditions which lead to them moving.

Governments sometimes deliberately create refugee flows as part of the process of achieving foreign policy objectives. Weiner terms this sort of emigration 'strategic emigration'.[6] In the past, colonial powers forced populations to move, to fulfil expansionist ambitions. For instance, the deportation of British convicts to Australia brought that landmass under the control of the British Crown and slavery forcibly moved West Africans to the Caribbean and the USA to strengthen the plantation based economies of that part of the Empire. Its replacement, indentured labour movements from British India to other parts of the Empire, was also designed to continue the economic benefits of slavery to the Empire.

Refugee flows are also a way of putting pressure on neighbouring states. They can be forced to yield to a demand of the sending country in return for a commitment to stem the refugee flow. The Duvalier regime in Haiti encouraged movement of their people to the United States, in order to get that country to increase development assistance and aid. In the early 1970s, the government of Pakistan forced huge refugee movement into India from East Pakistan, to use this flow as a means of getting India to stop providing assistance to the Mukti Bahini (the Bangladeshi freedom fighters).

Government policies do not always achieve the desired results, and can also have various unforeseen side effects. Such distortions of government intent can also create refugee flows. For instances the policies of the governments of Ethiopia and Sudan to contain insurgencies brought retaliatory action by the rebels, and the unintended result of these actions was to create a stream of refugees from both countries, comprised of people trying to escape the violence and consequent famine. Policies aimed at development and industrialisation can also have the unintended effect of inducing emigration. While these flows often remain internal to the country itself, they do sometimes spill over international borders too. Overgrazing combined with drought in the African Sahel, deforestation in rural Latin America, and dam building in India have all created refugee flows.

Government incompetence or inability to alleviate the effects of an 'act of God' like extended drought or floods creates an exodus. The drought induced famine in Ethiopia in the mid–1980s, and the inability of the government there to deal with its effects led to an outflow of Ethiopians. It must be noted that the majority of people displaced by natural disasters like famine, floods, earthquakes, cyclones or man-made disasters like Chernobyl or Bhopal stay within the boundaries of their own countries.

It should then be clear, that the creation of international refugee flows is only occasionally a product of an unforeseen cataclysmic event or natural disaster. In most cases, refugee movements are created by deliberate actions of governments, designed to achieve a variety of objectives, at home and abroad. Given this, it could be argued that distinctions made in the West between 'economic migrants' and 'genuine refugees' are less valid than they might first appear.

It is also worth noting that while the Universal Declaration on Human Rights grants everyone the right to exit from any country including their own, in fact this right is denied by many states. This right is blocked not only by the restrictions on entry enforced in all states, but also by restrictions on the right to exit imposed by many states. Frequently the very states that create forced emigration of some sections of the population are the same states that impose restrictions on the right of others to leave. For instance, while whole Afghan villages were being forced to flee to Pakistan, Afghani doctors were unable to exercise their right to exit (Dowty, 1987: 6). The Soviet policy of expelling dissidents while not allowing the bulk of the population the right to travel abroad is another example.

'Closing off free emigration is probably an essential policy for any regime that relies heavily on coercion' (Dowty, 1987: 6). They seek to compel the opposition to come to terms with political conditions by denying the option of escape. These regimes will often allow exit to those they cannot or do not want to assimilate, as previous examples show. The right to stay or leave is also sometimes seen as a debate between the interests of the state and those of the individual. States reserve the right to restrict the exit of those who owe it any debts or obligations like military service, on grounds of public health, safety and welfare, as well as 'national security'. Further, some states claim that they have made investments in individuals (such as education) and have a right to return on that investment, or compensation. For example, for some time the government of Romania permitted Jewish emigration only on repayment by the individual of the cost of her or his education. In recent years many governments have cited the brain drain as a reason for restricting exit. The effect of such arguments, and the policies they are used to justify is to allow a serious infringement of the right of individual liberty. The result of these policies is to create internal refugees, or refuseniks, who are persecuted, denied basic freedoms, and cannot be protected or assisted by any prevailing international norms or agencies that act to assist those who manage to escape.

## The international regime dealing with refugees

International practice on the treatment of refugees is based on the principle of non-refoulement. This broadly means, 'no refugee should be returned to any country where he or she is likely to face danger to life or freedom' (Goodwin-Gill, 1983: 69). This is a relatively recent concept in international law, and it first appears in an international treaty in 1933 in documents of the League of Nations. In the past it was common for kings or sovereigns to have reciprocal arrangements with each other for apprehending those who were dissenters. The concept gained currency in the mid-nineteenth century, a period of political turmoil and mass movement in Europe, and was seen as a reflection of the popular sentiment that those fleeing political persecution should be protected (Goodwin-Gill, 1983: 69–70).

Initial international efforts to deal with the problem of refugees began with the League of Nations and with the appointment of Fridtjof Nansen in 1921 as the first Refugee High Commissioner. The organisation took a group approach and defined refugees as those who were '(1) outside their country of origin and (2) without the protection of the government of that state' (Goodwin-Gill, 1983: 2). These were the criteria used to identify and assist Russians fleeing the Soviets and later those fleeing Nazi persecution in Germany. In the inter-war period, a body of refugee law also began to take root. The 1933 League of Nations' Convention relating to the International Status of Refugees and the 1938 Convention concerning the Status of Refugees coming from Germany provided limited protection for some uprooted peoples.

After the establishment of the United Nations, the work of assisting refugees was done first by the United Nations Relief and Rehabilitation Administrator (created in 1943), and then by the International Refugee Organisation, set up in 1946. But none of these agencies was entirely successful at dealing with the scale of the problems of displaced people created by the Second World War and the Holocaust. In 1950, the United Nations High Commission for Refugees was established, to deal with the more than one million still stateless people in Europe, five years after the end of the Second World War. And, in 1951, with the horrors of the Holocaust fresh in its mind the international community established the 1951 Convention Relating to the Status of Refugees. This was based on the principles enunciated in the 1948 Universal Declaration of Human Rights, which gives every person the right to exit from any country including their own, and the right to return to their own country. It also states in Article 14 that everyone has the right to "seek and enjoy in other countries asylum from persecution' (Goodwin-Gill, 1983: 5). The 1951 Convention established the widely accepted definition of a refugee, and in its various articles laid down the norms for the treatment of refugees.

Since the 1951 Convention related only to those displaced as a result of the Second World War, in 1967 the international community agreed the 1967 Protocol to extend the terms of the 1951 Convention to cover all refugees all over the world. It is these three instruments and the norms that they establish that still govern the treatment of refugees, by all signatory states.

The Convention spells out the kind of legal protection, other assistance and social rights a refugee should receive from states that are parties to the document. Their entitlement 'should be at least equivalent to freedoms enjoyed by foreign nationals living legally in a given country and in many cases to those of citizens of that state'.[7] Article 3 forbids states from discriminating against refugees on grounds of their race, religion or country of origin. The Convention demands that states should grant refugees the same rights as citizens in property matters (article 13), intellectual property rights (article 14), employment (article 17), self-employment (article 18), education (article 22) and public assistance (article 23). It also enjoins states to consider questions of family unity when granting asylum, and urges them to allow refugees to naturalise and become citizens as easily as possible. The Convention also outlines the refugees' obligations to the host state, which include compliance with all its laws and procedures.

Today much of the work of supporting and protecting refugees is carried out by the UNHCR, with the help of countries that are hosts to refugees, and other organisations. It is the primary United Nations agency concerned with refugees, and the norms it follows are based on the Convention, as well as on customs and practices used in practical situations on the ground. The role of the UNHCR varies from country to country. In third world countries, it may take the major burden of looking after refugees, from providing temporary accommodation, blankets, clean water, sanitation, food and medicine, and even education and training for long-standing refugees. This is particularly so when large numbers take refuge in a neighbouring country, in a relatively short space of time, to escape war or ethnic violence or famine. In industrialised countries its role is smaller, and it may simply be involved in assessing claims for refugee status on behalf of the potential host country. UNHCR is also involved in the process of repatriation of refugees to their home countries, and monitoring their safety in that environment. In general terms the UNHCR also bears some responsibility for monitoring the treatment of refugees and ensuring that signatory states act in accordance with the principles expressed in the instruments and documents they have signed up to. However, this must be done through diplomacy, discussion and moral and public pressure as there is no enforcement mechanism on which UNHCR can rely to force compliance from states.

---

**Box 4.1  The Office of United Nations High Commissioner for Refugees**

The Office of the United Nations High Commissioner for Refugees (UNHCR) was established on December 14, 1950 by the United Nations General Assembly. It is the leading humanitarian international agency charged with the care and protection of refugees worldwide. Its primary purpose is to safeguard the rights and well-being of refugees, enabling them to restart life elsewhere. It has offices in more than 120 countries and a budget in excess of one billion dollars annually.

The agency provides emergency relief in the form of housing, food, clean water and medical care to those displaced from their homes by conflict and persecution. It also helps in the resettlement and integration of refugees in their countries of asylum, and deals with repatriation of refugees back to their home country if circumstances permit. UNHCR monitors states' compliance with the 1951 Convention, and tries to ensure that refugees are treated in accordance with its terms. UNHCR assists not only refugees, but also asylum seekers and people displaced within their own countries.

UNHCR works with other UN agencies, organisations like the Red Cross and Red Crescent Societies, other governmental and non-governmental organisations to provide care and protection to refugees in all parts of the world. It acts as the conscience of the world on the treatment of refugees, and has twice been awarded the Nobel Peace Prize for its contribution.

---

It must be noted that none of these Declarations, Conventions, norms or practices actually guarantees anyone the right to asylum, only the right to seek it. The importance attached to sovereignty in the international system has meant that states must, in the final analysis be free to chose whom they will allow entry to their territory, and on what terms. Thus, the question of

whether someone is a refugee and should be treated as such by a state becomes an issue to be decided by the government and the courts of the country
in which refuge was sought. Nevertheless, these Declarations and Conventions form an important part of the international consensus on the treatment
of refugees, and they lay down an important universal principle that most
countries have come to endorse: that people who have a well-founded fear of
persecution have a right to leave their country, have international status, and
cannot be forcibly returned to their country of origin.

### How receiving states respond to refugees

Just as the creation of refugee flows is largely a product of states' domestic
and foreign policy objectives, so too the response to involuntary international
migration is also largely decided by the foreign and domestic concerns of
receiving governments. For a refugee to be accepted as such is a political
decision, and does depend to some extent on the relationship between the
sending and receiving countries. For instance, in the 1980s, the US Government
would not grant refugee status to Salvadorians fleeing civil war because to do
so would be to accept that a friendly government was indulging in human
rights abuse. Nicaraguans on the other hand were easily accepted as refugees
because of US opposition to the Sandinistas. Further it is worth noting that in
the period 1952–80, a refugee was defined in the US by the McCarran-Walter Act
(1952), as a person fleeing Communist persecution (Teitelbaum, 1980: 24).

The collapse of Communism has had a dramatic impact on Western governments' attitudes towards refugees. During the Cold War, when the Soviet
Union and its allies restricted emigration, the West's willingness to offer asylum and refuge to those who did manage to escape from the Communist
countries, was a weapon, albeit a small one, in its armoury. It reinforced the
belief that communist repression was worth resisting, and that those escaping such repression were worth assisting. With the removal of the Communist threat, which had dominated Western thinking for nearly half a century,
the commitment of Western countries to the concept of asylum collapsed.
Asylum, it appeared, depended upon the continued existence of a common
enemy confronted simultaneously by the refugee and the West.

If the government of the receiving country is happy to accept the refugees
into its territory, as for instance, the Indian and Pakistani governments were
during the population transfer that accompanied partition and independence,
such movements are not likely to become a source of conflict. When a government becomes unwilling host to a large refugee population, it is likely to
take steps to ensure that the stay of the refugees is temporary, and there is
every potential for conflict between sending and receiving countries in these
cases. The flow of East Pakistanis into India in the early 1970s and the movement of Afghans from their country to Pakistan in the 1980s are examples of

the latter situation. The receiving state will try to bring about a change in the policies of the sending country that led to the exodus, or failing that, try to bring about a change of government there.

One of the most widely used ways of doing this is to threaten to arm, or to actually arm, the refugees. Such a course of action has been taken up by various Arab governments towards the Palestinians, by the Pakistanis towards the Afghans, the Indians towards the Sri Lankan Tamils, the Americans to the Nicaraguan contras, and with the most far-reaching consequences by the Indians towards the East Pakistanis, resulting in the formation of Bangladesh. This strategy is not without risk. By strengthening a refugee group, the receiving country takes the chance that it will lose its ability to deal independently with the sending country, and that refugees will shape the host country's policies toward the sending country. This has happened to the Arab governments who have supported the Palestinians, the Pakistanis who supported the Afghan Mujahidin and later the Taleban, and to the Indians who supported the Tamils in Sri Lanka. Another response to a large refugee outflow is to directly intervene militarily to bring about regime change in the refugee producing country, as NATO did with its action in Kosovo, which ultimately led to the demise of the Milosevic Government in Yugoslavia.

The internal impact of refugee flows on the receiving country can be significant. In economic terms, refugees can be an immense burden to already troubled states, and in the short term they can cause quite serious distortions in the markets of the receiving countries, particularly with regard to escalating the prices of essential commodities. This is what happened in Iran in the aftermath of the Gulf War, when Kurdish and Shia refugees flocked into that country. In the long term, a third world country generally has to rely on the international community, usually through the offices of UNHCR to alleviate the burden on the economy, but is susceptible to the internal political tensions that difficult economic situations bring.

Long-term refugees can bring about changes in the society of the host country. In particular cases these can be dramatic, for example Pakistan's problems with increased drug addiction among its population, as well as the threats to law and order posed by the flourishing arms bazaars in Peshawar and elsewhere (what has been described as the 'Kalashnikov culture') are laid at the door of their Afghan guests. Large numbers of refugees can also be a driving force for change within the receiving country, particularly if they are ethnically similar to their hosts, or speak a common language. It was the fear that the Palestinians, who appeared to the rulers of Gulf States to be a potential threat to their traditional authoritarian culture, would have exactly this effect in the Gulf sheikdoms that has led these countries to import their labour needs from more distant countries with dissimilar people rather than allow large influxes of Palestinian refugees. The large Palestinian presence in Lebanon certainly contributed towards the destabilisation of that country.

In the long term, and certainly in democracies, it has become clear that once refugee (and other) migration takes place, whether intended to be permanent or temporary, it almost inevitably results in at least some refugees ultimately becoming citizens of the host country, and creating a cultural, linguistic, religious and possibly a racially distinct minority within the state. The existence of these communities has a substantial impact on social stability, economic prosperity and the internal politics of receiving states as well as on their relationship with the countries from where these communities originate.

Since September 11, the increased threat of terrorism has led to a particular concern regarding refugees. They are now perceived as constituting a possible 'fifth column' and thus a terrorist threat to states. Refugees from Muslim countries in particular, are regarded as a potential threat to Western states, and in response many states have stepped up the security vetting of asylum seekers, as well as taking other steps such as detention of some asylum seekers. The grounds for such a perception are arguably shaky as experience so far suggests that potential terrorists are more likely to use student or tourist visas to gain access to Western countries, as the 9/11 bombers did, rather than draw attention to themselves through entry as asylum seekers.

The preoccupation with the war against terror has only served to exacerbate an increasing hostility to asylum seekers in Western and particularly European countries, many of whom have substantial Muslim populations of immigrant origin. It has contributed to the post-Cold War drive to tighten the interpretation of 'refugee' and operate an ever-stricter regime for dealing with asylum seekers in these countries. The laws of asylum being what they are, states have considerable leeway in deciding whether people qualify for refugee status or not. The advanced industrial nations have come to stricter and stricter interpretations of these laws to enable them to minimise the number of people (mostly from third world countries) to whom they will grant refugee status. For instance, in 1998, only 11 per cent of asylum applicants in Europe were recognised as refugees under the 1951 Convention definition.[8]

The experience and response of successive British governments to increasing asylum applications since the beginning of the 1990s serves to make this point. Britain has been receiving growing numbers of asylum seekers since the early 1990s and as numbers have increased, the issue of asylum has become a highly politicised one. Currently, controlling the demand for asylum and reforming the processes in place to assess claims must rank as one of the major priorities of government. The impetus for this comes, at least in part, from spiralling numbers, the alarmist and negative attitude of the British tabloid press, domestic public opinion and the resurgence of the Right across Europe. The increasing cost of and length of time taken to assess claims for asylum and of supporting asylum seekers while assessments of their cases are made, is also a cause of concern.

Table 4.4 *Asylum applications submitted in selected industrialised countries in 2001 (Countries with more than 10,000 applications)*

| Country of asylum | Main countries of origin | Total asylum applications |
|---|---|---|
| United Kingdom | Afghanistan/Iraq/Somalia/ Sri Lanka/Yugoslavia | 88,300 |
| Germany | Iraq/Turkey/Yugoslavia/ Afghanistan/Russian Fed | 88,290 |
| United States | Mexico/China/Colombia/Haiti/ Armenia | 86,180 |
| France | Turkey/DRC/China/Mali/Algeria | 47,290 |
| Canada | Hungary/Pakistan/Sri Lanka/ Zimbabwe/China | 44,040 |
| Netherlands | Angola/Afghanistan/Sierra Leone/ Iran/Guinea | 32,580 |
| Austria | Afghanistan/Iraq/Turkey/India/ Yugoslavia | 30,140 |
| Belgium | Russian Fed/Yugoslavia/Algeria/ DRC/Iran | 24,550 |
| Sweden | Iraq/Yugoslavia/Bosnia-Herzegovina/Russian Fed/Iran | 23,520 |
| Switzerland | Yugoslavia/Turkey/Bosnia-Herzegovina/Iraq/FYR Macedonia | 20,630 |
| Czech Republic | Ukraine/Moldova/Romania/ Vietnam/India | 18,090 |
| Norway | Russian Fed/Croatia/Somalia/ Iraq/Ukraine | 14,780 |
| Denmark | Afghanistan/Iraq/Bosnia-Herzegovina/Yugoslavia/Somalia | 12,400 |
| Australia | Afghanistan/Iraq/China/ Indonesia/Fiji 12,370 | |
| Ireland | Nigeria/Romania/Moldova/Ukraine/ Russian Fed | 10,330 |

*Source: UNHCR website.*

**Table 4.5** *Number of asylum seekers arriving in the UK annually, 1990–2002*

| Year | Asylum applications |
| --- | --- |
| 1990 | 26,205 |
| 1991 | 44,840 |
| 1992 | 26,605 |
| 1993 | 22,370 |
| 1994 | 32,830 |
| 1995 | 43,965 |
| 1996 | 29,640 |
| 1997 | 32,500 |
| 1998 | 46,015 |
| 1999 | 71,160 |
| 2000 | 80,315 |
| 2001 | 71,365 |
| 2002 | 85,685 |

*Source: Home Office.*

The first element of the British government's decade-long attempt to reduce the number of asylum seekers involves trying to restrict the numbers arriving by creating obstacles to travel to this country. The imposition of visa requirements on nationals of countries producing the most refugees is a means to this end, as are measures put in place by the Immigration (Carriers Liability) Act 1987 and the Immigration and Asylum Act 1999. Airlines, ferry companies, train companies, coach operators and lorry drivers are fined £2000 for every passenger they carry who arrives without valid passport and visa.

The second element of the strategy involves making the experience of asylum applicants in the UK unattractive enough to deter others, through the use of detention, cutting eligibility for support, reducing levels of financial support, forcibly dispersing refugees to accommodation in areas of the country where they have limited or no access to community support and shortening the appeals process against unfavourable decisions regarding refugee status. The Immigrations, Nationality and Asylum Act 2002 in the UK makes plain the Government's intention to hold all asylum seekers in special centres until their cases are decided, not to permit them to work and to segregate them from the general populace by providing separate educational and medical facilities for asylum seekers and their children. Many of these actions bring the UK government perilously close to, if not in actual breach of, their obligations under the 1951 Convention, but domestic political compulsions are so strong that the government appears to be willing to take that risk.

The UK experience is not unique. The German government also responded with a comprehensive overhaul of its immigration and nationality laws in the face of huge immigration pressures from Germanic and other peoples from across Eastern Europe and the erstwhile Soviet Union, after the end of the Cold War. Several other European states have faced similar pressures, and responded with generally similar policies to restrict entry, to limit recognition of refugees and return people to so-called safe countries.[9] Denmark, for instance has created an extremely restrictive regime for dealing with asylum seekers, who are to be held in centres while their claims are processed, are not allowed to work, can only receive half the level of public assistance received by citizens, cannot marry while their claims are being heard and will have to wait seven years to acquire full Danish citizenship even if their claims to refugee status are accepted. Similar restrictive rules are coming into effect in other European countries like the Netherlands, France and Sweden.

Many European countries have seen a resurgence of the extreme right in politics as a consequence of public fear and unease about immigration and asylum. The rise of Neo-nazis in Germany, Le Pen in France, Jorg Haider in Austria, Pim Fortuyn in the Netherlands and the British National Party in the United Kingdom are all examples of the domestic political forces pushing European governments to take an increasingly hard line on asylum.

These immigration pressures have also prompted collective action from Western European countries. European Union states have tried to move towards a process of harmonisation of their refugee and immigration policies. This has proved a more difficult and slower process than they envisaged, but some fundamental agreements are now in place. The 1990 Dublin Convention (which came into effect in 1997) provided that an asylum seeker who has had his or her application rejected in one European country cannot seek asylum elsewhere in the European Union. Thus rejection by one member state is to be seen as a rejection by the European Community as a whole.

Most European Union states (with the exception of Ireland and the UK) have collaborated on developing a common visa and immigration policy, the Schengen Agreement, which harmonises rules for visa requirements, travel within the EU, and removes intra-European travel barriers. It also establishes a system of increased cooperation and information sharing between police and immigration authorities of member states, enabling states to cooperate on dealing with illegal immigrants, drug and people traffickers and security threats.[10] The Amsterdam Treaty of the EU also commits member states to striving towards developing a single European Refugee and Migration policy.

## Conclusion

Until the world is free of repression, conflict, political instability and economic inequality it is likely that refugee movements will continue. In an increasingly globalised world, with easy access to information, instant communication and cheaper travel the numbers of people on the move can only increase. However, it should not be thought that large-scale movements of people are a new phenomenon, rather they are a feature of human existence and have been intensified by 'industrialisation, colonialism, the emergence of nation states and the development of the capitalist world market' (Castles and Miller, 1997: 260). Refugee movements have always been a significant aspect of migratory movements in general.

The movements of refugees cast light on the divided nature of the contemporary world. In a larger part of the world – most of Africa, Latin America, and Asia – there is instability, violence, conflict and poverty to the extent that the protection of human rights in these areas is precarious and tenuous at best (Castles and Davidson, 2000: 230–1). By contrast, in Europe and the USA and a few other areas including Japan, Australia and New Zealand, people enjoy prosperity and democracy. Such stark contrasts are a striking indictment of the present age and they contribute significantly to refugee movements.

The response of most receiving countries to these movements makes it clear that they view those escaping persecution, brutality and misery as an increasing problem. However, it can be argued that such movements, whether refugee or otherwise can have beneficial effects for both the migrants and the countries to which they go. The migrants benefit from better standards of living, and higher levels of security and freedom from persecution. The host countries get a much-needed injection of labour and skills, and the possibility of vibrant multicultural democratic political life. Yet most receiving countries have taken a negative attitude to refugee movements, and responded by further punishing these already deprived and damaged people. Many are now considering a re-examination of the 1951 Convention and the obligations it puts on them, as a possible solution to their current problems.

But this would be to treat the symptoms, rather than the underlying cause. If there is to be a real reduction in refugee numbers it must, in the final analysis, come from an improvement in the conditions of life in the third world. Refugee movements show that the rich Western countries cannot maintain their isolation from, and remain untouched by the deprivation and instability of the third world. They provide a powerful argument for the sensible and whole-hearted participation of the powerful West in the development, both economic and political, of the third world.

### Notes

1 Refugees by Numbers 2002 Edition at www.unhcr.ch.
2 Number of asylum applications in 30 most industrialised countries 1992–2002 at www.unhcr.ch.
3 Refugees by Numbers 2002 Edition at www.unhcr.ch.

4 Refugees by Numbers 2002 Edition at www.unhcr.ch.

5 1951 Convention full text on www.unhcr.ch.

6 Weiner, M., 'The Political Aspects of International Migration', paper presented at the International Studies Association and British International Studies Association Joint Conference, London, March 1989, pp. 8–11.

7 1951 Convention Relating to the Status of Refugees Q & A, www.unhcr.ch.

8 Lecture by Anne Bijleveld, Director of Europe Bureau, UNHCR, at Cicero Foundation Debate on European Migration and Refugee Policy, Paris, 10–11 June 1999. Full text at www.cicerofoundation.org/lectures/p4bijl.html.

9 Lecture by Anne Bijleveld, Director of Europe Bureau, UNHCR, at Cicero Foundation Debate on European Migration and Refugee Policy, Paris, June 10–11, 1999. Full text at www.cicerofoundation.org/lectures/p4bijl.html.

10 For more information on Schengen Treaty see http://europa.eu.int/scadplus/leg/en/lvb/l33020.htm.

## Bibliography

Castles, S. and Davidson, A. (2000), *Citizenship and Migration*, London: Macmillan.

Castles, S. and Kosack, G. (1985), *Immigrant Workers and the Class Structure in Western Europe*, second edition, London: Oxford University Press.

Castles, S. and Miller, M. (1997), *The Age of Migration: International Population Movements in the Modern World*, second edition, London: Macmillan.

Cesarani, David (1996), *Citizenship, Nationality and Migration in Europe*, London: Routledge.

Cohen, R. and Layton-Henry, Z. (1997), *The Politics of Migration*, London: Edward Elgar.

Collinson, Sarah (1993), *Beyond Borders; Western European Migration Policy Towards the 21st Century*, London: RIIA & Wyndham Place Trust.

Collinson, Sarah (1995), *Migration, Visa and Asylum Policies in Europe*, London: Wilton Park Paper 107, HMSO.

Dowty, Alan (1987), *Closed Borders*, New Haven, CT and London: Yale University Press.

Goodwin-Gill, G. (1983), *The Refugee in International Law*, Oxford University Press, Clarendon.

Gordenker, Leon (1987), *Refugees in International Politics*, New York: Columbia University Press.

Gurtov, M. (1989), *Open Borders: A Global-Humanist Approach to the Refugee Crisis*, paper presented at the International Studies Association and British International Studies Association Joint Conference, London, March.

Hammar, Thomas (ed.) (1985), *European Immigration Policy: A Comparative Study*, Cambridge: Cambridge University Press.

Kritz, M., Keely and Tomasci (1981), *Global Trends in Migration: Theory and Research on International Population Movements*, New York: The Center for Migration Studies.

Sheffer, Gabriel, (ed.) (1986), *Modern Diasporas in International Politics*, London: Croom-Helm.

Teitelbaum, M.S. (1980), 'Right Vs. Right: Immigration and Refugee Policy in the

United States', *Foreign Affairs*, Vol. 59, No. 1, Fall, pp. 21–59.

Weiner, Myron (1989), *The Political Aspects of International Migration*, paper presented at the International Studies Association and British International Studies Association Joint Conference, London, March.

Weiner, Myron (1995), *The Global Migration Crisis: Challenge to States and Human Rights*, New York: HarperCollins College Publishers.

Zolberg, A. (1981), 'International Migrations in Political Perspective', in Kritz, Keely and Tomasci, *Global trends in Migration: Theory and Research on International Population Movements.*

Zolberg, A., Suhrke, A. and Aguayo, S. (1989), *Escape from Violence*, New York: Oxford University Press.

## *Websites*

UNHCR Websites (www.unhcr.ch):

  1951 Convention Relating to the Status of Refugees (Full Text).

  1951 Convention Relating to the Status of Refugees Q & A.

  Refugees by Numbers 2002 Edition.

Cicero Foundation www.cicerofoundation.org/lectures/p4bijl.html.

European Union website on the Schengen Agreement: http://europa.eu.int/scadplus/leg/en/lvb/l33020.htm.

# 5

# Terrorism

*Jon Gorry*

'Vote with a bullet. Vote early, vote often.' (*Dion Zdunic*)

Few issues, if any, in the politics of the world today can command attention with the same sense of immediacy, horror and tragedy as the idea and practice of 'terrorism'. Perhaps no single issue can generate as much controversy, engender such raw emotion, and demand the same sensitivity of touch. But the deliberate employment of political violence or the threat of political violence by sub-state actors, state-sponsored groups and powerful states in the pursuit of strategic goals has long been a permanent feature of the international system. 'War,' according to the nineteenth-century Prussian general von Clausewitz, 'is politics by other means' and terror as a method of conducting asymmetrical or low-intensity warfare has pre-biblical roots. As a basic political idea terrorism has thus remained relatively stable but its tactics are changing rapidly. Modern technology presents new opportunities and capabilities. An attack involving chemical, biological, radiological or nuclear devices is now a possible, even plausible, weapon of cheap mass destruction.

Taking the first six months of 2003 as an example, this issue had already devastated the lives of hundreds of people in dozens of states. Thus Chechen separatists, seeking national independence from Russia, killed fifty-four people and injured three hundred when their truck bomb rammed a government building in Chechnya. Thirteen people were killed and twenty-four injured when the Abu Sayyaf Group (ASG), the most violent of the Islamic separatist groups, planted a bomb in a crowded market place in the southern Philippines. In Tel Aviv, Hizballah ('Party of God'), HAMAS ('Islamic Resistance Movement'), and Palestine Islamic Jihad (PIJ) killed forty-three and injured over two hundred with three separate suicide bombings in their continued bid to destroy the state of Israel. In Florence, after a gun battle on a crowded commuter train, Italian police captured two members of the neo-Marxist Red Brigade. In Chicago the leader of the World Church of the Creator, a white extremist hate group, was arrested for plotting to kill a District Judge. In Northern Ireland one example of Loyalist paramilitary internecine warfare saw the Ulster Volunteer Force (UVF) assassinate a senior figure in the Red Hand Commandos. And an Egyptian customs officer died of anthrax poisoning after opening a suitcase thought to be part of a bio-terrorism plot bound for Canada. Elsewhere, the People's Revolutionary Militia (PRM) bombed the Hilton Hotel in Quito to protest the Ecuadorian government's austerity measures. The Revolutionary Armed Forces of Columbia (FARC), the oldest, best equipped and effective of Latin America's Marxist insurgencies, planted car bombs and targeted electricity pylons and reservoirs.

All these randomly selected examples suggest the diversity and spread of contemporary terrorist action. From the streets of Belfast to the slums of Lima, from the beaches of Sri Lanka to the *barrios* of Bogota, the areas in which terrorists operate appear without limit. Yet a tentative typology to help inform the general nature of the issue can still be drawn. First, much terrorism should be seen to have recognisable but geographically limited objectives. These objectives are first and foremost *political* (usually separatist, nationalist, ideological, religious or a combination of each) even if they are at times poorly expressed or articulated. Most of the above examples support this observation (HAMAS, UVF, FARC etc.). Second, some terrorists' objectives are not geographically limited and their *modus operandi* naturally crosses national boundaries. In the 1970s the Baader-Meinhoff Group's (also known as Red Army Faction or RAF) call for worldwide Marxist-Leninism was the most obvious example; today it is the wealthy Saudi dissident Osama Bin Laden and his Al-Quaeda (Arabic for 'The Base') network with their desire for global Islamic revolution. Such objectives remain political. In generic terms nonetheless, as rightly expressed by UN General Secretary Kofi Annan, *all terrorism* is a 'global threat with global effects'. 9/11 stands as a testament to this final categorisation.

In the early hours of Tuesday September 11 2001 a handful of Islamic militants armed only with knives and a total confidence in the righteousness of their cause drove two Boeing 737 airliners into New York City's tallest buildings. The World Trade Centre's twin towers – a quarter of a mile high testament to the might of the United States – collapsed and over 3,000 people from fifty-one different countries lost their lives. President Bush declared the attack an act of war. From here the USA embarked on what CIA Director James Woolsey termed the 'fourth world war' (following the First and Second World Wars and the Cold War) – an open-ended struggle against 'terrorism'.

A basic objective here is to demonstrate that terrorism became a salient political issue long before the twin towers. Undoubtedly horrific and portentous though it was, 9/11 by the standards of history was novel but not without precedent. The US Department of State's own statistics confirm this. According to the latest available figures, in the year 2000, 423 terrorist incidents were recorded. This compares to a 'low' of less than 400 recorded in 1975, and a 'high' of almost 700 such incidents in 1987. Indeed from the early 1960s we have witnessed somewhat of a renewal of enthusiasm for violence as a means of achieving a wide range of political objectives. (The global incidence of terrorism has almost doubled in the 1980s and 1990s.) As a political event in and of itself September 11 was thus not 'new under the sun' but rather the latest, albeit the most high profile and possibly the most audacious, in a long line of similar attempts to violently subvert the power of the state.

This chapter is divided into three sections. The first sets to demonstrate how terrorism as a political issue can and should be contested in definitional and moral terms. The second considers the terrorists' own rationalisation of political violence and the theoretical issues raised by this. The chapter concludes with further classification and typology, final comment, information on extracts quoted and suggestions for further reading.

## Who is the terrorist? What is terrorism?

To call someone a 'terrorist' is to give immediate notice that his or her beliefs and actions are beyond the pale of reasonableness. To describe an act as terrorist communicates its demonic character and immediately consigns it to the bin of illegitimacy. But to use the word terrorism and describe particular behaviour as terrorist is also to prejudge what are no less than substantive moral considerations inextricably linked to judgements of the behaviour in question. Few words, ideas or actions have the power to elicit the same passion. Reviled by the majority, defended by a minority, the very terms are sure to elicit a response from any audience.

For many the word terrorist has become a trigger-term attributed to all types of illegal political activity. Thus the powerful – those who determine civic, cultural and political value – delegitimise opponents – those who would re-write history – through language. Support is rallied for one position over another. Language is hijacked for political purpose and one man's 'terrorist' becomes another's 'freedom fighter'. Little wonder that the terms are keenly contested and/or resented. Indeed rarely will an individual admit to being a 'terrorist' or to supporting 'terrorism'. The participants tend to prefer 'guerrilla', 'freedom fighter', 'partisan', 'revolutionary' or a similarly respectable adjective from the lexicon of 'legitimate' political violence, each with their positive connotations of justified struggle against an occupying power or oppressive regime.

The Irish Republican Army (IRA), for example, use the word 'activist' and 'active service' to describe what the British media would label as 'terrorist' or 'terrorist outrage'. Irish Republicans tend to put inverted commas around the word terrorist in their newspapers to create distance between the activities of other people and themselves. Accordingly *An Phoblacht* (Republican News) reports the US campaign of 'economic, political and military terrorism' against the people of Cuba, French 'environmental terrorism' in the South Pacific, and notes Britain supplies arms to the 'terrorist regime' of Indonesia. The very word 'terrorist' was in fact first used just as the militants would prefer it: to describe a state or government. Its first recorded usage was by the celebrated parliamentarian Edmund Burke to describe the French revolutionary regime of the 1790s. Language matters, and how we use and respond to language matters most of all. Scholars are called to be particularly circumspect in this regard, perhaps to be less emotional, more detached and more reasoned.

From a scholarly perspective, however, there is little agreement as to the question of how a 'terrorist' or 'terrorism' can or should be defined. Some commentators argue that it is only sub-state actors and not the state itself that should be considered a proponent of terrorism. Still others believe that 'we ought not to begin by defining terrorism as a bad thing' (Teichman, 1989: 607) because to do so is 'to decide a normative issue by definitional considerations' and 'end the discussion before it begins' (Valls, 2000: 67). The subject certainly resists stable definition. Such confusion perhaps makes it more reliable to first consider the *effects* and *consequences* of a particular act of political violence rather than attempt to reach an intellectually coherent, objective, consensual definition of what particular *cause* is terrorist or otherwise.

The BBC's News Guide advises reporters that 'the best general rule' is to use the term 'terrorist' when civilians are attacked and 'guerrilla' when the targets are members of the official security services. But the tools of this particular trade have always been limited by circumstance. The Semtex-loaded-car, so the participants like to argue, is simply the 'poor man's Cruise missile' and 'collateral damage' a necessary and unavoidable casualty of war. However, if one at least considers the targeting strategy of an organisation it does become more possible to suggest the level of legitimacy or illegitimacy that can or should be invested in that grouping. Notwithstanding the possibility that terror can be a tactic of actors other than 'terrorists', when a group's *raison d'être* is to forward a cause by targeting civilians that behaviour must at once become *de facto* terrorist under any reasonable definition. In this way we are able to accept that a liberal democracy may perpetuate acts of terror or even sponsor terror (e.g. the USA was convicted by the World Court of committing acts of terrorism against Nicaragua during the 1980s), but this does not a terrorist organisation make. Yet when a dictatorship is based on terror and the dictator's rule is consolidated by terror it must become terrorist in and by its very nature (e.g. Nazi Germany, Stalin's Soviet Union, Saddam Hussein's Iraq). And an organisation that seeks change by utilising political violence is not first and foremost a terrorist organisation until its *modus operandi* becomes illegitimate because of violence against civilian targets e.g. the African National Congress (ANC) under apartheid in South Africa.[1] Thus, contrary to Teichman, terrorism can always be rendered a bad thing but not all forms of political violence become 'terrorist' simply because of the ends pursued. Terrorists become terrorists by the means of prosecuting their struggle;

not by whether we care to agree with the legitimacy of the ends sought (an independent Ireland, Basque country, Islamic republic etc.). The end very rarely, if at all, can ever be justified by the means. Just ends are rendered unjust through unjust means. This approach is a positive way of advancing the debate and the events of September 11 help to clarify the point.

Three facts mark 9/11 as being unusually noteworthy in this regard. First, the sheer number of people killed. This event was easily the greatest single act of terrorism anywhere any time in terms of the number of lives taken.[2] Second, it was significant in terms of its ramifications. We are now living in a world in which the USA has declared 'open season' on all 'terrorist' organisations and state sponsors of terrorism (Bush's 'axis of evil' – Iraq, Iran, Syria, North Korea and Cuba).[3] Finally, it was remarkable in terms of the strategy or tactic utilised. For the first time a loaded passenger plane was used as a weapon of mass destruction. This fact alone has undoubtedly created a sea change in our sense of security and vulnerability to attack.

The majority of fair-minded people would have little trouble in regarding September 11 as an act of terrorism (even if they were to argue about the cause and identity of the perpetrators). The mainstream would subscribe to a similar model as that suggested in the UK Prevention of Terrorism Act 1976, s.14 and define 9/11 as terrorism because it constituted 'the use of violence for political ends [including] any use of violence for the purpose of putting the public, or any section of the public, in fear.' Yet Roger Scruton has observed that this methodology in fact conflates two quite distinct ideas. On the one hand, the idea that violence is used to achieve political goals and on the other, political violence in order to generate or manifest fear in the public. Scruton concludes that what remains primary is the nature of terrorism as political violence of a random and arbitrary nature (1982: 460).

On terms such as these the twin towers attack can be defined as nothing other than terrorist. It was a clear example because its destruction was arbitrary in the sense that ordinary civilians were targeted. The workers in the World Trade Centre cannot reasonably be constituted as 'legitimate' political targets or combatants in a state of war. The act served to generate fear and loathing in wide sections of the West particularly America. 9/11 encouraged the view that no one was safe; all men, women and children are potential victims of terrorism. The political success of the operation (from Bin Laden's perspective) also encouraged the idea that al-Quaeda is invincible and the public beyond protection. Here the image of the anonymous, merciless, bomb-throwing madman becomes a potent one for generating fear, insecurity, and a sense of helplessness. Such analysis leads naturally into a consideration of what could urge people to engage in acts of such seemingly senseless barbarity.

## What drives the terrorist?

The reasons that drive individuals and groups to embrace terrorism are as varied and diverse as the number of terrorist organisations and the people in them. Different groups support different causes and have different reasons for fighting. On a basic level all are rebelling against conventional society in seeking a personal self-determination that allows them to forward a particular philosophy. All want to be listened to and not ignored. The more interesting issue is how these same individuals rationalise their use of violence to realise such goals. There are generic motivations at play and these can be accessed by reference to the theory known as 'propaganda by deed'.

The intellectual antecedents of 'propaganda by deed' are to be found among the nineteenth-century anti-state theorists writing at a time of revolutionary upheaval in the aftermath of the failed Paris Commune of 1871. Two Italian anarchists stand out in particular. The first, Carlo Piscine, wrote: 'The propaganda of the idea is a chimera. Ideas result from deeds, not the latter from the former, and the people will not be free when they are educated, but educated when they are free.' The second, Erico Malatesta who noted that successful revolution will always 'consist more of deeds than words'. To these sentiments may be added Marx's dictum that: 'The philosophers have only interpreted the world, in various ways; the point is to change it.' The belief underlying such sentiments is the notion that action always speaks louder than words, demonstrations are more effective than propaganda and ultimately 'war, war better than jaw, jaw'.

Political violence is adopted and designed to have a positive rather than negative impact on public opinion. It shows that a group or movement does not merely 'talk' but rather 'means business'. In other words, violent acts are used simply because they are rationalised as having more political effect than any amount of verbal argument. As a rule the perpetrators of such acts do not claim (at least rhetorically) that they seek political power for themselves. They see themselves as pioneers paving the way for others to follow. Their task is to act as a 'revolutionary vanguard' kick-starting a lethargic population to 'true consciousness'. Planting bombs and assassinating officials is supposed to coerce people into sitting up and listening. A radical violence that risks the terrorist's life – or creates martyrs in the case of suicide bombers – provides additional confirmation as to the righteousness of the cause and (theoretically) induces more people to join up. 'Propaganda by deed' is thus a form of political communication that seeks to connect at a level deeper than words the conviction that change is desirable, necessary *and* of course always possible.

Propaganda by deed constitutes both justification and strategy. Armed action is a signal of intent and a means of disrupting government. Because these struggles for 'hearts and mind' are protracted and the control mechanisms of the modern state so resilient, political violence is seen as a way of hastening political change. The assassination of state representatives undermines law and order while demonstrating the vulnerability of the rulers. The upsetting of public order by violent means, irrespective of the degree to which this is achieved or desired, aims at bringing the state's very legitimacy into question. The more 'successful' a bombing campaign the less capable a government is seen at protecting its citizens. Political violence demoralises the state (especially its officials and judiciary) to a point where the entire system is brought to the brink of collapse. The state's anti-terrorist measures, so the traditional argument goes, will push even a stable democracy into authoritarianism and so 'militarise' the situation. From there civil war occurs, driving even more support in the movement's direction. Violent struggle brings a state to a point of collapse more quickly than would otherwise be possible.

Recourse to lethal means is seen as legitimate 'counter-violence' in order to avenge the institutional or structural violence inherent within wealthy, well-organised and powerful states. 'Anti-system' violence thus exposes and challenges the violence that underlies and sustains state power. In these ways political violence is used to ignite the sympathy of the people. It becomes a symbolic act that energises the participants while having an emotionally galvanising impact on the citizenry. The liberation of society depends on smashing the current system in order to emancipate humanity from its 'false consciousness'. Violence is both the means to liberate 'old society' and an essential agent in the revitalisation of the 'new'.

The specific reasons behind the post-war (re)emergence of terrorism as a significant political issue are instructive. Paradoxically, the pacification of Europe in the late 1940s (particularly the early policy of détente between the superpowers) nurtured the conditions in which marginal political movements with extremist objectives could flourish on the fringes. As the Cold War escalated ideological differences became increasingly polarised encouraging people to take sides between Left and Right. France's near revolution of May 1968 and the Vietnam War (US involvement 1961–75) triggered the rise in support for many ideologically driven sub-state movements with violent agendas. Groups such as Britain's anarchist Angry Brigades, Italy's Red Brigades and their neo-fascist counterparts, West Germany's RAF and France's Maoist-inspired Action Direct all trace their roots to this time. The uneven nature of wealth distribution following post-war reconstruction created the pre-conditions in which, on one hand, middle-class idealists felt it necessary to question in political terms the 'new' moral, social, and economic order. And on the other hand, the working class became increasingly dissatisfied with their economic conditions and the growing gap between rich and poor, those who had and those who had not. In the case of recently established movements the use of violence in order to destroy existing liberal democracies was seen as necessary precondition for the creation and emergence of an equitable order.

During the Cold War period centuries old frictions within and between societies were overlooked or neglected. Regional and ethnic conflicts took second place to worldwide ideological confrontation. In the case of the older (pre-war) nationalist movements, such as Basque Fatherland and Liberty (ETA) and the IRA, the 'brave new world' was seen as illegitimate because it failed to address minority needs while cutting across unwritten legal and political traditions, customs, and norms of behaviour. In this light recourse to political violence against 'new tyranny' became a sacred duty or an 'ethic of responsibility'.

Arblaster (1977) has challenged several common misconceptions as to the motivation for terrorist activity. This is useful because it is often easier to determine what something is not, rather than what it is. He notes a number of common theoretical misunderstandings about the motivations of terrorists: that all terrorists are revolutionary or radical left-wingers; that terror groups always direct action against their own state or its agents; and that all terrorists are simply criminals and all terrorist activity criminal. Arblaster seems to be on solid ground with his first two observations: Osama bin Laden is not Marxist or left wing, and as an ostensibly Arab grouping, Al-Quaeda does not operate within its host country. But his final point of contention demands closer scrutiny.

There are generally four different positions held by people who argue the 'criminality of the terrorist' thesis. This theory concentrates on developing the essential notion that terrorism is a crime no different from murder. The political element is thus unimportant in categorisation. This is seen to be so because: first, terrorism involves the indiscriminate taking of life; second, the unjustified taking of life; third, the murder of innocent bystanders. And finally because the murder is committed by psychopathic personalities. All these assertions point to the proposition that terrorism is criminal precisely because it denies basic principles of decent civil society.[4]

We can certainly observe some terrorist incidents as indiscriminate but must also concede that other incidents are of a more discriminate nature. The destruction of the twin towers may have involved the indiscriminate taking of civilian life but assassination attempts on the Pope, several US Presidents, or even the British Cabinet in conference at Brighton were specific political acts on specific political targets. Indeed Anti-Tsarist elements in late nineteenth-century Russia, for example, would not 'attack' if the loss of innocent or illegitimate lives were possible. In the modern Middle East, Hizballah claim to target Israel's soldiers not her citizens. Such evidence suggests that some organisations do not target the public at large and so it could be claimed that their intention is not to engender widespread fear. This is precisely so because their targets and aims are more precise and specifically political. However there is also the argument that an attack on democratically elected figures, for example Thatcher's Cabinet, constitutes an attack on democracy or all of us. But it is possible to counter this by suggesting that political figures must take greater responsibility for state actions, and thus become more legitimate targets, than the average citizen. The point remains good: not all terrorist behaviour is indiscriminate.

When considering whether terrorism is nothing other than murder we are forced to consider whether a terrorist is able to justify his or her actions. Many terrorist campaigns are 'justified' as part of a wider nationalist struggle (e.g. the IRA or ETA) and orthodox or conventional political campaigning often runs parallel to a terrorist campaign. Moreover the issue of justification is rendered redundant or superfluous once the terrorists gain power. For example, the ANC were classified as murderous terrorists by the Apartheid state until they themselves became the government of South Africa and were thence hailed as heroes and 'freedom fighters'. It may be a cliché but it is clear that history has taught us again and again that yesterday's terrorist is today's statesman. Justification, in other words, is always relative to time and place.

The third point that needs to be considered is the idea that terrorists are criminals because they always murder innocent people. We are compelled to ask, in this context, who is innocent? Who or what, therefore, constitutes a legitimate target and who or what should be considered an illegitimate target? On one hand, this means establishing the level of innocence invested in the average citizen in the street, the innocence of the bystander, and on the other hand, distinguishing between the moral culpability and the moral responsibility of the rulers of a particular state. This is so because, as suggested above, we surely cannot judge the murder of despotic tyrants (tyranicide) in the same light as say the murder of everyday workers in New York. This is very important. There are two ways of unravelling such a Gordian knot.

First, we can simply conclude that terrorism is a form of murder if it involves the random killing of individuals with no direct responsibility for government or the security services. The problem with this is that the terrorist is able to retort that in a liberal democracy we are all morally culpable (at least indirectly) for our ruler's actions because we voted for them in the first place. Such conclusion also requires us to distinguish terrorism from other forms of warfare. This is because all war involves the taking of civilian lives. The Second World War for example saw millions of innocent people killed. Hundreds of thousands were lost in the nuclear strikes on Hiroshima and Nagasaki alone. Unless we are to argue that all war is terrorist (or terrorism is not war) we are forced to accept that both as a political practice and as a political issue all war can involve acts of terror whether that war is just or unjust. 'Collateral damage' is not limited to low-intensity conflict alone. As a political act whose consequences entails the death of bystanders terrorism is not unique and cannot be understood purely by reference to those killed. This is how the BBC-inspired argument above works. There is a good case to be made in favour of distinguishing between deliberate and non-deliberate, tactical and accidental targeting of civilians. If a civilian dies as a result of political action it does not make that action necessarily terrorist. In other words, there has to be a qualitative difference between a civilian shot in cross-fire during an encounter between an active service unit and the security forces, and a civilian being blown to pieces while shopping due to a bomb in the rubbish bin on a Saturday afternoon.

An alternative way of looking at this problem begins by first accepting that a civilian bystander is less responsible (i.e. more innocent, less of a legitimate target) than a politician, soldier or policeman. From here it is possible to decide whether a particular Government's actions invite violent response. If a state's behaviour involves the creation of great human misery, some may legitimately see recourse to violence as a legitimate option. Violence constitutes the lesser of two evils for those who would seek to change the views of those responsible for the creation of misery. If this position is to be upheld it is necessary to make a further distinction: one between the moral legitimacy (claim of innocence?) of different governments and regimes. This amounts to a distinction between just and legitimate regimes that may be liberal democratic, and unjust or illegitimate regimes that may be authoritarian or oppressive. If we are able to produce such a distinction we can then argue that the legitimacy of political violence rests on the character of the target regime. For example, many would agree that Nelson Mandela was not a terrorist but rather a freedom fighter because many South Africans saw little alternative to violence in opposing apartheid. The same may be said of Yasser Arafat and the claim of the Palestinian Liberation Organisation (PLO). However many would similarly argue that Loyalist or Republican violence in Northern Ireland is indeed terrorism rather than freedom fighting because the use of such violence is not so readily justified in a functioning liberal democracy. This is precisely because a liberal democratic government enjoys a wide degree of legitimacy on behalf of its citizens. It is generally understood that political conflict can be hammered out via the ballot box or judicial means. The very fact that there is regular voting is supposed to put a restraint on non-legal violence. By this logic an attack on the political leaders of a democratic state could be seen as an attack on the essence of the democratic process, the institutions embodied therein, and all citizens native to that country. An attack on an unjust, illegitimate tyrant who rules by force and coercion appears qualitatively different (i.e. more morally legitimate). From this perspective one could also suggest the murder of a tyrant would save lives (i.e. be the lesser of two evils). For example, the assassination of Hitler in 1939 would have saved the lives of millions and hence averted a greater evil from occurring. Yet one could perhaps retort that the policy of an oppressive regime is rarely dependent on one person – and who should be killed or who is responsible is not as straight-forward as one would like it to be (as demonstrated in the Nuremberg trial of Nazi leaders in 1945). This last argument, however, does not engender much support in the academy because of its reliance on hindsight.

The final element that constitutes the 'criminality of terrorism' thesis concerns the psychology of the terrorist. Are all terrorists really psychotic? Is terrorism caused by a mental disorder, or rather by an exceptional degree of political fanaticism? Readers would probably agree that explanations for terrorism are more likely to be found in a study of socio-economics and political commitments than in individual psychology. Some academics, however argue that terrorists must be deranged; that terrorists suffer from inadequate personalities and that they are mostly inadequate or rootless people. Yet this explanation does not satisfactorily give an answer to why such people engage in terrorism and not just violent crime. An element of 'political' purpose must be significant. Indeed such political purpose has to be the best way to distinguish terrorist groups from organised crime syndicates like the Mafia or the Colombian Drug cartels.

### Typology of terror and conclusion

Terrorism as a political issue and political practice has probably existed since humans began organising themselves politically. There are consequently many different ways of classifying terrorist groups and movements. Objectives, strategy, tactics, weapons, funding, effectiveness and so on, can all be used to compare or differentiate. Yet the way many authors assess these groups is not necessarily helpful. Not all classification advances understanding. Pre-1945 revolution has, however, had a massive impact on the form and structure of modern political violence. Two revolutions in particular stand out as being worthy of special mention: the eighteenth-century French and twentieth-century Russian Revolutions. It is useful to locate the modern roots of political violence in the context of these revolutions because they serve as important precursors and key reference points for the legitimisation of much modern political violence.

The French Revolution and its attempt to impose Enlightenment by force was a decisive turning point in the development of political violence. On one hand the vigorous French assertion of 'liberty, equality, and fraternity' (coupled with liberal ideas of self-government and nationalism) served as a lasting inspiration and a symbol of struggles for self-determination in all quarters of the globe. And on the other hand French attempts to impose their ideals by force caused widespread resentment and resistance both below the state and across state frontiers. Either way the French Revolution, by destroying the old regime by force, was a great catalyst for change. Moreover the 'reign of terror' attributed to the French Revolutionary regime in place broadly speaking between March 1793 and July 1794 is also identified by Edmund Burke and others as the first modern example of state-inflicted terrorism. However no single event, notwithstanding the French Revolution, has had such a decisive impact on the course of modern political violence as the 1917 Russian Revolution. The Russian

Revolution inaugurated the age of twentieth-century revolution and served as a symbol and point of reference for not only Marxists but also revolutionaries of all shades particularly in the anti-colonial struggles post-1945.

These revolutions have, in turn, left three categories with which we can distinguish between types of terrorist activity. First, state terror or a terrorism 'from above'. This is where governments and their agents employ terrorist methods against their own citizens. Since 1917 state terror has been practised widely by Russian, German, and British governments among others. The Black 'n' Tans are one particularly well-known example. This specially re-cruited auxiliary 'terror' force was sent to Ireland in 1921 by the British Government to combat support for Sinn Fein. Second, state-sponsored terror or terrorism 'across borders'. In other words, where governments in one country sponsor the violent subversion of other countries. As an example the CIA's efforts to subvert the Central American countries of Guatemala, Nicaragua, and El Salvador with personnel, arms and financing are well catalogued. Fi-nally, sub-state terror or a terrorism 'from below' where small groups organ-ise and pursue political violence of a lethal nature. Chomsky (1989, 2001) calls this 'retail terrorism' for it is the terrorism we most hear about and it is what most people think of and label as terrorism. In short, the terrorism of Al Quaida, the IRA, ETA, HAMAS, FARC etc.

Sixteen hundred years ago Saint Augustine, erstwhile bishop of the an-cient Numidian city of Hippo (present-day Annaba, Algeria), reported an en-counter between Alexander the Great and a captured pirate in his classic work *The City of God*. Alexander demanded: '"What is your idea, in infesting the sea?" And the pirate answered, with uninhibited insolence, "The same as yours, in infesting the earth! But because I do it with a tiny craft, I'm called a pirate: because you have a mighty navy, you're called an emperor"' (Augus-tine [1467] 1972: 139). Substitute a violent challenge to the state for pirate – a powerful state for emperor – and the saint's tale stands as an apocalyptic parable for one of the more relevant and pressing political issues in the world today.

Many academics have tried to offer definitions that help further our under-standing of what constitutes a terrorist, terrorism, or terrorist activity. It is undoubtedly a complex subject with no easy answers: all we can say with certainty is that all definitions are a product of varied academic backgrounds, perspectives, value judgements, and contrasting methodological standpoints. It is this very interplay of subjective factors and emotional response that makes the concepts difficult to define and approach. The concepts are slippery, much abused and their relationship with other forms of political violence and crimi-nal behaviour often ambiguous. Ultimately it is up to each of us as responsi-ble citizens to decide who is or isn't a terrorist. But these differences will remain ideological rather than semantic or etymological.

## Notes

1   Of course this is the rub of the argument and one that demands an act of faith in how we define 'legitimacy' and 'illegitimacy'. It is to say there has to be a qualitative difference between an organisation, though illegal and violent, conducting a campaign against an authority that prohibits alternative avenues of political protest (e.g. voting) and one whose recourse to violence is less circumspect. The classic example is the IRA ('Armalite' in one hand, 'Ballot Box' in the other) and the ANC (whose supporters, mostly black South Africans, were generally without the franchise).

2   In mortality terms, the next biggest outrage was the blowing up of an Air India flight over the Irish Sea in June 1985 where 329 lives were lost. More British lives were lost on September 11 than in any single Republican outrage.

3   9/11 is not unique as an act of terror that has led to war. The assassination of Crown Prince Franz Ferdinand, heir apparent to the Austro-Hungarian throne, on 28 June 1914 by a member of the Serbian 'Black Hand' led to the outbreak of the First World War in 1914. The attempted assassination of the Israeli Ambassador to London by Palestinians was given as reason behind Israel's invasion of the Lebanon in 1982.

4   The primary reason for the Republican 'hunger strikes' of the 1980s was Prime Minister Thatcher's determination to re-classify or down-grade IRA prisoners' special status. The British Government saw the prisoners as criminals while the Republicans saw themselves as 'prisoners of war' entitled to wear their own clothes (rather than prison-wear).

## Bibliography

Arblaster, M. (1977), 'Terrorism: Myths, Meanings and Morals', *Political Studies* Vol. 25, No. 3, pp. 5–24.

Augustine, S. [1467] (1972), *The City of God*, Harmondsworth: Penguin, p. 139.

Chalk, P. (1996), *West European Terrorism and Counter-Terrorism: The Evolving Dynamic*, Basingstoke: Macmillan.

Chomsky, N. (1989), *The Culture of Terrorism*, London: Pluto.

Chomsky, N. (2001), *9/11*, New York: Seven Stories Press.

Clutterbuck, R. (1994), *Terrorism in an Unstable World*, New York: Routledge.

Combs, C.C. (1997), *Terrorism in the Twenty-First Century*, London: Prentice-Hall.

Hoffman, B. (1999), *Inside Terrorism*, London: Indigo.

Kushner, H.H. (1998), *The Future of Terrorism: Violence in the New Millennium*, Thousand Oaks, CA: Sage.

Schmid, A.P. and Crelinstein, R.D. (eds) (1993), *Western Responses to Terrorism*, London: Cassell.

Scruton, R. (1982), *A Dictionary of Political Thought*, New York: Hill & Wang.

Stohl, M. (ed.) (1979), *The Politics of Terrorism: A Reader in Theory and Practice*, New York: Marcel Dekker.

Teichman, J. (1989), 'How to Define Terrorism', *Philosophy*, No. 64, pp. 605–17.

Thackrah, J.R. (1987), *Encyclopaedia of Terrorism and Political Violence*, London:

    Routledge & Kegan Paul.
Valls, A. (2000), 'Can Terrorism Be Justified?', in *Ethics in International Affairs*, Lanham,
    Rowman & Littlefield, pp. 65–79.
Valls, A. (ed.) (2000), *Ethics in International Affairs*, Lanham: Rowman & Littlefield.
Weinberg, L. (1989), *Introduction to Political Terrorism*, New York: McGraw-Hill.
Whittaker, D.J. (ed.) (2001), *The Terrorism Reader*, London: Routledge.
Wilkinson, P. (1977), *Terrorism and the Liberal State*, London: Macmillan.

# Part II
# Ethical and normative issues

# 6

# International morality

*David Morrice*

International morality is concerned with the moral evaluation of the behaviour of the various players in the international environment, including both states and non-state actors such as regional and international political organisations, transnational enterprises, and non-governmental organisations. Thus, the conduct of war, foreign policy and international trade are subject to moral evaluation. International morality is also concerned with the outcomes of processes in the international environment where the deliberate behaviour of organisations may be less apparent. Thus, the state of the world's natural environment, and the global distribution of resources are concerns of international morality.

The following questions illustrate the range of concerns of international morality.

- Is it the case (as the old adage has it) that all is fair in love and war? Are all wars immoral? Can there be a just war, which complies with moral standards indicating when it is proper to go to war and how it is proper to conduct war? Is nuclear deterrence, which involves a preparedness to bomb the civilian members of other states, morally justifiable?
- Do richer states have a moral obligation to help poorer states by, for example, giving aid, cancelling debt, or setting favourable trading terms?
- Should one state permit the sale of arms to another regardless of the use to which these are put? If there is evidence that the buying state is using the arms to terrorise some of its own citizens, should the sale of arms be halted?
- As pollution recognises no national boundaries, is a global authority required to deal with environmental issues? Should developed states seek to set limits on the environmentally damaging industrial growth of less developed states?
- Do states have an absolute right of self-determination, or can there be a moral justification for one or more states to intervene in the internal affairs

of another state to prevent an abuse of human rights?
- Do individuals have the right to move as they choose across state borders? Who is responsible, and to what extent, for the reception and welfare of refugees?

Moral thinking about the conduct of international relations is not new, but there has been in the past few years a marked increase in interest in the sorts of questions noted above. This may be attributed to a number of factors. Non-state actors such as Oxfam and Greenpeace have highlighted concerns about poverty and environmental damage across the globe. Globalisation has made people conscious of the interrelatedness of states and the worldwide impact of non-state actors. This in turn has brought to public attention the moral responsibilities of the various players in the global environment. The increase of international terrorism has sparked debate about the morality of such activity and the response of 'victim' states as they seek to deal with it, by, among other things, attacking foreign states thought to be sheltering terrorists. States have also adopted a moral stance on international issues which in the past have been treated as being free of moral significance. For example, Robin Cook, Foreign Secretary in the first New Labour British Government of 1997, declared his intention to pursue an 'ethical foreign policy'. This chapter seeks to outline the range of approaches to be found in international moral theory, and to consider the range of answers to the sorts of questions listed above.

### Types of normative international theory

There is a huge variety of opinion on international morality, but it is possible and convenient to distinguish three main sets of beliefs:

- realism, which doubts that morality has any part to play in international politics;
- communitarianism, which holds that communities, such as states and nations, are morally significant, and that moral principles apply within specific communities and between them only to the extent that they agree on this;
- cosmopolitanism, which holds that the whole world (cosmos) is a moral community, and that universal moral principles apply to all individuals, regardless of state and national boundaries.

Such a tripartite division of positions in international morality is not uncommon in the academic literature, although the precise identification of the three positions varies, and some wish to distinguish fewer or more positions (Beitz, 1999; Brown, 1992; Caney, 2001; Dower, 1998; Jones, 1999). An examination of the three positions identified will allow a consideration of their relationship and their worth in answering the sorts of moral questions already noted.

## Realism

Realism, like any other conceptual approach, represents and conceals a number of distinct and sometimes differing principles. However, for our purposes realism may be taken to mean the following:

- the main actors in the international environment are sovereign states;
- states are primarily concerned with the acquisition and maintenance of power as the means of preserving their security and pursuing their interests;
- moral values, which may be applicable in other spheres of life, are not applicable in politics; in so far as moral values are employed in politics they are masks of state self-interest.

These principles of realism may be illustrated with reference to a couple of classic political theorists who have been interpreted as realists. The renaissance scholar Niccolo Machiavelli, writing at a time of conflict between rival Italian city states, argues: 'when the safety of one's country wholly depends upon the decision to be taken, no attention should be paid either to justice or injustice, to kindness or to cruelty, or to its being praiseworthy or ignominious. On the contrary, every other consideration being set aside, that alternative should be whole-heartedly adopted which will save the life and freedom of one's country' (Machiavelli, 1970: 515). Here Machiavelli assumes that in international politics the survival of the state overrides all other concerns, including all moral concerns. Machiavelli argues for a distinction between the spheres of politics and morality, and holds that to do well in politics it may be necessary to forsake ordinary moral principles. He says: 'rulers who have done great things are those who have set little store by keeping their word, being skilful rather in cunningly confusing men; they have got the better of those who have relied on being trustworthy' (Machiavelli: 1988, 61).

Thomas Hobbes, writing at the time of the English Civil War in the seventeenth century, is considered to be another important realist. Hobbes characterises the natural condition of humanity, before the invention of politics, as a condition of war. Without a common authority to promulgate and execute laws, each individual has the right to make their own decisions about what is necessary for self-preservation. Hobbes acknowledges that such a condition of war may not have obtained for all, everywhere, but claims that in all times 'kings and persons of sovereign authority, because of their independency, are in continual jealousies, and in the state and posture of gladiators ... which is a posture of war' (Hobbes, 1991, 90). Independent sovereign states, with no common authority over them to maintain law, order and peace, make whatever decisions they feel necessary to defend themselves. In the absence of common, universal moral standards, states make subjective decisions about their self-preservation. For Hobbes, war consists not in actual fighting only, but in the known disposition thereto, and the causes of war are inherent in the supposed realities of human nature and the consequent state of nature.

Realism, as illustrated by the positions of Machiavelli and Hobbes, is vulnerable to a number of criticisms. First, realism is not amoral, dealing only with the facts of politics, but is, rather, a position which tends to contain a number of implicit moral assumptions, which are never substantiated by reasoning. For example, realism assumes that states have a right of self-preservation and that action to secure state integrity is good. Although he explicitly eschews moral considerations in politics, Machiavelli implicitly accepts the values of 'life and freedom'. Realism is thus inconsistent and contradictory.

Second, Jacques Maritain offers a sharp critique of the 'incurable division between politics and morality' articulated by Machiavelli, and the consequent 'illusory but deadly antinomy between what people call *idealism* (wrongly confused with ethics) and what people call *realism* (wrongly confused with politics)' (Maritain: 1953, 137). Maritain identifies a 'paradox' and an 'internal principle of instability' in Machiavellianism. The use of a supramoral art of politics, which assumes but abuses the moral values of citizens, will lead to the degeneration of their moral culture and practice. Continued deceit and trickery will lead eventually to the loss of citizens' trust in their state, to the point that it can no longer cynically exploit their trust. (Maritain, 1953: 141).

Third, the international environment is not as Hobbes depicts it. Cooperation between states, and non-state actors, is evident, and the modern world is not composed of separate, competing sovereign states, but is interdependent. Thus, states have learned to relate to one another in terms of mutually agreed values. The interdependence of the various actors in the international environment makes morality both necessary and possible.

### Communitarianism

Unlike realism, communitarianism does not deny the significance of morality in international affairs. Unlike cosmopolitanism, with its universal moral approach, communitarianism emphasises the moral significance of bounded communities, and so recognises limits to moral principles. Communitarians tend to argue that individuals are given moral identity by their communities; that the good of the community takes precedence over the individual goods; and that moral and political principles are embedded in, and limited to, specific communities (Morrice, 2000; Mulhall and Swift, 1996). In international affairs two types of bounded communities are significant and so worthy of consideration: states and nations.

## Morality of states

Hedley Bull, one of the great international theorists of the second half of the twentieth century, argues that the concept of a society of states, with the associated morality of states, occupies a space somewhere between the extremes of Hobbesian realism and cosmopolitanism (Bull, 1966: 37–9). Bull characterises the position as: 'co-operation among sovereign states in a society without government' (1966: 38). Bull acknowledges that the position is in part descriptive and in part prescriptive. The prescription covers the 'duties and rights attaching to states as members of international society'. (Bull, 1966, 39) Bull identifies the four main values of the morality of states as:

- the preservation of the society of states itself;
- the maintenance of the independence and external sovereignty of individual states;
- the maintenance and pursuit of peace (with the just war theory of when and how it is proper to wage war);
- the common goals of social life (security of person against violence; honouring promises and agreements; stability of possessions) (Bull, 1977: 15–21).

As in the realist model of international politics, national interest dominates the behaviour of states and the relations between them. But in the society of states model, states exist within a wider community, which takes on a distinctive moral framework for its members. That is, state self-interest may dictate that it is prudent to recognise the self-interest of other states and to maintain the international order, or society of states.

The morality of states position is vulnerable to a number of criticisms. First, it offers only a minimal response to the amoralism of realism. The position recognises the integrity of individual states in the making and adjudication of mutual agreements governing their interactions. But the position remains state-centric and fails to recognise the integrity of human beings, whose moral worth is not exhausted by their membership of a particular state. That which unites individuals as human beings may be morally more significant than that which divides them as citizens of particular, transitory states.

Second, the morality of states position enshrines the sovereignty and inviolability of states. This principle serves to defend states against perfectly proper moral judgement and remedial action. As Nigel Dower says: 'There are surely circumstances in which it is right for states, individually or collectively, to intervene in the internal affairs of other states, for instance over human rights violations' (Dower, 1998: 62).

Third, the notion that there can be no common moral purpose in international politics denies the need to take concerted action to deal with global moral problems. As Charles Beitz argues, the morality of states position stresses the autonomy of states and the security of the international community at the expense of issues of global distributive justice (Beitz, 1999: 181). Dower argues in similar vein: 'There are many issues especially to do with the environment which require the adoption of a common cause, well beyond what has traditionally been required. That is, for the sake of promoting or protecting a global common good, states ought to accept various forms of limitation to what they do' (Dower, 1998: 62).

### Nationalism

Nationalism is often seen as a sentimental, aggressive doctrine, which, although popular, is lacking intellectual justification. A number of contemporary theorists, of a generally liberal persuasion, have attempted a justification of it. Among these is David Miller, who offers a communitarian defence of nationalism. For Miller, 'Nationality is ... a powerful source of personal identity' (Miller, 1995: 68). He elaborates:

> nations are ethical communities. They are contour lines in the ethical landscape. The duties we owe to our fellow-nationals are different from, and more extensive than, the duties we owe to human beings as such. This is not to say that we owe *no* duties to humans as such; nor is it to deny that there may be other, perhaps smaller and more intense, communities to whose members we owe duties that are more stringent still. (1995: 11).

The particular rights and duties of nationality flow from a public culture, which is subject to change through debate and negotiation. That we have particularist, nationalist rights and duties is not to deny that we also have universalist rights and duties with regard to non-compatriots. Rather, we have other and additional, special rights and duties with regard to compatriots. Although Miller stresses the moral significance of distinct national communities, he does recognise the demands of international justice, involving 'a world in which nation-states are self-determining, but respect the self-determination of others through obligations of non-interference and in some cases aid' (Miller, 1995: 107).

Communitarian nationalism may represent a small advance on the older society of states approach in so far as the former is not limited to considerations of order and security. However, nationalism is not beyond criticism. First, Miller, and others, fail to explain what is so special about duties to nations and compatriots, given that nations are temporary, changeable constructs. Nationalism may remain the triumph of emotion over reason. As Onora O'Neill puts it: 'Why should the boundaries of states be viewed as the presuppositions of justice rather than as institutions whose justice is to be assessed?' (O'Neill, 2000: 4). Second, communitarianism renders all moral values relative to the communities in which they are shared. Thus, communitarianism cannot escape the profound problem of relativism, according to which all cross-community moral judgements are impossible and invalid. No community may properly criticise the values and practices of any other community, and no one may step outside of their particular community to form a universal and impartial moral perspective on an interdependent world. Third, communitarians fail to explain how one can render coherent all the various duties one might be said to hold to various communities. Perhaps it is necessary to recognise that although humans necessarily belong to various limited communities, it is their membership of the single universal community of humanity which gives them their unique moral identity.

### Cosmopolitanism

Cosmopolitanism holds that principles of morality apply between states, across national borders, and to all persons on the globe. Cosmopolitanism may take many different forms. This section outlines the basic principles of some important different forms, and indicates some lines of criticism of them. Although the philosophical foundations of cosmopolitanism may differ markedly, the conclusions of the various cosmopolitan theories are often similar. I conclude by considering criticisms of cosmopolitanism in general.

### Utilitarianism

Utilitarianism holds that behaviour is good in so far as it results in an increase in utility, which is understood as the ability to satisfy some human good, or benefit, or pleasure, or happiness. An action is bad if it results in a decrease in utility. Utilitarianism is a consequentialist doctrine, in that it is concerned with the outcomes or results, rather than the motives, of action. In the hands of Jeremy Bentham, one of the most famous exponents of utilitarianism, it is also an individualist doctrine, for individuals are considered best able to judge their own pleasure and so happiness. It is also for Bentham a maximising doctrine; to work out public policy from individual preferences one must aggregate them. According to Bentham, 'it is the greatest happiness of the greatest number that is the measure of right and wrong' (Bentham, 1988: 3).

If all individuals are to count, and all are to count as one, in calculations of utility maximisation, then utilitarianism is a cosmopolitan doctrine. Peter Singer provides a brief and clear utilitarian, cosmopolitan argument for aid giving. He starts with the basic utilitarian principle that 'suffering and death from lack of food, shelter, and medical care are bad'. He then clarifies the principle of obligation which follows from this: 'if it is in our power to prevent something bad from happening, without thereby sacrificing anything of comparable moral importance, we ought, morally, to do it'. This principle of obligation 'takes, firstly, no account of proximity or distance' and secondly 'makes no distinction between cases in which I am the only person who could possibly do anything and cases in which I am just one among millions in the same position' (Singer, 1979: 23–4). Singer does not accept the nationalist communitarian argument that we owe more to our compatriots than we do to strangers. His utilitarian principles recognise the moral significance of the interests of all individuals, and the obligation that is shared by all individuals to do what they can to relieve the suffering and augment the happiness of others.

Interestingly, Garrett Hardin offers what looks like a utilitarian argument against aid giving (Hardin, 1974). Hardin argues that giving aid to those who are starving will merely contribute to unsustainable population levels and growth, with the consequence that as more mouths chase a limited food supply all will eventually suffer to some extent. The very different conclusions reached by Hardin and Singer indicate that utilitarianism is not a reliable formula, but is dependent on a number of assumptions which will influence calculations and conclusions (including, in this case, dubious assumptions about the relation of food supply and population growth).

A more profound and widely recognised problem of utilitarianism is that the demand to maximise the good of the majority may threaten the good of the minority. That is, some individuals may be sacrificed for, or used as a means to achieve, the good of others (O'Neill, 2000: 123). This may involve a violation of basic rights, which utilitarianism tends not to take seriously. For example, it might be argued, on utilitarian grounds, that the dropping of atomic bombs by the USA on the Japanese cities of Hiroshima and Nagasaki in 1945 was justified by the calculation that although a number of civilians would be killed, this action would put an end to a war that, if it continued, would cause the death of even more. The problem with such an argument is that it assumes it is proper to sacrifice the ultimate good of some people in order to protect that of a greater number of others.

### Kantianism

Immanuel Kant's moral philosophy is concerned not with the consequences of acts, but with one's duty to act in right ways. Humans, as rational beings, are required to consider whether their will and action can be rendered universal. Kant expresses the 'categorical imperative' thus: 'I ought never to act except in such a way that I can also will that my maxim should become a universal law' (Kant, 1972: 67). The duty to think and act in this fashion applies 'to every member and to all members in equal measure' in a 'kingdom of ends' (Kant, 1972: 96). The reference to a kingdom of ends indicates that for Kant individuals must be treated as ends in themselves, and never as means to another end: 'that is, an end against which we should never act, and consequently as one which in all our willing we must never rate merely as a means' (Kant, 1972: 99).

Kant's approach is obviously universal, and when he considers international politics he does see the need for a cosmopolitan moral framework. However, Kant remains state-centric, accepting the existing state system, and arguing that a world government would be a source of conflict rather than the 'perpetual peace' which he sought. When he considers cosmopolitan rights of individuals, Kant limits these to what he terms 'universal hospitality', which 'means the right of a stranger not to be treated with hostility when he arrives on someone else's territory' (Kant, 1991: 105). This principle might be of some significance in the consideration of the treatment of refugees, but it is a solitary and limited cosmopolitan right.

Onora O'Neill presents a contemporary development of the work of Kant in the field of transnational justice. 'Any version of Kantian justice which has contemporary relevance will need to show that the principles of justice he identifies could be embedded in the institutions, practices and policies of a global political and economic system' (O'Neill, 2000; 139–40). The categorical imperative applies not only to individuals but also to collective agents. However, as O'Neill concedes, transnational justice is 'messy', because it is not always clear which agents or agencies (individuals, states, and various other corporate bodies of political, business and charitable natures) should be doing what to whom (O'Neill, 2000: 115). It is clear though that across the world poverty frustrates many people in the exercise of their rational autonomy, and it follows that those who are no so afflicted have a duty to do what they can to relieve the problem (O'Neill, 1986: 145).

If, as O'Neill argues, individual and collective agents have a duty to reject avoidable, systematic injury to humans (O'Neill, 1996: 167) then one could employ this principle to argue, for example: that no state ought to permit the sale of arms which it knows are to be used in the repression of innocent civilians in the buyer state; that no state or international organisation ought to provide to another state a loan with a repayment schedule which will militate against the maintenance of minimal living standards for the debtor state's citizens; and that no transnational enterprise ought to exploit the desire of poor countries for inward investment by locating or relocating there polluting industries which would not be tolerated elsewhere.

A couple of relevant criticisms of Kantianism may be noted. First, by stressing duty as the essence of moral behaviour, Kantianism tends to neglect consideration of the consequences of action, whether these outcomes are intended or unintended. Thus, Kantianism may take a somewhat limited view of morality and the things about which moral judgements might be made. Of course, a concern only with consequences is equally narrow. Second, with its stress on the need to render one's reason and will consistent with those of others, Kantianism may seem to recognise only duties to other humans, and neglect moral obligations to the non-human environment (Dower, 1998: 87).

### Natural law; human rights

Natural law, as a moral doctrine concerned with how humans ought to behave, is not to be confused with the laws of nature, which are physical laws concerned with how and why nature behaves the way it does. Natural law is natural in two ways: it concerns the good of humanity, which is usually conceived as the fulfilment of the given ends or goals of human nature; and it is known naturally by reason, which is the defining characteristic of human nature. The tradition of natural law thinking dates, perhaps, from the concept

of good as the fulfilment of human nature found in the work of Plato and
Aristotle. The doctrine was given coherent expression in the work of the Roman theorist Cicero, and received perhaps its fullest and most rigorous treatment in the work of the thirteenth-century theologian and philosopher St
Thomas Aquinas. Aquinas argues that human nature has certain proper ends,
indicated by natural inclinations, and that human reason can know these
ends and order human action so as to achieve them. In this way human
reason participates in a higher law, the eternal law by which God governs all
of creation.

One clear application of natural law in international politics is the theory
of just war. Aquinas, continuing a tradition of such thinking, takes the view
that not all war is bad, for there are certain moral wrongs which need to be
righted by legitimate acts of violence. On the other hand, war cannot be
unregulated and there are certain moral principles which apply to its conduct. For a war to be just, Aquinas argues, it must meet three conditions
(Aquinas, 1970, 159–60). First, the war must be declared by a ruler with the
authority to do so. Private individuals may not declare war and may not
mobilise others to fight their private causes. Second, war requires a just cause,
such as punishment for some wrong or restoration of some injustice. Third,
those conducting the war must have the right intentions: the achieving of
some good or the avoidance of some evil. The desire to hurt, the arrogance of
victory, and the thirst for power, for example, are not right intentions.

Working within the natural law tradition, the sixteenth-century Spanish
theologian and philosopher Francisco de Vitoria presents a clearly cosmopolitan approach to international politics. Vitoria believes there is a natural law,
which is discovered by human reason and which applies to all humans everywhere. He also recognises that humans are gathered in particular political
communities and are subject to the positive laws enacted by their legitimate
leaders. But according to Vitoria, all political communities are subject to what
he terms the *ius gentium*, or law of peoples, precisely because the whole world
is, as it were, a community which can sanction law (Vitoria, 1991: 40). The
*ius gentium* occupies a somewhat ambiguous space between natural and positive law, and so has an ambiguous binding force. But it is clear that according
to Vitoria, the *ius gentium* regulates the interaction of political communities.
Writing at a time when some European powers were exploring the globe and
encountering hitherto unknown peoples and communities, Vitoria believes
that the *ius gentium* has something to say about matters such as trading
relationships, the treatment of indigenous peoples, and the conduct of war.

Natural law thinking has been applied clearly to contemporary issues of
international politics, especially the issue of the morality of nuclear deterrence (Midgley, 1975; Finnis, Boyle and Grisez, 1988). As nuclear deterrence involves the conditional intention to use indiscriminate weapons of
mass destruction, which would kill not only combatants but also non-combatants, and as it is wrong, according to natural law, to destroy or intend to

destroy innocent life, so the defence strategies of nuclear powers are morally wrong.

Aquinas's doctrine of natural law clearly applies to individuals, and all individuals, but it is expressed not as a theory of individual human rights but as a moral law for individuals and communities. The theory of individual human rights (especially if they are seen as natural rights) emerges, partly, from the natural law tradition, in the more individualistic modern age. If rights belong to individuals, and if all individuals have the same rights, then it is clear that a political theory based on rights is cosmopolitan. A theory of cosmopolitan justice, based on a theory of human rights, is offered by Charles Jones (Jones, 1999). Jones presents his theory of rights as claims to right treatment based on vital human interests (1999: 83). All humans have an interest in, and therefore a right to, those resources necessary for a recognisably human life: food, shelter and health maintenance (1999: 58). Such subsistence rights constitute, says Jones, the moral minimum.

One common criticism of rights theory is that the identification of rights is not always matched by the identification of the duties of agents and agencies to deliver the rights (O'Neill, 2000: 136). Jones responds to such criticism and argues: 'rights function as a middle ground between human interests on the one hand, and duties attaching to individual agents and collectivities on the other. Rights-talk is the language in which connections between the two domains are made' (Jones, 1999: 57) Individuals, governments and other agencies have correlative duties to protect basic human rights (1999: 84). Jones argues, for example, that transnational corporations, although not designed to protect human rights, have a duty not to promote and sell products which, in some circumstances, are likely to cause ill health or death. It is wrong for certain companies to promote baby milk powder, in preference to breast milk, in less developed countries, where clean water is not always available to prepare the milk, and where impoverished mothers may be tempted to use insufficient powder (1999: 71).

### Criticism of cosmopolitanism in general

Cosmopolitanism as a general approach, regardless of its particular philosophical foundations, has attracted some criticism. Two such criticisms will be considered and answered. First, there is the concern that cosmopolitanism is an argument for monolithic world government, and that this threatens local, national and regional autonomy and ways of life. Zolo claims world government would be 'despotic and totalitarian', and against this 'regressive' vision advocates a view of international relations which takes account of their "complex' – that is to say, pluralistic, dynamic and conflictual – nature.' Zolo insists that 'diversity, change and differentiation should be conceived as the rule.' (Zolo, 1997: 166, xiv–xv). The second concern about cosmopolitanism is that the world government it seems to favour will not be truly universal, but, rather, simply the imposition of the will of the state or states with the greatest and necessary power. Zolo argues that any world government would entail the intervention of 'the great powers in the political, economic and social problems of other states, even against the wishes of their governments or of majorities or minorities within these countries' (Zolo, 1997: 166, xiv). An earlier realist critic of cosmopolitanism, Carr, argues: 'Power is an indispensable instrument of government. To internationalise government in any real sense means to internationalise power; and international government is, in effect, government by that state which supplies the power necessary for the purpose of governing' (Carr, 1970: 107). Thus, cosmopolitanism is seen as little more than covert imperialism.

The mistake that Zolo, Carr and other such realist critics of cosmopolitanism make is to assume that it entails world government, and that world government will be like state government on a global scale. Certainly cosmopolitanism recognises that there are global problems, of pollution and illness for example, which demand global solutions. Also, cosmopolitanism does challenge the long established and deep seated notion that state boundaries are morally sacrosanct, and that states should have a veto on political action. But cosmopolitanism does not entail world government; rather, it could justify government for the world. There is no need to assume that all decisions must be taken at only one – the highest – level. Cosmopolitanism is entirely compatible with the principle of subsidiarity, according to which decision making should be devolved to the lowest competent level. Global issues require global decision making, but many other issues are best dealt with at appropriate lower levels, including the regional, national and local. Rather than being seen as a threat to democracy and autonomy, cosmopolitanism could be seen as the inspiration for a restructuring of the present state system so as to make the world more responsive to its problems, more open to democratic decision making, and ultimately more just.

## Conclusion

The various political, social, economic and environmental problems of the contemporary world demand moral responses. Realism doubts that moral values are applicable in international politics, and so is incapable of formulating justifiable moral responses to these problems. Communitarianism, by grounding moral values in the shared beliefs of particular communities, is incapable of furnishing a comprehensive set of universally applicable moral principles. Only cosmopolitanism is capable of dealing adequately with the moral problems of an interdependent world. Cosmopolitanism has a number of philosophical foundations, not all of which are compatible. However, many of the moral conclusions reached by these various strands of thought are consistent, and so there is scope for agreement. Cosmopolitanism does not entail despotic world government or some form of moral imperialism.

Cosmopolitanism safeguards the moral integrity of all individuals, regardless of their community identity, while also allowing for the integrity of various legitimate communities. Most importantly, cosmopolitanism recognises the integrity of the greatest of all human communities, that of the whole human race itself.

## Bibliography

Aquinas, St Thomas (1970), *Selected Political Writings*, ed. A.P. D'Entreves, Oxford: Blackwell.

Beitz, Charles, Cohen, Marshall, Scanlon, Thomas and Simmons, John A. (eds) (1985), *International Ethics*, Princeton, NJ: Princeton University Press.

Beitz, Charles (1999), *Political Theory and International Relations*, revised edition, Princeton, NJ: Princeton University Press.

Bentham, Jeremy [1776] (1988), *A Fragment on Government*, ed. J.H. Burns and H.L.A. Hart, Cambridge: Cambridge University Press.

Brown, Chris (1992), *International Relations Theory: New Normative Approaches*, Hemel Hempstead, Harvester/Wheatsheaf.

Bull, Hedley (1966), 'Society and Anarchy in International Relations', in Herbert Butterfield and Martin Wight (eds), *Diplomatic Investigations*, London: George Allen and Unwin, pp. 35–50.

Bull, Hedley (1977), *The Anarchical Society: A Study of Order in World Politics*, London: Macmillan.

Caney, Simon (2001), 'Review Article: International Distributive Justice', *Political Studies*, Vol. 49, No. 5, pp. 974–97.

Carr, E.H. (1970), *The 20 Years Crisis, 1919–1939*, second edition, London: Macmillan.

Dower, Nigel (1998), *World Ethics: The New Agenda*, Edinburgh: Edinburgh University Press.

Elfstrom, Gerard (1990), *Ethics for a Shrinking World*, London: Macmillan.

Finnis, John, Boyle, Joseph and Grisez, Germain (1988), *Nuclear Deterrence, Morality and Realism*, Oxford: Oxford University Press.

Frost, Mervyn (1996), *Ethics in International Relations: A Constitutive Theory* Cambridge: Cambridge University Press.

Graham, Gordon (1996), *Ethics and International Relations*, Oxford: Oxford University Press.

Hardin, Garrett (1974), 'Lifeboat Ethics: The Case Against Helping the Poor', *Psychology Today*, No. 8, 38–43.

Hare, J.E. and Joynt, Carey (1982), *Ethics and International Affairs*, London: Macmillan.

Hobbes, Thomas [1651] (1991), *Leviathan*, ed. Richard Tuck, Cambridge: Cambridge University Press.

Hutchings, Kimberly (1999), *International Political Theory*, London: Sage.

Jones, Charles (1999), *Global Justice: Defending Cosmopolitanism*, Oxford: Oxford University Press.

Kant, Immanuel [1785] (1972), 'Groundwork of the Metaphysic of Morals', in H.J. Paton, *The Moral Law*, London: Hutchinson and Co.

Kant, Immanuel [1795] (1991), *Political Writings*, ed. Hans Reiss, second revised edition, Cambridge: Cambridge University Press.

Machiavelli, Niccolo [1531] (1970), *The Discourses*, ed. Bernard Crick, Harmondsworth: Pelican Books.

Machiavelli, Niccolo [1532] (1988), *The Prince*, ed. Quentin Skinner and Russell Price, Cambridge: Cambridge University Press.

Maritain, Jacques (1953), *The Range of Reason*, London: Geoffrey Bles.

Midgley, E.B.F. (1975), *The Natural Law Tradition and the Theory of International Relations*, London: Elek.

Miller, David (1995), *On Nationality*, Oxford: Oxford University Press.

Morrice, David (2000), 'The Liberal-Communitarian Debate in Contemporary Political Philosophy and its Significance for International Relations', *Review of International Studies*, Vol. 26, No. 2, pp. 233–51.

Mulhall, Stephen and Swift, Adam (1996), *Liberals and Communitarians*, second edition Oxford: Blackwell.

O'Neill, Onora (1986), *Faces of Hunger: An Essay on Poverty, Justice and Development*, London: George Allen and Unwin.

O'Neill, Onora (1996), *Towards Justice and Virtue*, Cambridge: Cambridge University Press.

O'Neill, Onora (2000), *Bounds of Justice*, Cambridge: Cambridge University Press.

Rawls, John (1999), *The Law of Peoples*, Cambridge, MA: Harvard University Press.

Shue, Henry (1996), *Basic Rights: Subsistence, Affluence and US Foreign Policy*, Princeton, NJ: Princeton University Press.

Singer, Peter (1979), 'Famine, Affluence and Morality', in P. Laslett and J. Fishkin, (eds), *Philosophy, Politics and Society*, fifth series, Oxford: Blackwell.

Tamir, Yael (1993), *Liberal Nationalism*, Princeton, NJ: Princeton University Press.

Vincent, R. J. (1986), *Human Rights and International Relations*, Cambridge: Royal Institute of International Affairs / Cambridge University Press .

Vitoria, Francisco (1991) [original date unknown], *Political Writings* ed. Anthony Pagden and Jeremy Lawrence, Cambridge: Cambridge University Press.

Zolo, D. (1997), *Cosmopolis: Prospects for World Government*, Oxford: Polity.

# 7

# Human rights

*Barbara Emadi-Coffin*

In April 2002, Amnesty International issued its *Annual Report* on abuses of human rights, which included information on the application of the death penalty. The report claimed that the number of executions worldwide had more than doubled in 2001, with 3,048 known cases in 31 countries. China, Iran, Saudi Arabia, and the United States accounted for approximately 90 per cent of the documented worldwide total (Amnesty International, 2002). Amnesty International has asked the United Nations Commission on Human Rights to call for a universal moratorium on the death penalty, arguing that it is both cruel and, in many cases, unfairly applied (Gumbel, 2002). Both conditions violate already existing international standards regulating the treatment of prisoners, such as the United Nations Convention Against Torture. In that same month, the Israeli Defence Force (IDF) intensified military operations on the West Bank aimed at eliminating Palestinian militias. In ten days of fighting, the army's helicopter gunships and tanks destroyed the Jenin refugee camp and attacked other towns. Nearly half the Palestinians who died in Jenin and who have been identified were civilians, including children. Afterwards, the International Committee of the Red Cross accused Israel of breaching the Geneva Conventions by recklessly endangering civilian lives and property during the assault on the camp and by refusing the injured access to medical personnel for six days (McGreal and Whitaker, 2002). In addition, the IDF prohibited journalists from entering the areas of conflict for several days (Huggler, 2002), thus restricting freedom of the press. In both of these situations, human rights advocates claim that the human rights of the individuals involved are being violated, and that national governments are refusing to abide by international law or other agreed international standards relating to the protection of human rights.

The concern shown for the individuals in each of these cases demonstrates the disquiet that has been felt within the international community since the Second World War about the failure of governments to respect the human rights of their citizens and the human rights of the citizens of other states. Herein lies the crux of the problem of human rights. Since the seventeenth century, it has been assumed in the West that one of the main purposes of the state is to protect the rights of its citizens. Since the nineteenth century, the rights of citizens of other states have been protected by international humanitarian law.[1] In the case of human rights violations, it is often that very body that is supposed to be protecting us, the state – our state – that is violating our rights. Whether it is the application of the death penalty, the torture of political prisoners, or the 'disappearance' of members of political opposition groups, the victims may find it almost impossible to ask for help from external sources because of the long-established principle of state sovereignty. This principle holds that states are the highest authority over their territories, and that non-intervention in the domestic affairs of states is a fundamental principle of international law. Since the Second World War, it has been argued that the only real protection for the rights of individuals will come from international law, but getting international agreement on which rights should be protected, and getting national governments to agree to these obligations, and to abide by them, has proven very difficult. In this chapter, we will examine the nature of human rights and development of international concern with respect for human rights, as well as the various categories of human rights and the problems these categories create for the development of an international consensus on human rights. Finally, we will examine national, international, transnational and individual political responses to the problem of the violation of human rights by national governments, and assess the adequacy of these responses.

### What are human rights?

One of the definitions of the word 'right' in the dictionary is that it is something to which one is entitled. In Europe and North America, the concept of rights is usually related to law, so that rights are things to which we are entitled and which are defined by law. Historically, in the West, the things to which we are entitled are certain freedoms or liberties. For example, the French Declaration of the Rights of Man of 1789 and the 1791 amendments to the American Constitution known as the Bill of Rights provide protection for liberties such as freedom of speech, freedom of religion, the right to private property, and the right to a fair trial. These rights provide individuals with protection from interference by the state or by other people. However, these rights belong to specific groups of people, in these cases, the French and the Americans, and were intended to provide citizens of these countries with protection from abuses of power by their governments.

The idea of human rights, in contrast, suggests that some rights should not be limited to any particular group, such as the French or the Americans.

The concept of human rights transcends any natural or socially-constructed divisions and applies to all human beings regardless of sex, national or ethnic origin, religion, sexual preference, and socio-economic class or caste. This assumption of the essential unity of the human species is based on the view, which can be traced back to the philosophy of the Stoics in classical Greece in the fourth to third centuries BC, that all human beings are similar in that they have an equal capacity to reason. By the ability to reason they meant the ability to discover for oneself what is right and what is wrong, and to over-come instinct. This is what makes people different from animals. For example, when animals are threatened, they follow the instinct to attack. People can, however, learn to resolve conflicts by ways other than fighting. Therefore, what makes an individual human is this capacity to reason, and through reason we can know what is required for a life of basic dignity.

Human rights are today thought to be part of what is essential for a life of basic human dignity. Those rights that are considered important enough to be human rights are assumed to have three characteristics. They must be universal, that is, they should apply to everyone in the contemporary world and they should apply throughout time, for example into the future. They must also be inalienable, so that it is impossible to surrender a right or trans-fer it to the ownership of another, for example, it should be impossible to sell oneself into slavery. Finally, human rights must be absolute. They should be more important than other considerations, such as the public interest or state sovereignty or cultural autonomy. Everyone is entitled to human rights, even if one cannot exercise them or enjoy them at a given point. They are some-times referred to as 'moral rights', because these rights ought to exist but may not in fact be enforced by positive (national or municipal) law. Legislation is needed to enforce human rights, but one's entitlement to these rights is not dependent on existing law. For example, it may be argued that prisoners on death row have in principle the right to freedom from cruel and unusual punishment and the right to life, even if they are not able to benefit from those rights while they are held on death row or when they are executed.

Concern with human rights can be traced back to the Enlightenment and the development of liberal philosophy in the seventeenth and eighteenth cen-turies. The American and French Revolutions in the late eighteenth century were based in part on ideas about 'natural rights', which developed from the work of John Locke (1960 [1690]) and included the right to life, the right to liberty, and the right to property. Later philosophers such as Thomas Paine (1973 [1791–92]) argued that if the state did not protect these natural rights, then the right of resistance was triggered. The outcome of these struggles was the codification of protection for natural rights in national legal frame-works such as the French and American constitutions. Later, in the nine-teenth century, attempts at finding international solutions to human rights problems included the international anti-slavery movement which resulted in the Declaration Relative to the Universal Abolition of the Slave Trade of 1815 calling on states to declare it illegal; the establishment in 1863 of the Red Cross, an early non-governmental organisation dedicated to caring for the wounded after conflicts; and the ratification of the Geneva Convention of 1864 which regulated the treatment of prisoners of war and of civilians in times of war. In the early twentieth century, concern with rights was evident in the suffragette movements in Britain and the United States, and in the limited powers held by the League of Nations to protect the rights of ethnic and national minority populations following border changes in Europe after the First World War. It was, however, the Second World War and the Holocaust in particular that re-directed international attention to the question of the protection of human rights. The Nuremberg and Tokyo Trials, involving Nazi and Japanese military leaders accused of crimes against humanity, were the first international response to the human rights abuses of the period. Since 1945, the international community has struggled with two aspects of the protection of human rights; first, to find a definition of human rights with which everyone, everywhere, can agree, and second, to find a mechanism to compel states to respect the human rights of their citizens.

### Three types of human rights

One of the main difficulties in the establishment of international agreement over the protection of human rights is that, since the eighteenth century, three different categories of human rights have developed. Table 7.1 shows the categories contained in the United Nations Universal Declaration of Human Rights.

The first category of rights is based on the natural rights tradition of the seventeenth and eighteenth centuries. The rights in this category are now referred to as civil and political rights. These are individual rights that provide freedom from interference by the state or other persons. Civil and political rights include natural rights like the right to life, the right to liberty, the right to security of the person, and the right to property, as well as other similar rights such as freedom of speech, freedom of the press, freedom of religion and freedom of conscience. Rights relating to the judicial system are included in this category, such as the right to freedom from torture, the right to freedom from arbitrary arrest and the right to trial by jury. Rights relating to our private lives, such as the right to privacy, the right to marry and the right to found a family are also part of this category. The importance of these rights is that they provide us with protection against the power of the government, and occasionally against the power of other groups. They provide us with a space in which we are able to think and live as we please, as long as we are careful not to infringe on the rights of others. The right to freedom of speech, for example, gives us the right to express ideas that others may not like, to say things that may even hurt the feelings of others, but it does not give us the

Table 7.1   *Rights included in the United Nations Universal Declaration of Human Rights*

| Civil and political rights Articles 1–21 | Social and economic rights Articles 22–28 | Collective rights Article 29 |
|---|---|---|
| 1 Equality of all humans 2 Equality of entitlement to rights in the UDHR 3 Right to life, liberty and security of the person 4 Freedom from slavery and the slave trade 5 Freedom from torture and cruel, inhuman and degrading punishment 6 Right to recognition as a person before the law 7 Equality before the law 8 Right to a remedy by national tribunals for acts violating fundamental rights 9 Freedom from arbitrary arrest, detention or exile 10 Right to a fair hearing by an impartial tribunal 11 Right to be presumed innocent until proven guilty 12 Right to privacy 13 Right to freedom of movement within each state, and right to return to one's own country 14 Right to seek asylum 15 Right to a nationality 16 Right to marry and found a family 17 Right to own property 18 Freedom of thought, conscience and religion 19 Freedom of opinion and expression 20 Freedom of peaceful assembly and association 21 Right to take part in the government of the country | 22 Right to social security 23 Right to work, to free choice of employment and to just and favourable conditions of work 24 Right to rest and leisure, including reasonable limitation of working hours and periodic holidays with pay 25 Right to standard of living adequate for health and well-being, including food, housing, clothing, medical care and social security 26 Right to an education, free at elementary stages 27 Right to participate in the cultural life of the community 28 Right to a social and international order in which the rights in the UDHR can be recognised | 29 Everyone has duties to the community in which alone the free and full development of one's personality is possible |

*Source: United Nation Universal Declaration of Human Rights [Resolution 217 A (III)], adopted by the General Assembly of the United Nations, 10 December 1948.*

right, for example, to tell blatant lies about others (forbidden by libel laws) or to produce or print pictures of children being harmed (forbidden by criminal law).

The second category of rights is known as social and economic rights. This category of rights has emerged from the socialist tradition of the nineteenth century, in which it was argued that political rights did not go far enough to truly liberate people, and that freedom for individuals from the most serious material deprivation was also required for a life of basic dignity. Social and economic rights include subsistence rights such as the right to adequate food, water, clothing and housing. The rights to an education and basic medical care are also considered significant. This category would also include the right to employment, the right to a just wage, the right to social security, the right to periodic holidays with pay, and the right to a clean environment. These rights are different from civil and political rights in the sense that they do not concern freedom for the individual from government intervention, but rather they require government intervention to ensure the designated entitlements. They constitute a claim on the government, rather than a restraint on government action. These rights provide the minimal physical conditions necessary to benefit from other rights, including civil and political rights (Shue, 1980). It is argued that those who lack even basic supplies of food and water, such as persons suffering from famine in Malawi, are unable to make use of any other rights such as the right to vote or the right to freedom of religion, because they may be too weak to walk to polling stations or to places of worship. Therefore, a guarantee of subsistence rights may be said to be a precondition for the enjoyment of all other rights.

The third category of rights is known as collective rights. The importance of the community rather than individual liberty as the source of freedom was emphasised by Rousseau (1973 [1762]) in the eighteenth century, and the notion of the rights of groups grew in importance during the period of decolonisation from 1947–65. The idea of collective rights is based on the view that groups are not always reducible to the individuals that make them up. Therefore, while all individuals in a particular group may have their individual rights fully enforced, it may be argued that the group, as an entity in and of itself, has rights that need to be guaranteed. Collective rights include rights claimed by groups, such as the right to national self-determination, the right to economic development, and the right to freedom from discrimination based on race, class or gender. These rights are said to be necessary because even in cases in which all members of the group enjoy individual rights, the group itself still lacks freedom. The easiest example to understand is that of national determination. In the case of the claim for the right to national self-determination for Scotland, it may be argued that although all Scots in the United Kingdom benefit from the right to vote, the Scottish nation itself (regardless of where each individual lives) will not be free until it is self-governing. Similar arguments apply to affirmative action policies designed to ensure that particular groups are more proportionally represented in education, business or public life. Although all women in the United Kingdom have the right to vote, the Labour Party in 2002 planned to institute women-only short lists in key parliamentary seats in order to increase the number of women who serve as MPs in England and Wales to 35 per cent of the party's total (Black, 2002). Therefore, although group rights sometimes derive from the rights of individuals, these rights to not apply to individual humans but to groups that are considered corporate individuals in themselves.

After more than three hundred years of the development of the concept of rights, there are now three ideas about what rights should be; civil and political rights, social and economic rights, and collective rights. While, in the abstract, many people would agree that the contents of these categories are all desirable goals, problems arise because it is very difficult to obtain an agreement among individuals and among states on which rights are so important that they should apply to everyone, everywhere and override all other considerations.

## Lack of international consensus

There are three main reasons for the difficulties in obtaining international agreement on the protection of human rights. The first is that states often do not want to be party to international legal agreements that will limit their autonomy. The second is that the three types of rights conflict in principle; they focus on different sorts of entitlements that sometimes contradict each other. The third is that this conflict in principle between categories of rights has found its way into practical conflict in international relations. The first reason for the inability to develop strong international agreements protecting human rights is the issue of state sovereignty. National governments are the institutions most often accused of the violation of human rights, and are also the institutions that will have to agree to treaties or conventions designed to eliminate human rights abuses. It is sadly the case that national governments are often reluctant to support international agreements protecting human rights. They are loath to agree to international instruments which would infringe on their freedom of action. Each government wants to be able to have its own institutional concerns, such as national security, the public interest or cultural autonomy, take precedence over other commitments. At times when international security or domestic order may be threatened, many governments wish to maintain the freedom to adopt policies considered necessary to the protection of what is defined as the national interest. Even the European Convention on Human Rights, one of the most effective international human rights agreements, provides for the possibility of contracting governments derogating from their obligations.[2]

In addition, some governments may fear that ratifying international agreements protecting human rights may leave them open to international criticism regarding treatment of their citizens. The failure of the United States to ratify the International Covenant on Economic, Social and Cultural Rights of 1966 is due to the reluctance of the US Congress to obligate the US government to deal with problems of homelessness and borderline (or actual) starvation (Brown, 2000: 85). The United States has also refused to ratify the Rome Statute of 1998 which established the International Criminal Court designed to prosecute genocide, war crimes and other crimes against humanity because it does not want members of its armed forces subject to the scrutiny of the court. Finally, any effective international agreement protecting human rights would have to allow external monitoring of a state's level of human rights protection. National governments often consider such monitoring as unacceptable intervention in their internal affairs, and will block efforts for monitoring or investigation to take place, as the government of Israel did in the wake of the April 2002 West Bank operation. The Israeli government demanded a veto of the UN investigating team's movements, the right to determine who attended official meetings, and a ban on the team outlining any conclusions in its final report on the events in Jenin (Usborne, 2002).

A second reason for the failure to develop an international consensus on the protection of human rights is the theoretical conflict between the different categories of rights, so that the pursuit of one category of rights may undermine the rights comprised in another category. Because these categories have emerged from different traditions of political thought, the entitlements they promote may at times clash with each other, so that there are tensions between individual rights and group rights and also between civil/political rights and social/economic rights. Here, a couple of examples may help clarify the point. First, the pursuit of a group right, such as the right to national self-determination, may result in the violation of the rights of individuals from minority ethnic groups if they are being 'ethnically cleansed' from the particular territory, a tension that was cruelly illustrated in the conflicts during the 1990s in the territories of the former Yugoslavia. In the second example, the political liberties in civil/political rights may conflict with the concept of economic equality inherent in social/economic rights. Here, the right to private property (including income from work) clashes with the need for national governments to increase taxation to provide subsistence benefits such as child benefit, income support, or national health services.

The third reason for the difficulty in generating international agreement over the protection of human rights is that the underlying differences in various categories of rights have come to play an important role in international conflict. The different categories of rights have come to be associated with different groupings of states, and have become one of the weapons that states in one bloc can use against another. Western Europe and North America have historically prioritised civil and political rights, while the communist regimes in Eastern Europe used to emphasise social and economic rights. During the Cold War, this provided opportunities for the USA and the Soviet Union to accuse each other of human rights violations. The USA was able to criticise the Soviet Union's violations of civil and political rights when it sent political prisoners to psychiatric hospitals and to labour camps, or refused to allow Jews to emigrate to Israel. The Soviet Union responded by pointing to the homelessness, the hunger, and the lack of national health care in the United States.

In the contemporary world, Western states continue to prioritise civil and political rights, while Third World states often prioritise collective rights like national development at the expense of individual rights. In recent years, this has provided the USA with many opportunities to criticise China for violations of civil rights such as the lack of freedom of religion and speech and the use of political prisoners as forced labour. In general, Western states, especially the United States, have drawn attention to human rights violations in developing countries that do not share their interests such as Nicaragua, Cuba, Mozambique, Iran after the revolution of 1979, and the Palestinian territories, while ignoring violations in developing countries with national governments that do share their interests such as Chile during the Pinochet years, Iran under the Shah, Turkey and Saudi Arabia as well as other countries considered strategically important such as South Africa during the apartheid period and Israel. In summary, it is issues such as national sovereignty and differing interpretations of the concept of rights that have made it extremely difficult to negotiate international instruments for the protection of human rights.

### Responses to human rights violations

What happens when violations of human rights occur? Despite the difficulties in trying to establish international agreement on the protection of human rights, responses to violations can come from states, either individual or multilaterally, from non-governmental organisations, and from individuals.

Individual states may try to encourage greater respect for human rights on the part of other national governments. This may be done through diplomatic channels, for example in cases in which the British government has contacted foreign governments about the rights of British nationals abroad. In the spring and summer of 2003, senior British officials were in close communication with US officials over the detention conditions and military trial of two UK nationals who fought against the Western alliance in Afghanistan and had been held by the US military in Camp Delta in Guantanamo Bay, Cuba. Pressure may also be put on other governments to improve their human rights record by economic sanctions such as withdrawal of foreign aid, making foreign aid conditional on improvement in the protection of human rights, or by boycotts such as the 1972 Jackson-Vannick Amendment which imposed restrictions on trade between the USA and the Soviet Union in response to the

Soviet ban on the emigration of Russian Jews to Israel. In a few cases, individual governments have undertaken military intervention to protect the rights of citizens of other countries, as Britain did in Sierra Leone in 2000, or more controversially, the golden parachute provided by the United States to coup leader General Cedras of Haiti for leaving the country during 1994–95.

A number of types of responses to human rights violations have also developed at the international level, including multilateral sanctions, human rights instruments (legal documents protecting human rights), the new International Criminal Court, economic development programmes, and humanitarian intervention. Many, but not all, of these responses are organised through the various bodies making up the United Nations. Multilateral sanctions involve agreements between two or more countries to cooperate on sanctions restricting aid, trade and/or foreign direct investment with third countries accused of human rights violations. Currently, multilateral sanctions in place include the slashing of bilateral aid packages to Burma by the United States and European Union governments and the UN-organised restrictions on aid, trade (except medical supplies) and foreign direct investment to Iraq in place from 1991 until 2003.

There are also a wide variety of international legal agreements that have been developed with the goal of protecting human rights. The United Nations Universal Declaration on Human Rights (summarised in Table 7.1) is probably the best known. There are many other instruments developed by the United Nations, such as the International Covenant on Civil and Political Rights, the International Covenant on Economic, Social and Cultural Rights, the Convention Against Genocide and the Convention Against Torture. Examples of other international agreements include the Geneva Conventions, which define the rights of both combatants and non-combatants during war, and the International Labour Organisation's Tripartite Declaration of Principles Concerning Multinational Enterprises and Social Policy, which encourages both national governments and multinational corporations to develop investment policies more sensitive to the rights of workers. There are also regional international agreements for the protection of human rights, the most effective of which is the European Convention on Human Rights. Other regional agreements include the African Charter on Human and Peoples' Rights, and the Inter-American Democratic Charter of the Organisation of American States.

The newly-created International Criminal Court is a permanent independent judicial body designed to prosecute human rights violations which fall under the protection of international humanitarian law (such as the Geneva Conventions) including genocide, war crimes, and other crimes against humanity. The reluctance of the UN Security Council to set up criminal tribunals for those accused of war crimes and genocide and the failure of national courts to prosecute alleged perpetrators of such crimes have led to the establishment of an international court which will be able to act when national courts are unable or unwilling to do so. In 1998, an international diplomatic conference adopted the Rome Statute of the International Criminal Court, which defines the crimes and how the court will work. The Rome Statute provides that the court will come into existence when sixty states have ratified the Statute. This occurred in April 2002, and the ICC came into being in July 2002. By July 2003, ninety-one states had ratified the Rome Statue (Coalition for the ICC, 2003).

There are many international development programmes, health programmes and humanitarian aid programmes aimed at promoting social and economic rights by alleviating famine, poverty and ill-health. For example, in Malawi the UN agency World Food Programme has been working with non-governmental organisations such as Concern Worldwide, World Vision, the Red Cross, and the Catholic Relief Services as well as national governments such as Britain and the United States to provide famine relief (Vidal, 2002). In Afghanistan, many organisations including the World Food Programme, US AID, the UN High Commissioner for Refugees, CARE, the Red Cross/Red Crescent, Medecins Sans Frontieres, and Refugees International are cooperating to deliver humanitarian relief.

Humanitarian intervention to protect human rights by UN-backed military forces is the most high profile category of international responses to human rights violations. Since the end of the Cold War, international military intervention into conflicts to protect the rights of civilians has been increasingly legitimised despite the implications for the principle of state sovereignty. In conflicts in places such as former Yugoslavia (1992–95), Somalia (1992–93), and Rwanda (1993–96), the United Nations Security Council has voted to send troops to help encourage reduction in the level of conflict and thus protect civilians from ethnic cleansing and/or starvation.

Solutions to the problems of human rights violations are also being sought at the transnational level, particularly by non-governmental organisations. Respect for civil and political rights is monitored by Amnesty International and Human Rights Watch, which try to educate people about political freedoms, help to publicise the violations of these rights, provide support for victims and lobby national governments on behalf of those who are denied civil and political rights. The promotion of social and economic rights is undertaken by groups such as Oxfam, Save the Children, the Salvation Army, Medecins Sans Frontieres and church-related groups that work on individual projects such as Oxfam's projects in villages in southern Africa and collaborate with other organisations, as in the example of Malawi above, to ensure that people have basic subsistence rights met. It may also be argued that environmental groups such as Greenpeace, Friends of the Earth and the Worldwide Fund for Nature, by encouraging protection of the environment help to protect social and economic rights by actively supporting demands for clean air, clean water, and biodiversity.

Finally, individuals can also contribute to the protection of human rights in a number of ways. First, as individuals, we can contribute money to groups like Amnesty International and participate in letter-writing campaigns on behalf of prisoners of conscience. Such campaigns have often resulted in the release of, or better conditions for, people who are imprisoned and mistreated because of the ideas they espouse. Second, we can support the work of individual journalists such as Robert Fisk, Fergal Keane and the Iranian photojournalist Abbas, who have courageously covered events in the Middle East, Zimbabwe, Northern Ireland, and elsewhere about which governments would prefer that we didn't know. Third, there are individuals who, because of their courage and determination, contribute substantially to international consciousness about the protection of human rights. Martin Luther King, the American civil rights leader; Nelson Mandela, the first South African president in the post-apartheid era; Mother Theresa, the Catholic nun known for her work with the poor in India; and Louise Arbour, the United Nations High Commissioner for Human Rights are examples of individuals who serve as international symbols encouraging respect for human rights.

### Evaluating responses to human rights violations

In this section, we will assess the solutions to the problem of the violation of human rights, and ask ourselves about the extent to which these solutions succeed in meeting the challenges presented. Here, we will examine the solutions used by individual states, by multilateral organisations, by transnational organisations, and by individuals. In evaluating these responses to human rights abuses, we will also be considering the question of why, if there are so many possible solutions, widespread violations of human rights still occur.

First, we examined the solutions provided by individual states, such as diplomatic pressure; economic sanctions, including the placing of conditions on or withdrawal of foreign aid; and unilateral military intervention. Although such strategies have sometimes achieved successes, as in the case of Irish government pressure on the British government to improve the treatment of IRA detainees, more often governments prefer to put the national interest ahead of human rights concerns, so that human rights issues are subordinated to other interests. The renewal of China's most favoured nation trading status in 1994 by the US Congress despite earlier objections by President Clinton on the grounds of China's human rights record, and the continuing support of the United States for Israeli policy in the West Bank and Gaza demonstrate the importance of economic, political and security issues relative to human rights concerns. Unilateral military intervention to protect human rights in other countries remains extremely controversial, not only because of the principle of state sovereignty, but also because intervention does not occur when many people feel it should, such as in former Yugoslavia in the early 1990s as the ethnic cleansing policies became known and in the continuing civil war in Liberia. Moreover, on some occasions, unilateral intervention in the name of human rights is often thought to be a cover for the promotion of other interests such as the protection of spheres of interest, the establishment of market economies or the control of oil supplies.

Second, we examined the responses which have developed at the international level to human rights violations, including multilateral sanctions, human rights instruments (legal documents protecting human rights), the new International Criminal Court, economic development programmes, and humanitarian intervention. Multilateral sanctions, while expressing the concern of the international community and creating resource and political issues for the government in the targeted country, are frequently very difficult to enforce because of the difficulties outlined above in getting governments to agree on what constitutes a violation of human rights as well as getting them to prioritise human rights above other national interests. For example, multilateral sanctions against South Africa during the apartheid period were undermined for many years because of the refusal of Britain and the United States to participate as a result of historical, political and resource considerations. Moreover, as in the case of the sanctions against Iraq during the 1990s, the government under pressure may divert the limited resources allowed to enter the country to the use of the government administration and the military, rather than allowing food and medical supplies to reach the civilian population.

In the period since the Second World War, dozens of international legal agreements protecting human rights have been developed at both the global and regional levels, thus providing international standards for the conduct of national governments in relation to human rights. Unfortunately, the enforcement mechanisms underpinning many of these agreements are very weak, therefore, although governments may become parties to such agreements, there are few sanctions available should governments not live up to their obligations. In the case of the United Nations Universal Declaration of Human Rights, there is no legal obligation to abide by the standards it contains, and the preamble merely states that individuals and organs of society 'shall strive ... to secure their ... recognition and observance'.[3] For other agreements which have a greater degree of obligation, such as the International Covenants on Civil and Political Rights and on Economic, Social and Cultural Rights, the enforcement mechanisms available to the Human Rights Committee and the Committee on Economic, Social and Cultural Rights which monitor the agreements are very slow and of limited effectiveness.

A very recent multilateral solution, the International Criminal Court established to prosecute those accused of genocide and other crimes against humanity who may escape prosecution in their own countries, only came into existence on 1 July 2002. However, the ICC Prosecutor will only be able to initiate investigations into situations in which the crime has been committed in the territory of a state party to the Statute or in which the accused person is a citizen of a state party to the Statute, so that the scope and effectiveness of the ICC will depend on the number of states ratifying the Statute. Ninety-one states have ratified the Statute as of July 2003, only about half of the states in the international system; notable among those who have not ratified the Statute are the United States, the Russian Federation, Israel, Algeria, Iran and Indonesia (Coalition for the ICC, 2003). In addition, although the UN Security Council may also refer cases to the ICC, the reluctance of the Security Council to investigate allegations of war crimes in the 1990s suggests that this is not likely to happen often (Coalition for the ICC, 2003).

International attempts to address issues of social and economic rights through development, health, and aid programmes often bring temporary relief to those most in need in the poorest or most conflict-torn parts of the world. Unfortunately, these programmes are unable to address the underlying causes of poverty, starvation and ill health including military and political conflict, the interests of multinational corporations in promoting GM foods and controlling generic pharmaceuticals, and ultimately, the effects of global capitalism. Globalisation has exacerbated particularly inequalities in wages, so that Third World workers are paid one-tenth of what workers in the West earn; and the disparities in relative prices, so that the price of a tractor manufactured in the USA keeps rising compared to the income of Third World farmers. Such tractors cost today three times what they did in the mid–1960s. Therefore, while hunger in a particular refugee camp may be alleviated by UN agencies, the reasons that families left their homes to go to the camp in the first place will still continue to cause problems for years to come.

The results of humanitarian intervention for the protection of human rights in the 1990s have not been entirely positive. Although the end of the Cold War in 1989 was supposed to signal the start of a new period of UN effectiveness in terms of peacekeeping activities and humanitarian intervention, most of the main examples of UN involvement in the early to mid-1990s lacked notable success. In many cases, such as UNPROFOR in former Yugoslavia, UNOSOM in Somalia, and UNAMIR in Rwanda, the protection of human rights was hampered by great power conflicts (former Yugoslavia), the desire for publicity and conflicting mission objectives (Somalia), and regional politics as well as a failure to understand the nature of the problem (Rwanda). Moreover, there are still international concerns that UN intervention may be used to promote the interests of the United States, as in Afghanistan in 2001, and perhaps even more worryingly, that the UN Security Council may be sidelined altogether, and that great powers may be tempted to intervene without UN backing, as the USA and the UK did in Iraq in the spring of 2003.

Transnational solutions such as those adopted by non-governmental organisations like Amnesty International, Oxfam, and Greenpeace have the advantage of being independent of the control of any national government, therefore the types of national interest that hamper individual state or multinational solutions do not create obstacles for these organisations. Such organisations may, however, be limited in their effectiveness by the failure of national governments to cooperate with them, for example, Amnesty International may not be allowed to visit prisoners of conscience, Oxfam may be unable to deliver food aid because of fighting, or Greenpeace may have their boats sunk by governments wishing to continue with nuclear testing. These organisations rely very much on international public opinion to help pressure governments into cooperating, and they are also entirely dependent on public contributions for their funding. Therefore, the actions of individuals, the media, and the state of the economy are critical to the ability of these organisations to make an impact in their area of concern.

It is, of course, individuals who suffer from violations of human rights, and it is individuals who make the greatest sacrifices for the promotion of human rights. In the West, we think of joining groups such as Amnesty International as part of our right to participate in the political process. In other countries, however, even belonging to groups like Amnesty or local action groups may be evidence enough for governments to detain, torture, or cause members to 'disappear'. Journalists who write or speak about human rights violations may find that their work is not published, that they are blacklisted from appearing as television guests, or that they lose their jobs, as many reporters and commentators found in the United States when they criticised human rights aspects of the US conduct of the 2003 Iraq War. Journalists who actively investigate human rights violations may even find that their lives are in danger. In July 2003, the Iranian-Canadian journalist Zara Kazemi died from head injuries suffered while in detention after photographing the outside of the notorious Evin prison in Tehran, the place where the Khomeini regime's political prisoners are detained.

Finally, those who serve as international symbols of support for human rights may also find that they are at risk. Aung San Suu Kyi, the leader of the National League for Democracy in Burma, suffered six years of house arrest for her activism. Nelson Mandela, one of the leaders of the African National Congress in the apartheid period in South Africa, spent more than thirty years in prison for his opposition to apartheid policies. Martin Luther King, president of the US civil rights group Southern Christian Leadership Conference from 1957–68, was assassinated in 1968 as a result of his activities. The claim that his death was a conspiracy involving the US government was upheld in 1999, when the jury in a civil case concluded that restaurant owner Loyd Jowers and governmental agencies including the City of Memphis, the State of Tennessee, and the federal government were parties to the conspiracy to assassinate Dr King.

A final problem in the search for solutions to the violation of human rights is the fact that not all governments agree that they need to meet international human rights standards of any kind. Some governments argue that such standards are examples of Western imperialism and violate the cultural autonomy of non-Western societies as well as undermine the attempts of governments to promote economic development. Ohn Gyaw, the Foreign Minister of the State Law and Order Restoration Council (SLORC) in Myanmar/Burma, has said that 'there are no compulsions or obligation for any country to sign the UN Convention on Human Rights. Like some other countries in Asia, we have to take into consideration our culture, ethos and the standards of development before accepting these declaration' [sic] (Free Burma, 2003).

This view stems from two beliefs about human rights. The first is that, because the idea of human rights is largely a product of Western European political philosophy, it is irrelevant, or even harmful, to other societies. This is the cultural relativist viewpoint, which argues that ideas about right and wrong must be judged within the context of the culture in which they developed. Pressuring non-Western governments to accept international human rights standards is therefore an act of domination or imperialism, forcing these societies to accept something that is foreign, and the adoption of such standards may dislocate traditional cultural or religious practices, such as the veiling of women. The second belief is that the need for economic development outweighs the individual rights of citizens. Some governments have felt that it is necessary to restrict individual rights as part of the effort to raise national income and living standards. In the most well-known example of this type, China in 1979 instituted the one-child policy (one child per family) in an effort to slow population growth and allow the government the opportunity to eradicate famine in the world's most populous country. Thus, the difficulties in protecting human rights stem not only from the limited effectiveness of the solutions currently available, but from the unfortunate fact that some governments feel that the idea of human rights is irrelevant to the interests of their countries.

### Conclusion

Today, the establishment of an international consensus on human rights seems as unlikely as ever. The New World Order (post-1991) claimed to have human rights and democratisation as a focus, but the increase throughout the last decade in intra-national conflicts characterised by ethnic cleansing has meant that human rights violations have been on the rise in many parts of the world. In addition, although the War on Terrorism since September 11 2001 has been concerned with the elimination of threats to personal security as well as to the national security of the United States and its Western allies, Western governments have ignored the civil liberties implications of anti-terrorist measures as well as the wider human rights abuses that have motivated, although do not justify, the actions of hijackers and suicide bombers. It is necessary for both governments and individuals to re-evaluate their priorities if further developments in the protection of human rights are to be achieved. Governments must be willing to push human rights concerns further up the foreign policy agenda, and connect human rights issues with other issues such as trade and military assistance. Moreover, Western governments should reconsider their foreign aid packages to developing countries. Rather than slashing foreign aid budgets to increase their own defence spending, the governments of the world's richest countries ought to fund projects for sustainable development in the Third World, which will both improve social and economic rights in poor countries and improve international security. Finally, it is individuals who can make the greatest difference in the protection of human rights. Citizens must increase the pressure on their governments, through voting and lobbying, to prioritise human rights issues in the ways suggested above. Consumers should express concern for the rights of workers in developing countries by buying Fair Trade tea, coffee, chocolate and clothes, and encouraging retailers who rely on sweatshop labour to change their subcontracting practices. Individuals can also make a difference by supporting non-governmental organisations such as Amnesty International and Oxfam in their campaigns for political and social justice. In the end, it is up to us. National governments and multinational corporations will not change their policies unless we demonstrate to them that human rights violations by any government, anywhere, are unacceptable.

### Notes

1  The sources of international humanitarian law are international treaties including the Geneva Convention of 1864, the Hague Conventions of 1899 and 1907, and the Geneva Conventions of 1949. The four conventions of 1949 cover the prevention of human rights violations during war, the prevention of mistreatment of prisoners of war, and the prevention of mistreatment of civilians during war. Additional protocols added in 1977 cover the protection of victims of international armed conflict and the protection of victims of non-international armed conflict (O'Byrne, 2003: 88).
2  The European Convention on Human Rights, Article 15, paragraph 1, states that 'in time of war or other public emergency threatening the life of the nation, any High Contracting Party may take measures derogating from its obligations under this Convention to the extent strictly required by the exigencies of the situation, provided that such measures are not inconsistent with its other obligations under international law'.
3  United Nations, Universal Declaration of Human Rights, General Assembly resolution 217A (III), 10 December 1948.

### Bibliography

Amnesty International (2002), *Amnesty International Report 2002*, Amnesty International Publications, accessed at http://web.amnesty.org/web/ar2002.nsf/home/home?OpenDocument, 18 July, 2002.

Black, E. (2002), 'Labour MPs Rebel Over All-Women Shortlists', *The Sunday Times*, 7 July, p. 5.

Brown, S. (2000), *Human Rights in World Politics*, Harlow: Addison Wesley Longman.

Coalition for the International Criminal Court, www.iccnow.org accessed 21 July 2003.

Colvin, M. (2002), 'Jenin: The Bloody Truth', *The Sunday Times*, 21 April, p. 23.

Donnelly, J. (1993), *International Human Rights*, 2nd edition, Boulder, CO: Westview Press.

Free Burma, www.ibiblio.org/freeburma/ accessed 22 July 2003.

Gumbel, A. (2002), 'China's Killing Spree Doubles World's Execution Toll', *Independent*, 10 April, p. 14.

Huggler, J. (2002), 'My Mother Ran For Help. A Soldier Shot Her in the Head', *Independent*, 11 April, p. 5.

Locke, J. [1690] (1960), *Locke's Two Treatises of Government*, ed. P. Laslett, Cambridge: Cambridge University Press.

McGreal, C. and Whitaker, B. (2002), 'Israel Accused Over Jenin Assault', *Guardian*, 23 April, p. 2.

O'Byrne, D. (2003), *Human Rights: An Introduction*, Harlow: Pearson Education.

Paine, T. [1791–92] (1973), *The Rights of Man*, Garden City, NY: Doubleday Anchor.

Rousseau, J.-J. [1762] (1973), *The Social Contract and Discourses*, trans. G.D.H. Cole, ed. J. Brumfitt and J. Hall, London: Dent.

Shue, H. (1980), *Basic Rights: Subsistence, Affluence and U.S. Foreign Policy*, Princeton, NJ: Princeton University Press.

United Nations, (1985), *Convention Against Torture and Other Cruel, Inhuman or Degrading Treatment or Punishment*, entered into force in March.

United Nations, *Universal Declaration of Human Rights* [Resolution 217 A (III)], adopted by the General Assembly of the United Nations, 10 December, 1948.

Usborne, D. (2002), 'UN Struggles to Salvage Mission to Enter Jenin', *Independent*, 29 April, p. 2.

Vidal, J. (2002), 'Malawi Faces Famine As Aid Dribbles in', *Guardian*, 30 April, p. 14.

Vincent, R. J. (1986), *Human Rights and International Relations*, Cambridge: Cambridge University Press.

# 8

# Gender

*Emma Clarence*

In the latter half of the twentieth century the idea of 'gender' became an increasingly important concept in politics. It challenged conventional ideas and stretched the traditional boundaries of politics and provided a different way of viewing the world and social and economic relations within it. Gender should not be simply equated with feminism, nevertheless the analysis which gender provides of such relationships clearly owes much to feminist analysis. As a concept what gender examines is the differences between women and men that are more than 'biological sex' incorporating ideas of masculinity and femininity. Thus, gender is concerned with the meaning of 'masculine' and 'feminine' and their role and influence as ideas within society. Moving beyond this gender has sought to explain why there are differences in the economic and social outcomes which men and women experience. It is in this explanatory role that gender is at its most powerful in contemporary politics. Furthermore, gender has served as a useful tool around which to focus campaigns on improving the role, status and access to resources of women within society as well as challenging the assumptions about the roles of both men and women within society.

The belief of female inferiority was the basis for the exclusion of women from participating in political life and it was not until the twentieth century (with one or two exceptions) that women were accorded legal, intellectual and moral equality with men. For example New Zealand granted women the vote in 1893 and Turkey in 1934; it was not until 1971 that Swiss women were able to vote. In the United Kingdom women over the age of thirty could vote or stand for parliament from 1918, although it was 1928 before such rights were extended to all women over twenty-one. Women also confronted significant difficulties in their desire for economic autonomy. Until a series of changes in the law in the United Kingdom between 1870 and 1882 any property a woman acquired either before or during her marriage belonged to her husband. The belief of female inferiority which such practices illustrate was not shared by all and the claim that people were of equal worth, regardless of their sex, became increasingly, although not universally, accepted.

Despite success in achieving the legal recognition of equal worth, perceptions have continued that women and men are *fundamentally different* beyond basic physical distinctions. The differences are no longer based upon the belief of female inferiority, but rather that there are characteristics and traits which women and men have that impact on their behaviour, skills and attributes. Such traits are considered to be important because, some have argued, they allow men and women to fulfil different roles which are complementary, even equal. However, such ideas and attitudes reinforce the unequal economic, political and social outcomes which are experienced by women and men in addition to subsuming them under the guise of 'different but equal'. They have also had a profound impact upon the way in which the roles men and women play within society are perceived and evaluated. These characteristics have been labelled 'masculinity' and 'femininity' and in order to address what they have come to mean, and the impact these have on people, the idea of gender has been developed. This chapter examines the meaning of gender, how the idea developed and explores its role and importance in contemporary politics.

## What is gender?

The words 'sex' and 'gender' are frequently used interchangeably; however, sex and gender have two very distinct meanings that need to be clearly understood. 'Male' and 'female' are the words that describe the *biological* sex of people which refer to the anatomical and biological differences that exist between men and women. It is important to recognise that the word 'sex' does not contain any assumptions about characteristics of people being linked to their sex, but is simply a biological description of a person. In contrast, gender refers to processes outside of biology; it goes beyond sex and focuses on ideas of masculinity and femininity (Tripp, 2000: 3). Broadly, it is the way in which 'sex [is] expressed in society in terms of behaviour' (Carver, 1998: 19). To be male does not necessarily mean to be masculine, nor does being female mean being feminine although there are particular traits that have become identified and associated with masculinity and femininity.

Gender is a relatively 'new' concept in the social sciences, whose origins can be traced back to the first half of the twentieth century. At first it was used primarily in the fields of anthropology and sociology and it was not until the late 1960s and 1970s, when feminist authors sought to explain why the economic and social outcomes experienced by women differed so markedly from that of men, that the idea of gender developed the political meaning and significance it has today (Oakley, 1997: 31–2). Gender is a contested idea and does not have a single, fixed definition. Some authors have argued that gender examines culturally driven assumptions and expectations about feminine and masculine behaviour. Thus, gender is a useful analytical tool which enables us to develop an understanding of how ideas of feminine and masculine behaviour develop and how they are reflected within societies. Others, however, have gone beyond that idea, claiming that gender is 'the *social* explanation of sex differences' (Oakley, 1997: 44). This position accords gender a far more powerful role. It is not simply a tool but actually an idea which explains why men and women achieve different outcomes across a range of social and economic experiences. Clearly the ideas are linked, although the second position gives gender a far stronger explanatory role than the first.

Extending the concept of gender even further is the belief that gender should take into account sexuality. This idea argues that gender should not be simply defined as 'masculinity' and 'femininity' but rather, that it should actually consider the idea of a multiplicity of genders. For example masculine heterosexuality and homosexuality should be identified as distinct genders rather than subsumed into the single category 'masculine' (Carver, 1998). If this idea is accepted then the number of genders is significantly larger than the simple binary of masculine and feminine. This not withstanding, the discussion in this chapter will treat gender as referring to masculine and feminine forms.

As with many political concepts language is important when talking about gender. Despite the conceptual differences that exist between the words 'sex' and 'gender', the word gender has entered into common usage, effectively replacing sex. It is not uncommon to see on surveys and forms: 'Gender: male or female', as if asking for a person's gender is somehow 'more polite' than asking for their sex. The fact that gender has edged sex out as a biological description is more than simply a change in language, it impacts upon the way in which the idea of gender is understood. By using sex and gender interchangeably the importance of the concept of gender is lost (Oakley, 1997: 52). Gender has a crucial role to play in explaining the differences that exist in the outcomes which women and men experience: in effect, it is a powerful tool for explaining inequality. If it is used inaccurately to talk about biological sex then its effectiveness as an explanatory tool is lessened.

## Gender and feminism

As a result of the perceived connections between women and gender there has been a tendency to consider gender as being synonymous with women (Oakley, 1997: 30). This is both a result of the historical development of the term and, as Oakley argues, 'because gender was invented to help explain women's position' (1997: 30). Given these factors, it is not unsurprising that a significant amount of the discussion on gender has developed from feminist debates. Broadly, feminism has sought to explain and address inequalities between women and men. In particular it has argued that women experience oppression *because* they are women and that this oppression is a result of systems of structures of male authority, commonly referred to as patriarchy. Feminism seeks both to provide an analysis and critique of patriarchy and to identify ways to improve the role and place of women within society. However within feminism there is disagreement as to how to end the patriarchal structures which oppress women and what they should be replaced with.

The discussion of patriarchy has been accompanied by significant debate around the ideas of equality and difference within feminism. Essentially the arguments revolve around two competing ideas; firstly, that women should be treated equally to men or secondly, that women are fundamentally different to men and that such difference should be recognised. The idea that women are equal to men has raised questions about whom women should be equal to and in what way. Men are not an homogenous group; like women, they are divided by class, ethnicity and other factors. A demand for equality is therefore problematic. Some feminists, notably liberal feminists, have argued for legal and political equality between men and women. Such formal equality would allow women to compete with men for the same resources on the same terms. This idea has been rejected by other feminists, including socialist and radical feminists, who have claimed that such a narrow definition of equality does not go far enough because it ignores forms of oppression which women may experience based on, for example, class and/or ethnicity. However, ideas of equality with men are not accepted by all feminists. Rather, it has been argued that the differences that exist between men and women need to be recognised. Those who support the claim of difference reject the idea of equality with men because of its failure to recognise sex/sexual differences and claim that such differences cannot be ignored or subsumed into ideas of equality. The equality or difference debate finds echoes in discussion of gender and in the political responses to gender debates.

Feminism has made an important contribution to our understanding of politics by identifying a (false) divide between the public and private worlds which individuals inhabit. Historically, there was a perception that a divide existed between the private sphere of home, family and personal relationships and the public sphere of politics and public employment. Men played a role in the public sphere, while women were confined to the private sphere. The divide was seen as being a 'natural' divide with women responsible for the areas in which they were considered to be competent, notably the home and children. However, feminists have argued instead that 'the personal is political' and have rejected the naturalness of the divide. The argument maintains that the line between politics and personal life cannot be drawn; that all aspects of our lives can be political. This is not to say that the divide was rigid; however, it served to delineate the boundaries between what was the interest of politics and what was not. By challenging that divide our understanding of politics is broadened.

Feminism does not have a single position on gender and the idea of gender itself has its critics. For many feminists the idea of gender is crucial in explaining inequality. It rejects the way in which inequality has been structured as being 'natural' in favour of recognising that ideas of masculinity and femininity are actually constructed ones, based upon the *expectations* and *assumptions* of the societies in which people live. Thus, gender can be both learnt by individuals and ascribed by the social and cultural environment individuals inhabit. However, while some feminists have argued for the importance of gender, other feminists have rejected it because they argue that it fails to incorporate the power relations required to adequately reflect society (Oakley, 1997: 50). It does not give enough weight to the idea that power is experienced differently by men and women. By claiming that gender is a cultural construction then the issue of oppression, so central to many feminist thinkers, is side-stepped and discriminatory structures are in fact hidden behind ideas of gender differences (1997: 52). Accordingly, some feminists think that gender weakens the idea of oppression rather than strengthens it, although this is disputed by those who maintain that gender relations can also be seen as relationships of power and inequality between men and women (Peterson and Runyon, 1999: 5).

### Learning gender

The stereotypes which have arisen surrounding men and women provide a useful pointer to the way in which ideas about gender have become part of common understanding of the way men and women should behave. Men are rational, ambitious, strong and aggressive while women are emotional, passive, fragile and consensual. It is easy to find instances where such stereotypes are not accurate but by considering what is meant when the words 'feminine' and 'masculine' are used highlights the way in which certain traits have become linked to one or the other. It also raises the question that if gender is not natural, but is rather learnt, how are such ideas developed and inculcated?

The view that some modes of behaviour are natural to men or women – such as that women are 'naturally' nurturers whilst men are 'naturally' providers – has been rejected by many feminist sociologists in favour of the idea of 'gendering'. Gendering refers to the processes by which men and women take on and internalise particular ways of behaving that are deemed to be appropriate to their sex. The characteristics that are considered to be 'masculine' and 'feminine' are created by the societies and cultures in which people live. They are inculcated and learnt as individuals actually perform 'prescribed gender roles' (Peterson and Runyan, 1999: 5). Each time a girl is encouraged to 'play house' or to participate in 'passive' games and activities and a boy to play competitive or aggressive games certain ideas about gender roles are being taught. It is important to remember that gender does not see difference as being 'natural'. These ideas are not uncontested.

The distinction made between sex and gender is one that has been challenged because of the divide it creates between the body and consciousness: sex is the body while gender is found in the consciousness (Gatens, 1991). Such ideas reject the notion that gender is learnt on a number of different grounds. Firstly, the idea of gendering can be coupled with that of 'degendering'; if gender is learnt then it can be 'unlearnt'. This idea was particularly popular during the 1970s when there was a belief in (re-)education as a way of bringing about social change. It can still be seen in the minority practice (mainly in the USA) of attempting to alter an individual's sexual orientation through a process of education. Secondly, gender fails to recognise the importance of the body in the process of gender identification. Sex and gender cannot be distinguished because the body has a profound impact on the way in which individuals are perceived and treated.

Accepting the idea that gender is a social and cultural construction it is clear that the meanings given to masculinities and femininities vary and differ between cultures and over time. Accordingly, the social, cultural and historical contexts in which gender differences exist have to be recognised if gender is to be effectively understood. There is not a series of differences that can be identified and used to measure or examine gender, and its associated differentials in outcomes, across all times and all countries. Rather, gender is a conceptual framework through which to examine the social, political and economic world in which people live and accordingly, when studying politics with gender as a consideration, it is necessary to be aware of cultural, historical and other differences. Clearly, the processes of 'gendering' take place across all aspects and parts of society – hence the cultural and social context – however, one area which has been identified as being of central importance to learning gender identities is the family. The role of the family is crucial because it is an arena in which gender relations are reproduced and maintained. Despite the changes that have occurred in patterns of employment, assumptions about roles both inside and outside the house are rooted in ideas of appropriate gender roles. Constructions of the family are imbued with ideas and assumptions of gender roles (Vogel, 1998: 29).

The 'traditional' family model – of man as breadwinner, woman as carer – persists in the conceptions of families. It remains an expectation that women will be the main carers for children; 'house husbands' are unusual and at best are viewed with mild bemusement. Even in those cases where both men and women are in full time work, women are confronted with very different expectations about their responsibilities and activities based upon gender assumptions. Newspapers and popular magazines report on the competing demands women confront as they seek to find a balance between work and home. Men, however, appear not to be faced with the same need to balance the competing demands of work and family. This is a simple example of the way in which social expectations highlight gender differences; men are not 'meant' to be the main carers – that role belongs to women.

The perceptions of appropriate gender roles in this case are clear and link neatly to ideas of what is feminine or masculine behaviour. Such behaviour is not only reinforced by the society and culture in which people live but the state can play a powerful role in directing ideas of gender. The state is not a neutral actor in gender relations; using policies and laws the state can influence or reinforce the meaning given to ideas of gender. For example, maternity leave was something which was first granted to women; men were not considered to need the time away from work to adjust to the significant changes that occurred following the birth of a child. Changes have taken place which grant men two weeks paternity leave in the United Kingdom, although this should be compared to the statutory allowance of twenty-six weeks for women. In this example the state is playing a crucial role in constructing or reinforcing ideas of gender, specifically that women are responsible for caring for children. While this may appear to be a statement of 'fact' it is necessary to go beyond the reality and look at how and why that assumption is maintained. Why is it that we assume only women will take care of babies? Why aren't men the main carers of their children? The concept of gender offers an explanation by highlighting the way in which gender is learnt through performing particular roles (in this case mother as carer, father as breadwinner) and reinforced not simply by society but by the state.

This is not to claim that the state is responsible only for reinforcing particular gender roles. The state can also play a role in mediating gender relations by changing policies and laws so that they are 'gender neutral', in that they neither privilege nor discriminate on the grounds of gendered behaviour – perceived or otherwise. Alternatively, the state may recognise gender and the differences it creates and seek to obviate those differences. Another option is where the state actively seeks to effectively deconstruct gender roles by, for example, breaking down the distinctions between the 'breadwinner' (masculine) and 'carer' (feminine). This would have far-reaching and radical consequences as the notion of gender itself would ultimately be compromised. It is, therefore, perhaps unsurprising that this option is not often evident in the activities of states (Sainsbury, 1996).

Economic outcomes provide an example where gendered social expectations have been met by attempts to change the way in which gender impacts upon women. The argument that women do less well in terms of pay and promotion because they bear children is one frequently put forward to explain the differences in economic outcomes between men and women. While it is an indisputable biological fact that women have children; it is the social construction of that role as mother/carer, rather than the biological fact itself that economically disadvantages women (Bryson, 1999: 47). Although women continue to be economically penalised for having children (in terms of, for example, overall lower pay and a lack of promotion opportunities, or the inability to develop an adequate retirement pension) there have been attempts to address areas of major concern. If there is inadequate childcare provision research indicates that overwhelmingly it will be women who stay at home to care for children, despite the fact that childcare is an issue for both men and women. The provision of childcare in the United Kingdom is still inadequate in meeting the expressed needs of women (Women and Equality Unit 2002: 68) and there is a strong reliance upon the private sector to meet childcare needs. In other parts of western Europe, including the Scandinavian countries, Belgium, France and Italy, there is less pressure on childcare provision due to more generous parental leave provisions and/or the provision of publicly funded childcare. As a result of campaigns to highlight the impact of such underprovision, particularly upon women, governments have, over time, been forced to respond to demands for adequate childcare by making it increasingly available.

The term 'gender gap' is used to refer to the differences in outcomes that exist between men and women, particularly with reference to employment and income. While across much of the Western world 'equal pay for equal work' has been achieved as a legal right, it remains an, as yet, unattained goal. Women continue to earn, on average, less then men and they are still concentrated in certain sectors of the labour market. It is not simply income, but also status, which has a gender dimension. Those employment sectors which are considered to be 'feminine' (e.g. teaching, nursing, etc.) are both rewarded less than other sectors and viewed as having lower status than those which are seen as being predominantly male which are considered to have greater status and remuneration (Steans, 1998: 11). Even when women work in sectors which are not 'feminised' they invariably find themselves earning less than men. Through using gender as a tool it is possible not simply to identify the pay differences that exist but to explain them.

Ideas of childcare and unequal rates of pay between men and women may appear to be concerns relevant only to the developed world. However, gender is also a useful explanatory tool when applied in developing countries. Issues such as access to resources, not simply financial resources such as pay, but also land, education and healthcare, as well as how power is distributed within society, can all be examined through a gender framework. The assumptions regarding the roles individuals play are also relevant. The importance of the social, cultural and historical contexts of gender need to be remembered when it is being used trans-nationally. It should also be noted that ideas surrounding gender can be problematic outside of Western states. In particular, 'gender-equity' can be viewed as a 'Western liberal' concept that is not applicable within a non-Western setting. This can raise difficult challenges for western governments and institutions which work in a non-Western environment as to the extent to which they use, or even impose ideas of, gender in the programmes and policies they may be encouraging and implementing. Should, for example, funding for education be dependent upon both girls and boys receiving equal access? While this would appear to ensure gender equity in terms of access to education such a demand has wider implications for who does what work within a wider social context. What happens if boys are removed from assisting with farmwork to go to school? What happens if the only member of a family earning money is a girl who should be at school? These are difficult decisions and highlight the way in which gender can be easily subsumed within wider considerations surrounding poverty as well as the need to recognise cultural and social difference when considering gender.

## Men and gender

It is clear that gender refers to more than simply women and goes beyond feminist ideas and includes men as well as women. According to theories of gender it is not simply ideas of femininity that are socially and culturally constructed but also ideas of masculinity. Two key points can be identified: first, gender explicitly incorporates men and secondly, gender is learned. Despite the explicit desire to incorporate men into the idea of gender there can be little doubt that at the level of both domestic and international politics gender has been understood primarily with reference to women.

The tendency to consider gender and women synonymously, a result of the historical development of gender, also raises interesting and important questions about the way in which ideas of 'male' and 'masculinity' remained unquestioned and unproblematised. Men appear to be granted the status of 'normal', while women are not; for example, 'women's studies' are not posited against 'men's studies'. Instead 'women's studies' are seen as being something conducted outside of 'mainstream' politics. In failing to recognise the importance (or even existence) of men when discussing gender, in effect to use 'gender as a synonym for women', many of the difficulties already identified return. If gender has nothing to do with men, then women are again problematised and marginalised. By recognising that gender is more than women or feminism it is possible to acknowledge the constructed nature of masculinity and to consider gender in a very different way.

Accompanying the way in which maleness is normalised in politics is the relationship between masculinity and femininity. Femininity and masculinity do not exist independently of each other; they are implicitly or explicitly defined against each other. This is not to imply that a balance exists between those ideas or that they coexist equally. Rather, the dichotomy between 'masculine' and 'feminine' is an unequal one whereby a hierarchy, in which certain traits and modes of behaviour are valued and prioritised above others, has been established. By privileging one, the other is effectively denigrated. In the 1997 *Human Development Report* the United Nations reported that 'no society treats its women as well as its men' (United Nations Development

Programme, 1997). Such a finding highlights the way in which men have been, and continue to be, privileged over women.

Gender analysis has highlighted the problems and difficulties women confront because of the assumptions about their roles. It can also challenge the assumptions made about men and the roles they play. Presuming that men are not carers has the potential to impoverish both themselves as individuals and the relationships they have with others. Crucial to considering gender is to see people as individuals, rather then as a collection of roles. Such a consideration would contribute to people being able to fulfil their potential – something which is central to the way in which gender as a concept is being operationalised in politics (Equal Opportunities Commission, 2003).

## Gender and politics

Having established what gender is and how it is maintained, it is necessary to establish *why* it is important in the study of politics and *how* it contributes to our understanding of the political world. How politics is defined has important implications for what is studied and what is deemed to be outside the field of what should be studied. While any definition of politics is essentially contested and debated, the predominant focus has been on states, governments and institutions. Interactions between people as individuals have not been part of that definition – politics has effectively been confined to events and issues and how governments (and individuals within the government) have responded to them. In such a narrow definition it is clear that much has been left out. One area that has been marginalised is gender and by bringing it in, it is possible to view politics and the political world very differently.

Although the idea of public/private spheres has been convincingly challenged by feminists with their claim of 'the personal is political', the idea of the divide remains important because it plays a role in structuring the way in which individuals are expected to behave within particular spaces. The gender traits most commonly associated with masculinity and femininity are linked to ideas firmly rooted in the assumption that the public world is a masculine one and the private world a feminine one. The challenge to the public/private divide not only allowed women to be brought into clearer focus in politics but it also enabled the politicised understanding of the concept of gender to enter the political world.

By challenging the view that politics is more than states and governments the historically narrow definition of politics is contested. The private sphere that was not part of the study of politics, and indeed continues to be ignored by some, emerges as a political arena. In doing this, the way in which women have been marginalised, if not excluded, from the study of politics is identified. No longer are women something outside of politics; rather they can be brought to the centre of politics and accompanying them the idea of gender can also enter the debate. Although this is what gender could have done for the study of politics it should not be assumed that this is what has necessarily taken place.

Despite the advances women have made in the political and economic spheres it remains that, in terms of politics, men and women have a differential access to power. Given the use of gender as an explanatory tool it would appear correct to think that gender plays a valuable role in addressing issues of power, exclusion and unequal outcomes. So why has it remained marginalised from mainstream politics? Arguably, the marginalisation of gender is a product of the historical development of the study of politics. The public and private divide provides one explanation; politics takes place in the public sphere and was historically a male domain. Thus, the study of politics was about men. Other reasons that have contributed to the marginalisation of gender are that men have dominated the field of political research and that the absence of gendered approaches has not been recognised. The study of politics was, and arguably still is despite decades of gender-focused research, dominated by a particular view of the world which effectively privileges masculinity and male views of the world. Furthermore, it is a view that has failed to acknowledge that by studying politics with gender in mind not only do we learn things about women, but we also learn about men.

Gender is important because it plays a central role in life opportunities and social relations. It is not something that is experienced intermittently; it shapes how an individual experiences social and economic outcomes. How it is experienced will depend not only on the social and culture forces in existence, but how an individual is affected by other social relationships, such as class or race. To cross the boundaries (that is for a man to display feminine attributes, or a women masculine attributes) is ultimately negative for both men and women. Women are seen as having 'lost' their femininity (with a suggestion of unnaturalness and/or homosexuality) and men may find their (hetero)sexuality challenged. The centrality of gender in shaping the lives of individuals should not, and can not, be isolated from political understanding.

Not only is gender important in politics because it allows us to learn about social and economic outcomes between men and women, but because it goes to the heart of politics and allows us to focus on a central issue within politics – power. As Peterson and Runyan argue 'Gender is about power, and power is gendered' (1997: 7). To acknowledge that 'gender is about power' is to place gender at the heart of politics and political analysis – it focuses on gender relations within society and highlights the masculine dominance that continues in the way in which power is exercised. Thus, gender is not only crucial in the development of an understanding of the way in which women's lives are affected by social conventions, assumptions and expectations but in the nature of the dynamics of power itself within societies.

Nor is it simply about gender as power between men and women. The fact that gender can be moulded by politics indicates that in turn gender can seek to shape politics and political interactions (Randall and Waylen, 1998: 1). Power, and all its dynamics, are present in that relationship. However, it is important to recognise that gender is not simply about one particular set of actors or goals. Resistance offered to feminist ideas and feminist goals cannot be ignored in the study of politics and gender. As Walby states 'Gender politics ... are not only the activities of women asking for greater equality, but involve anti-feminist responses' (Walby, 1997: 156). It is clear that gender can provide a different framework through which to examine and consider the political world and that it is a concept that challenges the way in which politics is viewed.

Gender, as we have already explored, is useful for examining and explaining differences in access to political power and political outcomes. However, it can be more than an analytical tool. In its identification of differences it becomes a focus around which to campaign and lobby for change. National and international communities have not been able to ignore the emergence of gender and gender related issues although the way in which states and institutions have responded to the idea of gender has seen it focused predominantly on women. The United Nations Decade of Women (1976–85) accompanied by global conferences in Mexico City, Copenhagen, Nairobi and Beijing is indicative of the way in which gender has been pushed onto the international agenda. Such meetings have also been accompanied by other activities by the United Nations (including conventions on the elimination of sex discrimination and the declaration on women's equal rights), which have addressed gender based inequalities (Petersen and Runyan, 1999: 11). In turn, national governments have also become increasingly aware of the need to consider and respond to gender issues in the policy process. This awareness has been raised by individuals and organisations who have campaigned for gender to be taken seriously as an issue which affects both men and women as well as by those working within governments and institutions on the impact of gender inequality on wider society. On the whole, governments and institutions have not fundamentally challenged gender assumptions but have instead sought to ameliorate the worst inequalities that have developed as a result of gender differences. While such events are important in raising the differences in outcomes that men and women experience and undoubtedly make small inroads into addressing the imbalances which exist, the often evident focus on women does little to acknowledge masculinities in gender.

At the UN Decade of Women Conference in Beijing in 1995 it was decided that the idea of 'gender mainstreaming' would be encouraged and promoted around the world. Gender mainstreaming is the attempt to bring gender into the heart of what governments and institutions do. In the context of policy making it means that the implications of a policy are examined with explicit consideration for associated gender issues; any potential negative outcomes should be recognised and resolved. For example, altering the times at which the school day starts and finishes has an impact not only on the school staff, but also on parents. What that impact is, and how it affects the various people, would need to be considered. Do the changes presume that there is always an individual available to collect a child? How do the changes impact upon other responsibilities an individual may have? Gender mainstreaming does not only take place at the national level, international organisations and institutions such as the United Nations and the development agency Oxfam have also sought to ensure that their policies and programmes are sensitive to gender issues by implementing gender mainstreaming guidelines.

Gender mainstreaming is a positive recognition of the importance of gender for both men and women. However, it does not necessarily mean that gender inequalities are meaningfully addressed, simply that there is an acknowledgement of the need to consider gender in the design and implementation of policies. For gender inequalities to be addressed other strategies would need to be used that explicitly challenge the structures and behaviours which maintain them. Such a challenge requires both men and women to work together if gender equity is to be realised.

### Conclusion

To understand gender and its role in politics it is necessary to recognise that it is both a concept and a tool which can be used to challenge the roles of men and women. As a concept gender has recognised and sought to explain the differences which men and women experience in their economic and social roles. From this it has enabled a wide range of organisations, institutions and governments to acknowledge and consider how such differences can be addressed. Even before the adoption of the idea of gender mainstreaming at the 1995 United Nations World Conference on Women, gender was an issue gaining increased consideration as to its impact within wider society.

In terms of understanding gender within the study of politics it is an issue that has to be understood and studied as part of politics rather than as something separate from it. To do the latter is to construct gender issues as secondary ones, effectively marginalising gender, rather than recognising its centrality and importance. By placing gender at the heart of the study of politics, not only is it possible to develop a deeper understanding of women and their experiences, but also of men and of politics itself. In failing to recognise the potential of gender, contemporary political research is inadequately examining the political world.

Gender continues to make a valuable contribution to the study of politics. It also plays a central role in contemporary politics around the world. By addressing the assumptions about the roles of both men and women within wider society not only are the political, social and economic inequalities which women experience brought to light but the way such assumptions also impact upon men can be identified. As a result an awareness of the role of gender assumptions, and an attempt to address them, has the potential to play a transformatory role in improving the social and economic experiences for both men and women.

### Bibliography

Bryson, V. (1999), *Feminist Debates: Issues of Theory and Political Practice*, London: Macmillan.

Carver, T. (1998), 'A Political Theory of Gender: Perspectives on the "Universal Subject"', in V. Randall and G. Waylen (eds), *Gender, Politics and the State*, London: Routledge, pp. 18–28.

Equal Opportunities Commission (2003), *Introduction to Gender Mainstreaming*, www.eoc.org.uk/EOCeng/EOCcs/AboutEOC/01.asp.

Gatens, M. (1991), 'A Critique of the Sex/Gender Distinction', in S. Gunew (ed.), *A Reader in Feminist Knowledge*, London: Routledge, pp. 139–57.

Gunew, S. (ed.) (1991), *A Reader in Feminist Knowledge*, London: Routledge.

Oakley, A. (1997), 'A Brief History of Gender', in A. Oakley and J. Mitchell (eds), *Who's Afraid of Feminism: Seeing through the Backlash*, London: Hamish Hamilton, pp. 29–55.

Peterson, V. and Sisson Runyan, A. (1999), *Global Gender Issues*, Oxford: Westview Press.

Randall, V. and Waylen, G. (eds) (1998), *Gender, Politics and the State*, London: Routledge.

Sainsbury, D. (1996), *Gender, Equality and Welfare States*, Cambridge: Cambridge University Press.

Segal, L. (1990), *Slow Motion: Changing Masculinities Changing Men*, London: Virago.

Steans, J. (1998), *Gender and International Relations: An introduction*, Cambridge: Polity Press.

Tripp, A. (ed.)(2000), *Gender: Readers in Cultural Criticism*, Basingstoke: Palgrave.

United Nations Development Programme (1997), *Human Development Report 1997: Human Development to Eradicate Poverty*, http://hdr.undp.org/reports/view_reports.cfm?type=1&start=1&subyear=1997.

Vogel, U. (1998), 'The State and the Making of Gender: Some Historical Legacies', in V. Randall and G. Waylen (eds), *Gender, Politics and the State*, London: Routledge, pp. 29–44.

Walby, S. (1997), *Gender Transformations*, London: Routledge.

Women and Equality Unit (2002), *Key Indicators of Women's Position in Britain*, London: Department of Trade and Industry.

# 9

# Religion

*Jeff Haynes*

This chapter will examine the extent and nature of religion's interaction with politics, and assess its contemporary political significance. It will look at the interaction of religion and politics in Western, former Communist and developing countries. It will conclude by considering the likely importance of religion in politics in the twenty-first century.

Until recently it was widely believed that modernisation – the shift from 'traditional' to 'modern' society, involving a fundamental change in the nature of people's occupational roles and asociated values – would lead to both the privatisation of religion, that is, its withdrawal from the public realm and to a more secular society in which religious issues were no longer widely deemed to be of public concern. Given such expectations, it was a surprise to many when, in 1978–79, Iran's Islamic revolution swept away the pro-Western regime of 'Shah Pahlavi. Now, a quarter century after the Iranian revolution, around the world religious actors with political goals are very common. A key question is: what are the political consequences of the involvement of religion in politics? The short answer is that they are variable. On the one hand, religion sometimes has a pivotal influence on political outcomes. For example, in Africa, Latin America and Eastern Europe in the 1980s and 1990s, leading figures in various churches – notably the Catholic Church – were instrumental in regional turns to democracy. On the other hand, religious actors cannot always influence political outcomes in the way they would like. For example, in Algeria during the 1990s, Islamic fundamentalists were unable to force the secular-minded, military-backed government to stand down, despite a civil war that has cost around 120,000 lives.

So numerous were the examples of religious resurgence around the world that an American commentator, George Wiegel claimed that an 'unsecularization' of the world was occurring (Huntington 1993: 22). By this he meant not 'only' an *apolitical* respiritualisation but also a geographically widespread religious political involvement. Religious actors with political goals were especially prominent in, but not restricted to, developing countries in Africa, Asia, Latin America and the Middle East. In the latter region, encouraged by the Iranian Islamic revolution of 1978–79 and the continuing Arab–Israeli conflict, there was widespread Islamic militancy (Husain, 1995). In South Asia, an explosion of militant Hinduism in officially secular India helped to transform the country's political landscape with Hindu fundamentalists, predominantly in the Bharatiya Janata Party, of particular political importance. In addition, relations deteriorated between Muslim Pakistan and Hindu India in the early 2000s, although this may not have been primarily a religious problem. Turning to South East Asia, in Thailand newly politicised Buddhist groups and parties emerged in the 1990s, while in Africa there are numerous recent examples of the political involvement of religion. First, there is Nigeria, a country which, politically and socially, is becoming increasingly polarised between Muslim and Christian groups; secondly Somalia, riven for years by clan fighting, also has a strong Islamic fundamentalist political movement; third, Sudan, has been torn for many years by a civil war between Arab Muslims and Black African Christians and other non-Muslims. In the developed world too, notably in the USA, Eastern Europe and the Balkans, there are recent examples of the political involvement of religion. The list of examples could be extended, but the point is clear: at the beginning of the twenty-first century there are few regions of the world where religion is not a factor in political conflict.

## Religion and politics in global context

Before attempting to explain why the recent political resurgence of religion has occurred, the key terms 'religion' and 'politics' should be defined. Politics may be defined as the pursuit of power to achieve social, ideological or diplomatic purposes. Defining religion is more difficult, but there are two main approaches. First, religion is either a system of beliefs and practices related to an ultimate being and the supernatural or beliefs and practices that are regarded as sacred and inviolate in a society. Second, in practical terms and for purposes of wider social analysis religion may be approached as a body of ideas and ethical norms known as a theology. From this may be derived either an ethical code, a formal institution, such as a church or mosque, or a social group or movement or even all three. There are two basic ways in which religion can affect the temporal world: first, by what it says and, second, by what it does. The former relates to its theology or doctrine, the latter to its social activity and its importance as a mark of identity. These may gain or seek influence through a variety of both institutional and informal links, such as political parties and church–state relations.

Analytically, it is necessary to distinguish between religion at the individual and group levels. Only with regard to the latter is it normally of political importance. From an individual perspective, religion may be thought of as a set of symbolic forms and acts, which relates people to the ultimate conditions of their existence. This is the *private*, spiritual side of religion. In this chapter, however, we are more concerned with *group* religiosity, whose claims and pretensions are *always* to some degree political as religion always has consequences for value systems. Group religiosity is manifested politically in collective solidarities and, frequently, in inter-group conflict, focused on either shared or contested images of the sacred, or on differences of culture or class, any of which may become political issues. Let us consider this question further with reference first to the developing world, then the West and finally, former communist Eastern Europe.

### The developing world

After the Second World War, decline of religious faith and growing secularisation in Western Europe fitted neatly with the idea that technological development and the application of science to overcome perennial social problems of poverty, hunger, and disease would result in sustained progress for all. And in this process, it was believed, religion would be an inevitable casualty.

One of the main tenets of what became known as modernisation theory was that societies would both secularise and develop as they modernised and industrialised. A key focus in this regard was the 'developing world', a shorthand expression covering more than one hundred non-Western countries. It was invented in the 1960s to describe two groups of countries: first, a large group of economically underdeveloped, then decolonising countries in Africa, Asia and the Middle East, and second, Latin American states, mostly independent since the early nineteenth century, yet still economically weak. In the 1960s and 1970s, many Latin American countries experienced the emergence of liberation theology, a set of religious ideas also concerned with issues of socio-political division and class struggle. Liberation theology was an intensely political phenomenon, a response to the appalling social and political conditions widely found throughout Latin America. Central to the concept was the notion of dependence and underdevelopment; the use of a class struggle perspective to explain social conflict and justify political action; and the exercise of a political role to achieve both religious and political goals.

Despite common histories of mostly European colonisation there are notable differences between developing countries. For example, such economically diverse countries as the United Arab Emirates (GNP per capita of US$18,220 in 1998), South Korea (US$7,970) and Mozambique (US$210), or politically singular polities such as Cuba (one-party communist state), Pakistan (military dictatorship), and India (multi-party democracy), are all classified as developing countries. However, to some observers, the economic and political

– not to mention cultural – differences between such countries outweighs their purported similarities.

Nevertheless, opinion surveys over time in countries across the developing world indicate that there is a high proportion of religious believers in virtually all. Why should this be the case? It is sometimes argued that social upheaval and economic dislocation, connected to the processes of modernisation, have stymied secularisation. The 1980s and 1990s were, for many people in the developing world, a period of social, economic and political transition. The consequence, it is claimed, is that many people in developing countries are now rediscovering the religious dimension to group identity and politics, that is, there is a contemporary 'return' to religion. This is said to be a consequence of six interrelated developments:

1  inconclusive and/or unsatisfactory modernisation;
2  disillusionment with secular nationalism;
3  problems of state legitimacy;
4  political oppression and 'incomplete' formation of national identity;
5  widespread socio-economic grievances;
6  erosion of traditional morality and values.

The simultaneity of these crises is said to provide an especially fertile environment for the growth of religion with political goals.

However, it is important to understand that there are numerous historical examples of political religion in the developing world, especially during and after Western colonisation. European rulers often sought to introduce secularisation which frequently led to a religious backlash in which Hinduism, Buddhism and Islam all went through phases of intense political activity. Immediately after the First World War, religion was widely employed in the service of anti-colonial nationalism in Africa, Asia and the Middle East. Pakistan was founded as a Muslim state in 1947, distinct in religion and culture from Hindu-dominated India, while Buddhism was of great political importance in the struggle for liberation from colonial rule in Burma and Vietnam. As already noted, in the 1960s and 1970s in Latin America liberation theology also gained widespread political significance. In the 1970s, political religion became of great importance in a number of developing countries, including Iran, Afghanistan and Nicaragua. Overall, these developments suggest that political religion in the developing world has a long history of opposition to unacceptable secular regimes and is not a new development in our time. Rather, it should be understood as a series of historical responses to attempts by the state to limit the political influence of religion.

In the aftermath of independence, modernising politicians, often influenced by Western ideologies, filled the void left by colonial administrators. However, the secularisation process they promoted did not, for the most part, bring development. Instead, it resulted in the attempted transplantation of alien Western institutions, laws and procedures that collectively aimed to

---

### Box 9.1 The Iranian Revolution

Because of Islam's pivotal role, the overthrow of the Shah of Iran in 1979 was one of the most spectacular political upheavals of recent times. The outcome of the revolutionary process was a clerical, authoritarian regime. The Shah's regime was not a shaky monarchy but a powerful centralised autocratic state possessing a strong and feared security service (SAVAK) and an apparently loyal and cohesive officer corps. Unlike earlier revolutions in other Muslim countries such as Egypt, Iraq, Syria and Libya, Iran's was not a secular, left-wing revolution from above, but one with massive popular support and participation. The forces which overthrew the Shah came from all urban social classes, different nationalities and ideologically varying political parties and movements, but an Islamic Republic was eventually declared. The Muslim clerics (*ulama*), organised by the Islamic Republican Party came to power, established an Islamic constitution and dominated the post-revolutionary institutions.

The Iranian revolution was internationally significant in a number of ways. It was the first since the French Revolution of 1789 in which the dominant ideology, forms of organisation, leading personnel and proclaimed goals were all religious in appearance and inspiration. The guide for the post-revolution Iranian state was the tenets of the Muslim holy book, the *Quran*, and the *Sunnah* (the traditions of the Prophet Muhammad, comprising what he said, did and approved of). While economic and political factors played a major part in the growth of the anti-Shah movement, the leadership of that movement (the clerics) saw the revolution's goals primarily in terms of building an Islamic state in which Western materialism and political ideas would be rejected. Over time, this was to be of major importance in the context of Iran's generally poor international relations with the West.

The radicals within Iran's ruling post-revolution elite began to lose ground following the death of Ayatollah Khomeini, the revolution's charismatic leader, in June 1989, just months after the end of the bloody Iran–Iraq war (1980–88). As it became clear that Iran's government was in dire need of Western investment, technology and aid to help build its revolution, the pragmatic state president, Hashemi Rafsanjani, and his political allies seemed to gain ascendancy. The lesson of this was that even a successful Islamic revolution cannot succeed in splendid isolation. Iranians, like people everywhere, hoped for improving living standards. They were not content with increased Islamicisation of state and society, which many perceived as little more than political and social repression behind a religious facade.

---

erode, undermine and eventually displace traditional, holistic religio-political systems. Such modernisers saw their countries as politically, socially and economically backward and, as a result, they believed that what was needed was to emulate the secular model of progress pursued successfully by Western capitalist or Eastern communist countries. Over time, however, the credibility and legitimacy of both secular socialism and secular capitalism was often seriously undermined. This was because these ideologies widely failed to deliver the promise of economic and political development and national integration.

Poorly implemented modernisation programmes often proved incompatible with traditional religious practices, as growing numbers of people left the rural areas for the cities, often because of land and employment shortages. While the social, political and economic impact of displacement and urban migration is extensive and complex, it is highly likely that dislocations of large numbers of people from rural communities, and the reforming of personal relations in urban areas, opened the way to renegotiation of allegiances to traditional institutions. Where modernisation was particularly aggressively pursued – for example, in Iran – religious backlash occurred. In summary, post-colonial governments of developing countries typically followed policies of nation-building and expansion of state power, equating secularisation with modernisation. However, by undermining traditional value systems, often allocating opportunities in highly unequal ways, modernisation produced in

---

### Box 9.2  The Bharatiya Janata Party (BJP)

Hindu nationalism, from being just one of the diverse currents of Indian politics in the 1960s and 1970s, focused politically in the BJP, began to project itself as the party of the future in the 1980s. Between 1989 and 1991 its share of the vote tripled to 20 per cent to become the strongest official parliamentary opposition to the Congress Party since independence. Between 1990 and 1995 the BJP won power in the National Capital Territory of Delhi and in six of India's twenty-five states – four in the Hindi-speaking belt of north India and two on the west coast. Of the 119 BJP members in the 545-seat Lok Sabha (Lower House of Parliament) in 1995, 106 came from these areas, while the party held only 8 of the 220 seats in the eastern and southern regions of India. Yet, in the 1996 general election the BJP's share of the vote did not increase much above the 1991 figure, only to 23.5 per cent. But this was enough to give it and its allies 188 seats, that is, more than a third of seats on less than a quarter of the vote. The geographical unevenness of the Hindu nationalist support reflected the plural character of the Indian political scene. However, the 1996 result also confirmed the steady polarisation of Indian society. Congress lost seats heavily in the north, west, and south, although it managed to maintain its position in the east of the country, hanging on to thirty-six seats. The share of the vote for Congress declined from 48 per cent in 1984 to just over 28 per cent in 1996. The fading of Congress in the first three regions was hastened because of the failure of India's Muslims to vote, as they traditionally did, for the Congress Party. In the 1995 round of state elections, most

many ordinary people a deep sense of alienation, stimulating a search for an identity that would give life purpose and meaning. Many believed they could deal with the unwelcome effects of modernisation by presenting their claims for more of the 'national cake' as part of a group. Often their sense of collective identity was rooted in traditional community religion. The result was a focus on religiosity, with far-reaching implications for social integration and political stability. This was not a 'return' to religion, but the rational utilisation of religious belief in pursuit of socio-political goals.

A consequence has been that many states in the developing world have sought to make it very difficult for political religion to organise. In most Muslim countries, for example, Islamic fundamentalist parties are either proscribed or heavily infiltrated by state security services. Algeria's Islamic Salvation Front (FIS), the Islamic Tendency Movement of Tunisia, Hamas and Islamic Jihad in Palestine, the Islamic Party of Kenya, and Tanzania's Balukta were all banned in the 1990s. Others – including the Partai Persatuan Pembangunan of Indonesia, the Parti Islam Se Malaysia and Egypt's Muslim Brothers – are controlled or infiltrated by the state. On the rare occasions when such parties

---

Muslims voted against both the BJP and Congress in favour of candidates or parties with secular credentials. This helps explain the rout of the ruling Congress party in 1996 and again in 1999: many Muslims identified the party with pro-Hindu sentiments, particularly because of the demolition of the mosque in Ayodhya in 1992.

Partial scepticism was not enough to prevent the BJP's relentless electoral progress. Like Christian fundamentalists in the USA or Islamists in Turkey, the BJP was not able to achieve power on its own. The BJP's chief difficulty lay in persuading those who were unimpressed by its nationalistic agenda that its political aims had a wider applicability in India's pluralist society. The BJP did not manage to convince non-nationalist politicians following its failure to form a government, and the second largest party – Congress (I) – was able to put together a ruling coalition that survived into 1997.

In the early 2000s the BJP dominated the political landscape of north and west India; it has found the south and west of the country a tougher nut to crack. This is because it is regarded as a mainly northern party, intent on imposing its narrow version of the Hindu tradition at the expense of alternative regional traditions. In the 1996 elections the BJP and its allies only managed to acquire a handful of seats in the south and east. Compare this to the 180 it gained – of the 323 on offer – in the north and west. In these regions, its communalistic programme, perceived by many Indian secular intellectuals as the expression of primordial sentiments indicative of the underdeveloped nature of the people concerned, was obviously highly appealing to millions of Indians.

are allowed openly to seek electoral support they are often reasonably successful. Examples include the FIS's electoral victories in 1990–91 and that of
Turkey's Welfare Party (Refah Partisi) in the mid-1990s. Refah won the largest share of the vote (21 per cent) of any party in the 1995 election before
achieving power a year later in coalition with a right-wing secular party, the
True Path. Later, in 1999, Refah was thrown out of government and banned.
In sum, parties such as the FIS (Algeria) and Refah (Turkey) have been
electorally popular because they offer the disaffected, the alienated and the
poverty-stricken a vehicle to pursue beneficial change.

In India, there is strong electoral support for Hindu nationalist parties –
and not only from the poor and marginalised. Shiv Sena jointly ruled Bombay
(Mumbai) and Maharashtra state with the Bharatiya Janata Party (BJP) during the 1990s.

Nationally, the BJP is the largest political party, eclipsing the country's
traditionally dominant Congress (I) Party. In Buddhist Thailand, on the other
hand, a Buddhist reformist party, Santi Asoke, had some electoral successes
in the early 1990s. The point is that parties like Shiv Sena, the BJP and Santi
Asoke all have a wide appeal as viable alternatives to ruling parties which
they characterise as corrupt and inefficient. In sum, when people lose faith in
the transformatory abilities of secular politicians, religion often appears a
viable alternative for the pursuit of beneficial change. It has widely enabled
religion to re-emerge into the public arena as a mobilising, normative force.


## The West

The West is usually understood as 'Europe or Europe and North America'.
However, what is commonly meant by the term implies more than a statement about geography. It is also about science and a certain set of ideas.
Arguably the modern West was born as a reaction against cultural relativism,
expressed in the development of a set of absolute truths in both science and
philosophy. In western thought science, in the form of abstract and general
axioms, principles and theories, provides an important model of modern rationality and modernity. In this outlook, there is little room for a formal political voice for religion. Consequently, it is surprising to many that religion has
become involved in at least some Western countries, where it was thought to
have withdrawn from the public arena.

The key development involving religion and politics in the West was the
progress of secularisation. Secularisation means a significant diminution of
the influence of religious concerns in everyday life. It has been one of the
main social and political trends in the West, especially in Western Europe,
since the Enlightenment (1720–80). It was long believed that as a society
modernises it inevitably secularises – that is, it becomes more complex, a
division of labour emerges whereby institutions become more highly special-

ised and, as a consequence, are increasingly in need of their own technicians. To many, secularisation was the most fundamental structural and ideological change in the process of political development, a global trend, and a universal facet of modernisation. As Western societies modernised there was a demystification of religion and a gradual, albeit persistent, erosion of religious influence in public affairs. The end result of secularisation, a secular society, is where the pursuit of politics takes place irrespective of religious interests.

Secularisation has gone hand in hand with separation of power between church and state in the USA and much of Europe. This situation developed over time, with an important symbolic moment being the 1648 Treaty of Westphalia. This agreement brought to an end the Thirty Years War and the religious wars between Protestants and Catholics which followed the Reformation. The Westphalian settlement established the rule that it was for secular political leaders to decide which religion would be favoured in their polity. What this amounted to was that the emerging states of Western Europe tended to be more or less religious monopolies of one religion or another, as well as increasingly the homes of self-conscious national groups. Autocratic rulers saw religious conformity as an essential underpinning of their rule, necessary to maintain the existing social political order in their favour.

The tendency towards rulers' absolutism and the growth of nationalism were both greatly affected by the French Revolution of 1789. In France itself, the Catholic Church, which had retained much of its wealth, social influence and political power after the 1648 Treaty of Westphalia, came under attack from radicals and revolutionaries. The division between them and the Church was not bridged during the nineteenth century and by the end of that period the rise of socialism and communism helped to diminish further the Church's influence in the political battles fought between socialists, liberals and conservatives in Western Europe. While the Church retained much power in Italy, Spain, Ireland and elsewhere, the overall effect of the growth of nationalism and secular politics in Europe was to diminish the Church's political power in relation to secular rulers.

In sum, an extraordinarily high level of secularisation now marks the countries of Western Europe, including Britain. What this implies is that, in Britain and more generally in Western Europe, religion is now widely privatised. Religious privatisation means that religious organisations shall not have the *right* to be actively engaged with matters of public concern or to play a role in public life. In Britain, the social decline of institutional religion is reflected in the following:

- most mainline churches have increasingly serious financial crises because the numbers of believers willing to pay sufficient sums for their upkeep is falling;
- falling numbers of religious professionals coming into the churches;
- declining church membership. Less than 2 per cent of English people

regularly attend services of the established church, the Church of England.

Britain is a constitutional monarchy exhibiting several different types of arrangement between the State and the mainline Christian Churches. The Anglican Church is the national English church established by law. Its head – 'defender of the faith' – is represented in Parliament by bishops in the House of Lords. The Queen of England is both the constitutional head of State and formal head of the Anglican church. The monarch does not, of course, exercise the *real* authority enshrined in these offices: the Prime Minister and the Archbishop of Canterbury, respectively, are the effective heads of these offices. The Church of Scotland is also an established church, although Presbyterian in its organisation and free from government interference. There are no mainline Churches in Wales or Northern Ireland.

Formally, Britain is a Christian Protestant society with other religious denominations present. In reality, however, Protestantism has given way to secularism based on a rationalism common to most of north west Europe. This subsequent dual character of British society – Christian but secular – is evident in the composition of several major institutions in the country. In a constitutional sense church and state are not separated in England, although in practice state and church are neither estranged nor very closely connected. But they are tightly bound together as a result of Britain's island-history which separates the country from continental experience.

What this amounts to is that in Britain, as elsewhere in Western Europe, the political and the religious have to a considerable degree disengaged from each other. This is a process that reflects a continuing process of decline of institutional religion's social significance. A consequence of religion's declining social significance in Britain is that religious elites – such as the Archbishop of Canterbury, head of the Anglican Church – have lost a great deal but not all, political and cultural significance. Political rulers and their policies in the main no longer need the direct or indirect legitimation of religious elites – although this is not to say that political leaders – such as Tony Blair or George Bush – do not *prefer* to have their support. In sum, both comparatively and historically speaking, the opinions and interests of religious elites have become marginal to the major social forces operative and determinative in Western European countries, including Britain. This decline in the prestige and influence of religious elites in Western Europe corresponds to the secularisation of social structure and of culture – including the diminished import of religious symbols – and the accompanying privatisation of religious institutions that normally accompany economic and political modernisation.

This was not universally true, however, even in Europe, a region long thought to be inexorably secularising. The civil war in the early 1990s in Bosnia-Herzegovina between Croats, Serbs and Bosnian Muslims was a de facto religious conflict. Each combatant identified religious and cultural (not ideological) allies, respectively, in Germany, Russia and the Arab-Muslim world.

In the late 1990s civil war in Kosovo was fought between ethnic Albanians and Serbs, a conflict between Muslims and Christians, with the former allegedly aided by co-religionists from the Middle East. In the USA, sustained attempts by the New Christian Right to mould and drive the political agenda underlines the growing socio-political significance of religion. Finally, in Israel, the growing political significance of Jewish fundamentalist groups, especially the ultra-Orthodox Shas party, is manifested in their appearance in the ruling coalition government.

The point is that two phenomena are simultaneously taking place in many Western countries. There is an increase in various forms of spirituality and religiosity and, more readily and openly than in the recent past, churches are willing to articulate their views on political and social issues. Casanova (1994) suggests that this is occurring because churches are no longer willing to be sidelined as states' jurisdictions have expanded into areas historically under their sole control. In relation to the first issue, the question is, are people becoming personally more religious while their societies are becoming collectively more secular? Three main arguments have been offered in support of this contention: first, religion is replacing secular ideologies that have lost popular appeal; second, the popularity of religion is cyclical; and third, new religious movements are a response to the impact of modernity and/or postmodernity. Let us examine each argument.

First, it is argued that people are turning to religion in response to a decline in the attraction of secular ideologies, such as communism and socialism (Hallencreutz and Westerlund 1996). People are sometimes said to 'need' to believe in something, especially in the context of the post-Cold War international instability, sometimes referred to as the 'New World Disorder'. The argument is that decline of radical secular ideologies has meant that people have (re)turned to religion to (re)discover a religious dimension to group identity. While superficially attractive, the main problem with this explanation is that religion has not returned only in the 1990s and early 2000s. Rather, in some countries – the USA is the archetypal example – politicised religion has become increasingly important since the 1960s (Coleman 1996).

Second, some argue that there is a periodic collective 'thirst' for religion (Sahliyeh 1990). That is, religion has been a significant factor in a number of socio-political mass movements in the West over the last thirty years, including the American civil rights movement, the Northern Ireland struggle for dominance between Loyalists and Nationalists, and the so-called 'Moral Majority' in the United States. To many people, 'this-wordly' answers to the meaning and purpose of life periodically appear alienating and unsatisfying and, as a result, religious beliefs intermittently find fresh relevance and power, perhaps within new structures and patterns of belief. However, what needs to be explained is why should religion enjoy a periodic resurgence? What set of factors needs to be in operation to trigger this development? These questions are difficult to answer and are not satisfactorily answered by the proponents of the cyclical theory of religious resurgence.

Third, the contention is that people in the West are becoming 'more' religious, not less; that is, secularisation is being reversed. The argument here hinges partly on surveys showing both growing attendance at religious services as well as increased sales for religious books. It is also dependent on the fact that large numbers of new religious movements have emerged, including the fast-growing 'charismatic' Christian phenomenon unattached to any strong doctrinal or denominational tradition. Charismatic Christianity is a widespread non-denominational tendency and movement offering devotees spiritual excitement, with belief in divinely-inspired gifts of glossolalia (i.e. 'speaking in tongues'), healing and prophecy.

While, for many Charismatics, religion and politics 'should' be kept separate, they are not alone in eschewing political involvement. Various manifestations of new religious and spiritual phenomena, such as New Age spirituality,

---

**Box 9.3 The New Christian Right in the USA**

The 'New Christian Right' (NCR) in the USA comprises several strands of conservative – predominantly Protestant – Christianity. It can be divided into fundamentalist, evangelical and Protestant strands. The NCR worldview involves a 'scripturalist' form of religious piety that affirms the central relevance of the Bible for day-to-day behaviour and the regulation of all aspects of individual and social behaviour. Despite its apparent 'old fashioned' outlook, in fact the NCR is a modern phenomenon, a response to contemporary conditions and events. The NCR is primarily opposed to what it perceives as unwelcome aspects of modernisation, especially a widespread decline in moral values. There has been a remarkable upsurge in the disaffection and politicisation of such theologically conservative Protestants over the last thirty years. Many seem to act on their beliefs – for example, in relation to attempts to prevent legal abortion – with militancy. More generally, this is the voice of theologically-conservative Christians, united by a shared 'born-again' experience, who regard the USA's travails (Vietnam, abortion, drug addiction, etc) as punishment for alleged departure from traditional Judaeo-Christian morality. Such Christian conservatives strive to uphold what they perceive as desirable 'traditional values', while regarding legal abortion, the absence of prayers in state-run schools and teaching the theory of evolution as opposed to creationism as manifestations of an unacceptable liberalism. Among such people, most claim to have had a born-again experience.

Scientology, exotic Eastern religions like the Hare Krishna cult, 'televangelism' and the renewed interest in astrology are not particularly relevant for the social sciences or for the understanding of modernity as they do not present major problems of interpretation. Instead, they fit within expectations of established theories of secularisation and can be interpreted within that framework. The point is that such religious manifestations are neither normal phenomena, examples of 'private' religion, nor do they challenge – or wish to challenge – dominant political and social structures (Haynes 1998). Because such religious phenomena are, typically, rather apolitical, what they really show is that many people are interested in spiritual issues. In sum, the contemporary multiplicity of extant religious phenomena belie the claim even in respect of highly secular countries that there has been a widespread loss of interest in religious meaning – and that innovative religious forms are gaining ground, often at the expense of traditional religions. But from a political perspective new religions are rarely important.

The NCR includes around 20 per cent of the adult population of the USA, that is, some 40 million people and is dominated by white Protestants. While found in all parts of the United States, it is concentrated in the so-called 'Sun Belt' and, more generally, in the southern states. Over time, the NCR has become a powerful political force, deriving its funds both from its members and from big business. Reflecting the NCR's importance, underpinning President Bush's preparations for war against Iraq in 2003 was a carefully devised mission, one that was about both an imperial and Christian-values projection. This vision was the work of two key figures, Paul Wolfowitz and Karl Rove, and propelled within the President's cabinet by Vice-President Dick Cheney and Defense Secretary Donald Rumsfeld. It marked the assent of a two-pronged approach to achieving key US foreign policy goals. While it is often argued that the 2003 war with Iraq was primarily an attempt to secure its oil for US commercial interests, it is plausible to contend that ideologues such as Rove and Wolfowitz did not share such a view and, as a result, were not primarily concerned with foreign policy as a profit-making exercise. Instead, they represent an unexpected alliance between the Texan Republicans who, with George W. Bush in the driving seat, have taken over the US administration and, on the other hand, a faction among the East Coast intelligentsia whose key goal is the achievement of power.

Rove formulated and ran Bush Junior's presidential campaign. When Bush became President, Rove became a focal point of a Texan coterie that connected the Bush family, the Republican Party, the NCR and the oil industry. This alliance managed to achieve not only a 'Texanisation' of the national Republican Party but also the unquestioned ascendance of Rove to become chief policy adviser in the White House.

## Former Communist Eastern Europe

As in the USA, there has also been a prominent political role for religion in former communist Eastern Europe. For example, in Poland, Catholic priests achieved considerable political importance in the late communist and post-communist order (1980s and 1990s), while the Pope, a Pole, has involved himself in political and social issues, such as the campaign to reduce developing countries' debt, as well as fierce denunciations of birth control. He and the Vatican were also involved, sometimes as key players, in the events leading to the end of the Cold War and the fall of communist regimes. In Poland, there was a close association between national opposition to Soviet dominance and the national Catholic church. This led to the development of a religio-nationalist subculture that fed off a merger of nationhood, language and religious affiliation. Despite years of governmental repression and anti-religious campaigning, an anti-Soviet and anti-state linking of Church and nation were highly consequential for the demise of Poland's communist system in the early 1990s. Identification of the Polish nation with Catholicism was so strong during the communist era that loyalty to the Church was viewed as a question of patriotism. The Catholic Church was never cowed by the authorities in Poland, and dissidents openly used the Church as a focal point for opposition.

In Russia, the Orthodox Church emerged from communism as an actor of major social and political importance. Following the dissolution of the Soviet Union, religious institutions – especially the national church, the Russian Orthodox Church – quickly and unexpectedly regained a position of popular influence. Since the late 1980s, Russia has experienced a religious revival and the Russian Orthodox Church has been resurrected as a national symbol. However, this has not been reflected in growth in the Church's involvement in political discourse: there is no Church party, no Church-endorsed parliamentary candidates nor, at election times, clear preference for one presidential candidate. Instead, the Church appears to be most interested in fighting to retain its hegemonic position vis-à- vis other denominations in the face of what it regards as aggressive proselytisation campaigns from foreign – mostly Western – churches. Elsewhere, in various Russian republics – notably Chechnya and Dagestan – Islamic fundamentalists fight against the Russian government, which has deployed thousands of troops to try to thwart them.

Given that former communist Eastern Europe, one of the areas said to be experiencing a religious revival, is a region where religion was, until recently, strongly controlled and marginalised by the state, it is perhaps unsurprising that it assumed a higher profile, once the state's restraints fell away. However, does it mean that religion necessarily assumes a higher political profile simply because it is possible for people to practise their religion more openly than before? The answer is, no. As we have already seen, the Russian Orthodox Church does not involve itself extensively in political controversies despite a popular, post-communist increase in religious affirmation and practice in Russia. Russian society may now be highly religious at the level of individual belief, but this has not led to an institutionalised political role for the Church. This may be because it has not found it easy to change its behaviour after a long period – since the Bolshevik revolution of 1917 – when it was in thrall to the communist state.

Before the overthrow of communist governments, the countries of Eastern Europe were characterised by church–state relations where the latter dominated the former. Following the example of the Soviet Union, after the Second World War the new communist regimes made serious attempts drastically to reduce the social status and significance of religion. Such regimes were 'anti-religious polities', making serious attempts to throttle religion. No religious organisations had the right to be actively engaged with matters of public concern or to play a role in public life. Churches were to be strictly liturgical institutions; that is, their only permitted role was the holding of divine services. The point is that the communist regimes saw that it was impossible to eliminate religion completely so they begrudgingly allowed people to practise their religious beliefs in private. On the one hand, this constituted a kind of promise that the authorities would respect the privacy of people's religious faith and practice. On the other, it was normally no more than a camouflage for a policy of aggressive religious repression.

Before the democratic revolutions of 1989–90, church–state relations in Eastern Europe fell into two broad categories – 'accommodative' and 'confrontational'. The accommodative style involved compromise on both sides and there were rules of the game to which each side adhered. Church officials would strive to avoid criticising government policies in order to be left in peace, while some even collaborated with state security. Church and state were in confrontational mode when they argued over the premise for their mutual relations and operated in the absence of a modus vivendi; neither side felt able to make serious compromises. In this situation, state hostility towards religion was overt and scarcely disguised. Consequently, churches would often be thrown into postures of defensive defiance. Czechoslovakia and Poland offer perhaps the best examples of prolonged confrontation between state and church. In Czechoslovakia, after a communist-led *coup d'état* in 1948, there was bitter confrontation between the state and the Catholic Church. The authorities had to proceed with considerable caution against the Church in Poland because it enjoyed a great deal of popular support, with over 90 per cent of Poles being Catholic and in East Germany against the Protestant clergy and some lay members.

More frequently however state–church relations oscillated between confrontation and accommodation. For example, in East Germany they were confrontational from 1948 until 1971; after that there was more accommodation. In the USSR, the Russian Orthodox Church also experienced periods of both accommodation and confrontation and state policies of repression were apparent between 1917 to 1943, 1958 to 1964 and 1975 to 1985. They were interspersed with periods of relative church–state harmony.


## Conclusion

Globally, the recent political impact of religion falls into two – not necessarily mutually exclusive – categories. First, if the mass of people are not especially religious – as in many Western countries – then some religious actors have sought a renewed public role. This is often because they believe that society has taken a wrong turn and, as a result, requires an injection of religious values to put it back into equilibrium. In other words, religion has tried to deprivatise itself, so that it has a voice in contemporary debates about social and political direction, while aiming to be a significant factor in socio-political deliberations.

Religious leaders seek support from ordinary people by addressing certain crucial issues, such as the perceived decline in public and private morality and the insecurities of life, the result of an undependable market where, it is argued, greed and luck appear as effective as work and rational choice. In sum, religion's return to the public sphere is moulded by a range of factors, including the proportion of religious believers in society and the extent to which religious organisations perceive a decline in public standards of morality and compassion.

In many developing countries, on the other hand, most people are already religious believers. Attempts by political leaders to pursue modernisation led religious traditions to respond. Following widespread disappointment at the outcomes of modernising policies, religion serves to focus and coordinate opposition, especially – but not exclusively – that of the poor and ethnic minorities. Religion is often well placed to benefit from a societal backlash against the perceived malign effects of modernisation.

And what of the future? If the issues and concerns that have helped stimulate 'a return to religion' – socio-political and economic upheavals, patchy modernisation, increasing encroachment of the state upon religion's terrain – continue (and there is no reason to suppose they will not), it seems highly likely that religion's political role will continue to be significant in many parts of the world in the twenty-first century. This will partly reflect the onward march of secularisation – set to continue in many countries and regions, linked to the spread of globalisation – which will be resisted by religious professionals and followers, albeit with varying degrees of success. This suggests that we are set to experience a period of religious reinterpretation – spurred by changes both within individual countries and at the global level. This suggests that those who neglect religion in analyses of contemporary and comparative politics do so at their peril.

## Bibliography

Casanova, J. (1994), *Public Religions in the Modern World*, Chicago, IL and London: The University of Chicago Press.

Coleman, S. (1996), 'Conservative Protestantism, Politics and Civil Religion in the United States', in D. Westerlund, *Questioning the Secular State: The Worldwide Resurgence of Religion in Politics*, London: C. Hurst & Co., pp. 24–47.

Hallencreutz, C. and Westerlund, D. (1996), 'Anti-Secularist Policies of Religion', in D. Westerlund, (ed.), *Questioning the Secular State. The Worldwide Resurgence of Religion in Politics*, London: Hurst, pp. 1–23.

Haynes, J. (1998), *Religion in Global Politics*, Harlow: Longman.

Huntington, S. (1993), 'The Clash of Civilizations?', *Foreign Affairs*, Vol. 72, No. 3, pp. 22–49.

Husain, M.Z. (1995), *Global Islamic Politics*, New York: HarperCollins.

Sahliyeh, E. (1990), 'Religious Resurgence and Political Modernization', in E. Sahliyeh, (ed.), *Religious Resurgence and Politics in the Contemporary World*, Albany, NY: State University of New York Press, pp. 1–16.

### Note on bibliography

Casanova (1994) examines religious 'deprivatisation' in the contemporary world. Coleman's (1996) chapter is a useful survey of the socio-political importance of the American 'New Christian Right'. Hallencreutz and Westerlund (1996) is a useful contribution to the debate about secularisation. Haynes (1998) surveys the contemporary importance of religion around the world. Huntington (1993) is a discussion of the claimed civilisational clash between the West and Islam. Husain (1995) identifies a global Islamic resurgence and seeks to explain it. Sahliyeh's (1990) contribution assesses the importance of, and reasons behind, the contemporary religious resurgence.

# 10

# Debt, aid and development

*Graham Harrison*

### Context and origins

*Terms and definitions*

The terms debt, aid and development each draw our attention to a particular part of the world. Collectively, these terms frame the issue of the position of the Third World in global politics today. There are many controversies concerning how we define the Third World – and indeed whether the term *Third World* is a useful one (Bayart, 1991; Escobar, 1995) – but we will adopt the term here if only to work with a familiar vocabulary and to make a reasonably clear definition of this world region. The Third World contains a large and diverse group of countries which share two key features: a recent and continuing history of domination by Western states and a relatively high degree of poverty. Geographically, we are concerned with the majority of states in Asia, Africa and South America.

An equally contested term, *development* (see Box 10.1), is as widely used as it is poorly defined. Most people associate the term with notions of economic growth, or perhaps 'progress' in a more general sense. But how does it relate to levels of inequality? Does development involve political, social or cultural change as well as economic growth? How do we balance the costs and benefits of 'progress' however defined? This is not the place to engage with these issues, but they do require us to be clear at the start what we mean by development. Here, development is defined as a process of economic growth which generates a general improvement in people's well-being.

As we shall see, development in the Third World is far from a *local* issue, a concern for each Third World country as a separate social unit. Rather, 'development' requires us to look at more generalised or systematic patterns in *global* political and economic relations. The most important question is: what kind of relations exist between the Third World and the First World? This

---

**Box 10.1  Defining development: some key contributions**

'However development is defined, it must involve the accumulation of capital' (Leys, C. 1994)

'What has been happening to poverty? What has been happening to unemployment? What has been happening to equity?' (Seers, D. 1973)

'It is now clear that more than a decade of rapid [economic] growth in under-developed countries has been of little or no benefit to perhaps a third of their population.' (Chenery, H. *et al.* 1974)

'If we achieve the "quantity" goals and neglect the "quality" goals of development, we will have failed' (P. McNamara, President of the World Bank)

'Human development is a process of enlarging peoples' choices... development has two sides: the formation of human capabilities such as improved health, knowledge and skills – and the use people make of their acquired capabilities for leisure, productive purposes or being active in cultural and political affairs' (UNDP 1990)

'[The] expansion of freedom is viewed as both (1) the primary end and (2) the principal means of development.' (Sen, A. 1999)

*(various sources, with help from Leftwich 2000)*

---

brings us to the issues of debt and aid. A pivotal feature of international politics is the massive accumulation of *debt* by Third World states. Most of these states have borrowed money from agencies such as the World Bank and IMF, First World governments and private lenders. During the early 1980s, levels of debt became so high as to lead to a debt crisis in which the sustainability of Third World debt was drastically called into question, especially after Mexico and Brazil defaulted on their debt repayments from 1981. *Aid* includes all grants from First World states, non-governmental organisations (NGOs – about which more later), and international agencies such as the World Bank, to Third World states which have 'development' as its broad purpose (i.e. military aid and emergency/famine relief are not included here). Aid takes four more concrete forms:

- grants from donor states (Overseas Development Assistance);
- contributions from citizens channelled though non-governmental organisations ('charity');
- loans with subsidised rates of interest ('soft loans');
- 'technical assistance' in which donors pay for personnel, training or information soft/hardware.

Aid has been seen as the central way in which First World states contribute to the development effort in the Third World, although one must be very careful about the normative and sometimes more openly moralised ways in which aid is framed. We will return to this issue in the next section.

We are interested in this chapter, therefore, in the nature of development in the Third World and the way in which processes of development have generated international political issues around debt and aid. From hereon, we shall use the term 'development' to encapsulate all three of the terms in the chapter title, unless otherwise stated.

### A global historical context

Once we have a basic understanding of our terms, the obvious question is: what makes development an important contemporary issue in world politics? In order to begin to answer this question, we need to understand how these issues were generated, that is, how they came to prominence in the first place. For our purposes, we can briefly sketch out some key global changes that have made development issues so central to contemporary world politics. Firstly, in the early 1980s, there emerged a strong backlash against the state's involvement in the economy and a renewed faith in free market capitalism. This led many First World governments and international agencies to reduce their support for development plans by Third World states and to argue that opening up to global market economy was the principal path to development. Secondly, the end of the Cold War in the late 1980s made First World states (especially the United States) more discerning in their aid policies: they no longer felt it necessary to give aid to states merely to keep them within the Western sphere of influence.

These general changes have interacted with a more specific set of changes within the Third World, which can be summarised as a *crisis in development*. For many countries, the 1980s was the 'lost decade' of development, a period in which economic growth rates slowed considerably or even turned negative. There are some key aspects to this crisis.

Global economic change has had a detrimental impact on the Third World. Demand for key Third World exports has fallen in some cases, and the prices of almost all traditional Third World exports has fallen (Tiffen and Barratt Brown, 1992). Oil price rises in 1973–74 and 1979 had complex but generally detrimental effects on Third World economies' position within the world (Bromley 1991, Chapter 4). The shift towards free market capitalism, mentioned above, created a new form of economic management known as monetarism. This kind of economic policy led to a sharp increase in global interest rates which made international borrowing more expensive. Indebted Third World states found that the cost of sustaining loans increased rapidly: between 1979 and 1981, global real interest rates rose between 10 to 15 times (Engberg-Pedersen *et al.*, 1996: 3). Finally, for many countries – especially in

Africa – levels of direct foreign investment (that is, investment in production by transnational companies) fell. There were some important exceptions – notably in south east Asia – but generally foreign direct investment became oriented increasingly towards Europe, North America, and south east Asia. In sum, the global political economy changed significantly during the 1980s in a way that was disadvantageous for much of the Third World (Hoogvelt, 1997).

But, there is one final part of the puzzle which is vital to an understanding of the origins of the crisis in development. Third World states themselves had failed to achieve development. Development projects managed by Third World governments displayed high levels of inefficiency and perhaps corruption. Often development plans were *imposed* on people, making the supposed beneficiaries resent and resist state planning, asking: for whom does 'progress' take place? In this sense, the failure of development was also a failure of many Third World states to act developmentally and in the interests of their citizenries.

To summarise, having understood the meaning of development we have sketched an answer to the question: why have development, debt, and aid become such important issues for global politics today? But, the more thoughtful reader will already be wondering how we *interpret* the issues raised by this brief historical survey and will be aware that it is one thing to describe the emergence of development as an issue, and another to *analyse* it.

## Analysis, concepts and interpretations

It is important to study development with an awareness of the high degree of controversy and occasional polemic that surrounds the issues of aid and debt. In other words, we have a 'political issue' in two senses: an issue of interest to political science, and an issue mobilised by politicians and others within the realms of power. A clear separation between the two is ultimately impossible, but an awareness of these two senses may immunise us from cynical evocations such as 'the debt crisis' and 'aid fatigue' that one finds in the words of politicians and newspaper editorials. As political scientists we will engage with these controversial issues by assessing the way they are interpreted within/ through three broadly defined theoretical approaches to politics. These approaches are liberalism, nationalism, and radicalism.

### Liberal interpretations

Liberals are united by a belief that economic organisation and decision making is generally best left to the market. The pro-market stance of liberals is at once *technical* – that is, based on the modelling of a free market as efficient and socially beneficial – and *normative* – that is, based on a moral judgement about human nature and what *ought* to be. With respect to the latter, liberals believe in the underlying ability of individuals to think and act as rational and self-interested agents.

How do liberals engage with the issues of debt and aid? The answer for the former is fairly clear, but for the latter, we need to work a little harder. So, let us start with the easy part! For liberals, the debt crisis is an expression of the fact that states are poor developmental actors. It is Third World states that have run up such high levels of indebtedness, and they have done so in order to boost their own capacity to manage the economy. But, because states distort and block the free movement of supply and demand (the market mechanism described as an 'invisible hand' by Adam Smith), their interventions can only be inefficient and damaging for society as a whole. Deeper still, Third World states generate such a profusion of regulations that individual incentives and entrepreneurial activity are strongly suppressed. Thus, for liberals, the debt crisis is the product of the 'bloated' 'authoritarian' or even 'vampire' state, the latter producing an image of a state that sucks the lifeblood from individual freedom and productive activity. A clear statement of this account of the debt crisis can be found in the World Bank (1981).

Whereas the debt crisis is seen clearly as proof positive of the deep liberal distrust of the state, the issue of aid generates a less clear liberal judgement. There are two key themes running through liberal arguments, one negative and one positive. Negatively, aid is seen as allowing states to avoid the necessary reconciliation with powerful market forces, because aid allows states to boost their own wealth and grandeur against popular well-being. In the sharp words of Peter Bauer (1979) 'aid is a phenomenon whereby poor people in rich countries are taxed to support the lifestyles of rich people in poor countries'. Positively, aid is seen as a means to *promote* liberal reforms. This is the basis of the World Bank and International Monetary Fund's wedding together of a faith in the free market and their own massive discretionary allocation of soft loans to indebted states (Williams and Young, 1994). In essence, the World Bank in particular believes in liberal ideals and sees loans and grants as a way to promote the realisation of these ideals. Clearly these two perspectives on aid are not compatible; the second 'World Bank' approach is most prevalent. In sum, liberals interpret the development crisis as an argument for the *releasing of the free market* in the Third World, but aid can be part of the problem or the solution. The key issue for liberals here is: what role does the state play in market processes?

### Nationalist interpretations

Nationalism here is related to arguments in the defence of Third World states. Nigel Harris (1986) terms this particular form of nationalism as 'third worldism'. The point of departure is that Western powers, especially during colonialism, exploited and impoverished Third World societies and that the most effective way to deal with the legacy of injustice that this has created is through the policies and actions of independent Third World states.

Thus, for nationalists, the state is all-important – not as a burden on individuals and markets but as a liberator, a representative of the national interest, a defender of the rights won with independence. Unsurprisingly, then, much of the discussion of debt and aid is filtered through the issue of *sovereignty*, that is, the right of states to determine the rules for their own national societies. The debt crisis is seen as an *assault on the state*: debt weakens the state's capacity to act in the interests of the nation. Attention is paid to the way global economic relations (noted in the previous section) *imposed* a debt crisis from outside on indebted states.

In this view, indebtedness is a condition that enables a raft of external interventions in national affairs. It is in this sense that nationalist approaches understand aid. Aid and debt re-scheduling are mechanisms to allow external agencies to intervene in Third World states. *In extremis*, aid allows non-governmental organisations effectively to take over the running of certain aspects of governance while the World Bank and IMF survey and invigilate macroeconomic policy. In sum, nationalists interpret the development crisis as a crisis for the Third World state and the sovereignty it attempts to assert in the face of powerful external forces.

### Radical interpretations

This interpretation is the most awkward, attempting as it does to include a diversity of approaches based in a critique of capitalism as a global system of politics and economics. There is in fact a significant cross-over with the nationalist approach, as much (but not all) of the nationalist argument reads as left-leaning. In the radical view, the development crisis is an expression of the contradictions and tensions of capitalism (Brett, 1985). In essence, capitalism, as a global system, is based in the generation of inequality and impoverishment. The debt crisis is a result of attempts to smooth over these processes of differentiation and the failure of these attempts.

Here, the World Bank and IMF attract much attention: these organisations are seen as international institutions charged with managing the tensions of global capitalism. The World Bank in particular lends large amounts of money to Third World states to promote capitalist modernisation in the Third World (Payer, 1982) in order to increase levels of international trade and investment. This works to generate new capitalist elites in the Third World and new markets for Western transnational companies (Payer, 1991).

Radical interpretations have also made a critique of the state, more or less well integrated with arguments about markets and class relations. There are two aspects to radical arguments about the state which are relevant here. Firstly, Third World states are seen not as protectors of the post-colonial nation, but as social elites which frequently have their eye on the riches to be gained by global integration. Secondly, First World states – especially the United States – employ arguments about development merely to obscure their own self-seeking agendas. A strong argument here is that the United States has historically had far more influence over the World Bank and IMF than any other state and has worked its foreign policy through these institutions. It is these powerful imperialist state interests that also underlie the workings of aid. Radicals criticise the image of neutral or humanitarian aid, identifying instead a series of state interests behind aid allocation. The most often cited examples are Israel and Egypt – two countries with relatively high levels of income per head of population (relatively low levels of humanitarian need) receiving the highest levels of US aid in the world. Since the Camp David accords in 1978, these two states have been vital US allies in the turbulent geopolitics of the Middle East. For radicals, aid is imperialism by another name. In sum, radicals see the development crisis as a crisis in the capitalist global political economy in which real markets create inequality, capital exploits workers, and powerful capitalist states discipline Third World states and societies.

These three interpretations give us a sense of how the events and processes that created the crisis in development have been related to broader frameworks in political thought and debate. Readers have to make their own choices as to which form of analysis best interprets the evolution of the crisis in development. In the next section, we investigate some more specific issues that have emerged from analyses of aid and debt.

### Out of the development crisis? Aid and structural adjustment

Each interpretation has embedded within it a normative statement about how the development crisis *should* be solved. Indeed, it is worth noting explicitly that none of the three 'camps' denies that there is something seriously wrong with the development project. Rather than follow each of three perspectives on solutions to the development crisis (the basic features of which have just been outlined), we will now return to a sharper distinction between development, aid, and debt. Once the Third World entered a development crisis during the 1980s, it became clear that the two principal mechanisms through which international actors might address the crisis would derive from strategies of debt management and aid disbursement. In this sense, we can see debt and aid as the two arms of the global response to the crisis in development. Let us take each in turn.

#### *Debt management*

*Structural adjustment* is a general term to describe a set of policies that have been implemented in Third World states as a solution to the debt crisis. These policies are all embedded in the liberal interpretation noted above; they are concerned with three key aims:

- to reduce the role of the state;
- to develop markets;
- to open national economies to global economic forces.

Structural adjustment programmes (SAPs) are funded by the World Bank and IMF. Indebted states need to implement SAPs in order to ensure that the World Bank and IMF re-schedule debts and/or provide new finance to keep national economies afloat. As such, new loans and aid are often *conditioned* on the adoption of a structural adjustment programme, and SAP has – in one form or another – constituted the core of all economic policy in the vast majority of indebted Third World states.

The obvious and pressing question is: does SAP work as a solution to the development crisis? Answers to this question are diverse and at times polemic, and need to be broken down into more specific issues.

Has SAP generated economic recovery? Surely, this is the key question. If SAP has not generated recovery, how can it present itself as 'developmental'? Unfortunately, assessment is made complex by two conditions: the difficulty in comparing the performance of SAP against a counterfactual, that is, an assumption about how a country would fare if there had been no SAP; secondly, the difficulty in separating the effects of SAP from other processes within a society, for example a drought or civil conflict. Nevertheless, the best that we can say about SAP is that its results have been mixed. It is true that Latin America has experienced economic regeneration in the 1990s, but in the first place, regeneration has not moved Latin America's economies back to pre-debt crisis levels (Green, 1996) and in the second, as the examples of Mexico in 1994–95 and Argentina in 2002 have shown, recovery has not ended high levels of indebtedness or economic turbulence and vulnerability. It is also the case that high debt repayments and aspects of SAP have directly caused Latin America's poor economic performance (Weeks, 2001). In sub-Saharan Africa, SAP's record is less strong still: the 1980s, in which there were no robust signs of economic recovery (Schatz 1994) were followed by patchy economic recovery in a few states. In Asia, the record is very mixed, but it is noteworthy that states that avoided policies resembling those of structural adjustment fared better than others before and during the Asian crisis of 1998.

Has SAP improved general well-being? Remember that development is defined in terms of economic growth and some measure of general well-being among a population. Perhaps SAP has been lukewarm on economic recovery but stronger on a more equitable distribution of resources or opportunities within a national society? Here, the evidence is quite stark. SAP has failed to address the powerful processes of differentiation which capitalism has produced in most Third World states (Adepojou, 1993; Onimode, 1989). In Brazil, the number of absolute poor increased by ten million from 1979 to 1985 (Altvater *et al.*, 1991: 145). It was this 'social deficit' in SAP that led the United Nations Children's Fund (UNICEF) and others to criticise SAP and call for a 'human face' to adjustment (Cornia *et al.*, 1987). Nevertheless, specific policies which come under the structural adjustment umbrella, such as the introduction of user fees for water, continue to attract critical attention from those concerned with the well-being of the poor majorities in Third World states.

Has SAP solved the debt crisis? Structural adjustment has not succeeded in bringing countries out of debt. What has happened, in fact, is that SAP has restructured the 'crisis' of indebtedness of the early 1980s into a regime of debt, based in partial write-offs of debt, debt rescheduling, and the contracting of new loans to roll old debt over. Structural adjustment programmes are designed on the back of donor and creditor funding which allows this regime to work. More recently, SAP has been integrated into Poverty Reduction Strategy Papers which have for many countries brought further debt write-offs as these states achieve Highly Indebted Poor Country (HIPC) status.

It would seem, then, that structural adjustment has not 'worked'. Limited and partial successes have been overwhelmed by the continuing high levels of poverty, debt, and inequality in most of the Third World. And, this is after twenty years in which structural adjustment has been the global orthodoxy for the Third World. For most critics, one fundamental problem with SAP is that it is based on a liberal faith in the developmental prospects of the free market. While liberals take a model of the free market as equitable and efficient as their premise, others have seen in market relations differentiations and inefficiencies that have led to increasing levels of inequality. Where there is no 'level playing field', freeing up markets can only work in favour of those best placed to exploit them for their own ends, whether these groups be national elites or transnational companies. Underlying many criticisms of structural adjustment as a developmental project is a disquiet that SAP is driven mainly by the World Bank and IMF, both international banks with a close relationship with the governments of developed Western states. This global institutional positioning of the World Bank and IMF immediately raises the suspicions of those who are concerned with the life chances of extremely impoverished communities in Third World states. In light of this, perhaps the renewed thinking on aid policy during the 1990s provides a more hopeful developmental solution.

### Aid disbursement

Although World Bank and IMF soft loans contain an aid component, we shall concentrate here on the aid policies of Western states and NGOs such as Oxfam, Care, and Save the Children. For Western governments, aid policy is in the first place, declared as developmental: it is officially about economic growth and improvements in well-being. For some governments, development policy has encroached on Treasury decisions, leading to attempts to cancel bilateral debt (that is debt owed by one country to a single donor country). In the last ten years or so, and especially since the New Labour government in Britain, aid priorities have focused around a new set of concerns:

- environmental sustainability;
- gender equality;
- good governance;
- poverty alleviation.

Good governance relates to the degree of transparency and efficiency in Third World government policy making and execution. For individual Western governments, good governance also involves a concern to promote democratisation. In respect to poverty reduction, the UK Government's Department for International Development (DFID) has pledged to halve the number of absolute poor by 2015, along with other development agencies. Praiseworthy goals as these are, we need to make two important comments which put Western aid policy in perspective. Firstly, very few of the wealthiest states have achieved the United Nations target of dedicating 0.7 per cent of Gross Domestic Product (GDP – a measure of national income) to overseas development assistance: the UK figure was 0.312 per cent from 1989 to 1994 (Cumming, 1996: 494). Secondly, aid disbursement closely follows the decisions of the World Bank and IMF: states receiving particular favour with these two also, by-and-large, receive favour from Western state aid programmes. As such, aid policy is in fact tied in with the success or otherwise of structural adjustment. Loans and grants are closely interlinked.

But, what of NGOs? NGOs have a very different image to both the World Bank and Western states, although they are just as much international actors. NGOs are seen as more 'grassroots' organisations; by which I mean that they are seen as working with communities, happier to engage on a local and small-scale level, and more concerned with humanitarian concerns. NGOs are not-for-profit organisations which provide relief during social disasters such as famine and civil war. NGOs operate projects 'on the ground' in the Third World – funding health centres in villages, sanitation projects in urban outskirts, or new agricultural techniques in the countryside. This is why some have dubbed NGOs the 'democratisers of development' (Clark, 1991)

We should note that the NGO sector has grown precipitately during the 1990s so that some NGOs have developed into institutions resembling transnational corporations: controlling millions of dollars, organised into a head office and branches, containing their own publicity and communications departments and so on. The larger NGOs control considerable resources and work in many countries. For example, Oxfam-UK raised £124.3 million in 2001/2, spending £114.9 million on development (Annual Report 2001/2); this does not include resources from Oxfam's other national branches that have established themselves in the USA, Australia, Canada and elsewhere since the original office in Oxford was set up. As the NGO sector grows, some observers question the extent to which the image of grassroots development remains relevant. Furthermore, a very significant trend of the 1980s and 1990s is that donor governments have ploughed more of their aid budgets through their 'own' NGOs: 'it might well be asked if an organisation that receives more than half its funding from government sources ... can actually be considered a "non" governmental organisation' (Smillie, 1997: 563).

Perhaps the best way to understand the intricacies of aid is to think about an 'aid complex'. In Fig. 10.1, arrows represent aid resource flows, although the flows of information that accompany these resource flows are more complex and flow in both directions. Furthermore, this diagram relates strictly to aid flows, not other forms of resource transfer which could reveal mechanisms through which flows from the Third World to the First, such as debt repayments which can outweigh aid receipts. The three boxes Citizen-donors, NGOs and 'Target' population highlight the basic aid relationship that most

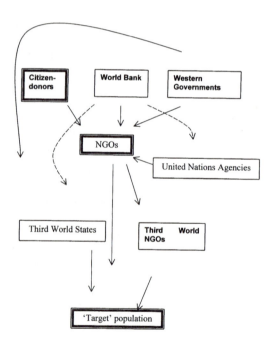

Figure 10.1 *The aid complex: a schema*

people are aware of. Both the World Bank (Fox and Brown, 1998) and United Nations agencies (Gordenker and Weiss, 1997) have recently contracted NGOs to carry out development projects. The notion of an aid complex draws our attention to the diversity of aid flows and the interactions of different agencies involved in aid provision: the patterning of aid resembles a network, although it is a network of *hierarchies*. For some, a kind of aid complex has developed to 'mop up' the damage caused by structural adjustment or state collapse in the Third World (Duffield, 1993).

Moving more closely to the question of the *effectiveness* of aid, we should note that until recently, little systematic work had been carried out in this area, and recent work has been intensely debated. In respect to the key aim of poverty reduction, a balanced judgement is given by White: 'what evidence we do have on aid's impact [for poverty reduction] is not encouraging' (2001: 1058). Some have discussed specific aspects of aid giving, for example its capacity to promote democracy (Crawford, 1997). A recent set of research writings from the World Bank has discussed aid effectiveness in terms of its effectiveness in supporting SAP-style reform and economic growth (Collier and Dollar, 1998). This research puts an emphasis on *political will* in the Third World state: aid only 'works' in states which seem to be motivated to follow structural adjustment programmes as their own, rather than as externally imposed policy. This relates to a broader criticism of aid, technically known as 'moral hazard'. The argument here is that aid giving produces perverse incentives that encourage recipient governments to avoid pro-development reform. Rather than encouraging a government to carry on with adjustment reforms, aid can potentially provide a government with the means and incentive to *avoid* implementing reform – at least for as long as it can draw on aid or convince external agencies that it is doing its best (Mosley *et al.*, 1991).

How can we make sense of the issues evoked by structural adjustment and aid provision's limited success? Structural adjustment has failed to regenerate the developmental project in the Third World because the market forces that SAP relies on have not provided stable and equitable economic growth in the Third World. Aid has attained a degree of success, but one must recognise that, in the final analysis, aid programmes and the NGOs that champion aid-led models of development cannot really rise to the challenge of development in that region of the world that contains three-quarters of the world's population. At this point, we can draw out some of the key characteristics of global politics that frame the nature of development and its limits:

- the failure of Third World states successfully to promote development;
- the power of Western states (and agencies dominated by them) to promote their own interests over and above those of Third World societies;
- the predominance of liberal ideals of economics and development (commonly known as *neoliberalism*) and the failure of this 'model' in much of the Third World.

So, where do we go from here? There is one other kind of agency which has engaged with the global development agenda which has expressed a different approach to debt and development.

### Drop the debt

A powerful and global campaign to drop the debt emerged in the build-up to the millennium, which has continued into the new century. Basing its politics on a humanitarian and moral call to drop all debt to severely impoverished and indebted societies, Jubilee 2000 used the notion of 'jubilee' and its old (Christian) meaning as a time to forgive outstanding debt, to call on the World Bank, IMF, and developed world governments to 'wipe the slate clean' and from thereon, tackle poverty with a greater degree of seriousness and radicalism. The campaign became a transnationalised campaign involving rallies and political lobbying, and it certainly pushed Western governments towards more debt write-off. What is interesting analytically here is the emergence of a kind of *global civil society* in which the development agenda is not solely the preserve of public institutions such as UN agencies, states and the World Bank, but also involves citizens from around the world, mobilising on a specific set of issues and working at several levels: in the Third World, in Western states, with international organisations and with NGOs. For many of those disheartened by the crisis in development and the neoliberal response, campaigns such as Jubilee 2000 are the 'green shoots' of a progressive development model.

### Conclusion: development prospects

Debt has not gone away, despite the 'crisis' developing since the 1980s. And, although aid levels appeared to have reached a plateau, aid policy remains an intensely discussed aspect of global politics. These two issues have produced an *internationalised development discourse* which has been produced by an increasingly diverse set of actors: the standard map of development (states from the First and Third World and the World Bank) has been made increasingly complex by the emergence of NGOs (First and Third World), campaign groups and UN agencies. If we accept that the liberal notion of international development is found wanting, we can hope that this diversity might break the dominance of neoliberalism and open the discussion of development to a more broadly based and imaginative discussion. This is all the more pressing in light of the following issues:

• The category 'Third World' has become far less meaningful. Extreme poverty exists in regions of *all* states. Poverty and powerlessness are now truly global issues (Thomas, 1999).

- Many development problems are global problems: environmental degradation, security and conflict, resource use, and migration are issues that do not respect state boundaries. Solutions must be based on international political action.

In a sense, globalisation has made development more forcefully a global issue. Discussions about global politics must necessarily engage with the issues of this chapter.

## Bibliography

Adepojou, A. (ed.) (1993), *The Impact of Structural Adjustment on the Population of Africa: The Implications for Education, Health and Employment*, London: James Currey.

Altvater, E., Hubner, K., Lorentzen, J. and Rojas, R. (eds) (1991), *The Poverty of Nations: A Guide to the Debt Crisis*, London: Zed Press.

Bauer, P. (1979), *Dissent on Development*, London: Weidenfeld and Nicolson.

Bayart, J. F. (1991), 'Finishing with the Idea of the Third World: The Concept of the Political Trajectory', in J. Manor (ed.), *Rethinking Third World Politics*, London: Longman, pp. 51–71.

Brett, E. A. (1985), *The World Economy Since the War: The Politics of Uneven Development*, Houndmills: Macmillan.

Bromley, S. (1991), *American Hegemony and World Oil: The Industry, the State System and the World Economy*, Cambridge: Polity Press.

Chenery, H., Ahluwalia, M. and Bell, C. (1974), *Redistribution with Growth*, Oxford: Oxford University Press.

Clark, D. (1991), *Democratizing Development*, London: Earthscan.

Collier, P. and Dollar, D. (1998), *Aid Allocation and Poverty Reduction*, Policy Research Working Paper 2041, Washington DC: World Bank.

Cornia, G., Jolly, R. and Stewart, F. (1987), *Adjustment with a Human Face. Vol. 1, Protecting the Vulnerable and Promoting Growth*, Oxford: Clarendon.

Crawford, G. (1997), 'Foreign Aid and Political Conditionality: Issues of Effectiveness and Consistency', *Democratization*, Vol. 4, No. 3, pp. 69–108.

Cumming, G. (1996), 'British Aid to Africa: A Changing Agenda?', *Third World Quarterly*, Vol. 17, No. 3, pp. 487–501.

Duffield, M. (1993), 'NGOs, Disaster Relief and Asset Transfer in the Horn: Political Survival in a Permanent Emergency', *Development and Change* Vol. 24, No. 1, pp. 131–57.

Engberg-Pedersen, P., Gibbon, P., Raikes, P. and Udsholt, L. (eds) (1996), *Limits of Adjustment in Africa*, London: James Currey.

Escobar, A. (1995), *Encountering Development : The Making and Unmaking of the Third World*, Princeton, N.J.: Princeton University Press.

Fox, J. and Brown, L. (eds) (1998), *The Struggle for Accountability: The World Bank, NGOs, and Grassroots Movements*, London and Cambridge, MA: MIT Press.

Gordenker, L. and Weiss, T. (1997), 'Devolving Responsibilities: A Framework for Analysing NGOs and Services', *Third World Quarterly*, Vol. 18, No. 3, pp. 443–56.

Green, D. (1996), 'Latin America: Neoliberal Failure and the Search for Alternatives',

*Third World Quarterly*, Vol. 17, No. 1, pp. 109–22.

Harris, N. (1986), *The End of the Third World*, Harmondsworth: Penguin.

Hoogvelt, A. (1997), *Globalisation and the Postcolonial World*, Basingstoke: Macmillan.

Leftwich, A. (2000), *States of Development*, Cambridge: Polity Press.

Leys, C. (1996), *The Rise and Fall of Development Theory*, London: James Currey.

Mosley, P., Harrigan, J. and Toye, J. (1991), *Aid and Power: The World Bank and Policy Based Lending*, London: Routledge.

Onimode, B. (ed.) (1989), *The IMF, World Bank and African Debt*, Vols 1 and 2, London: Zed Press.

Payer, C. (1982), *The World Bank: A Critical Analysis*, New York: Monthly Review Press.

Payer, C. (1991), *Lent and Lost: Foreign Debt and Third World Development*, London: Zed Press.

Schatz, S. (1994), 'Structural Adjustment in Africa: A Failing Grade so Far', *Journal of Modern African Studies*, Vol. 32, No. 4, pp. 679–92.

Seers, D. (1973), 'What are we Trying to Measure?', *Journal of Development Studies*, Vol. 8, No. 3.

Sen, A. (1999), *Development as Freedom*, Oxford: Oxford University Press.

Smillie, I. (1997), 'NGOs and Development Assistance: A Change in Mind-set?', *Third World Quarterly*, Vol. 18, No. 3, pp. 563–77.

Thomas, C. (1999), 'Where is the Third World Now?', *Review of International Studies*, Vol. 25, pp. 225–43.

Tiffen, P. and Barratt-Brown, M. (1992), *Short Changed*, London: Pluto Press.

United Nations Development Programme, UNDP (1990), *Human Development Report*, New York: Oxford University Press.

Weeks, J. (2001), 'Latin America and the "High Performing Economies": Growth and Debt', *Journal of International Development*, Vol. 12, pp. 625–54.

White, H. (2001), 'Will the New Aid Agenda help Promote Poverty Reduction?', *Journal of International Development*, Vol. 13, pp. 1057–70.

Williams, D., and Young, T. (1994), 'Governance, the World Bank and Liberal Theory', *Political Studies*, Vol. 42, No. 1, pp. 84–100.

World Bank (1981), *Accelerated Development in Sub Saharan Africa: An Agenda to Action*, Washington DC: World Bank.

# Part III

# Practical policy issues

# 11

# Environment

*James Radcliffe*

## The environment in context

The concept of the environment covers a wide range of issues of both local and international significance. By its nature the environment is everything around us, and how we deal with it is of increasing importance. It provides a wide range of problems to governments, including problems that cross national boundaries and present states with the difficulty of engaging with neighbours on resource issues and their allocation. Debates about, and concern with, the impact of industrialisation have been part of a long-standing alternative agenda within the history of political writing since the early days of the Industrial Revolution and the writings of Thomas Carlisle. However, the emergence of contemporary ideas associated with a broader environmental movement are linked to the period beginning in the early 1970s and the Stockholm Conference on the Environment in 1972. The emergence of resource limits and issues of sustainability was a key trigger to the development of new ideas concerning humanity's impact on the planet.

These emerging trends have meant that there are different approaches to the environment, which writers such as Andrew Dobson have tried to differentiate. For Dobson (1999) there needs to be a clear distinction between what he calls *environmentalism* on the one hand and *ecologism* on the other. Essentially the distinction is between an environmentalism, which is concerned with controlling the impact of humanity on the natural world, and a more radical ecologism, which sees environmental problems as symptomatic of broader social and economic structures that are the causes of environmental decay. Consequently, the political and social issues identified by ecologism are more radical in their potential impact on human activity. As such the political consequence of adopting this more radical approach has been identified as having a life-style component to its solutions rather than more narrowly traditional political responses.

One aspect of this debate centres on the meaning of Deep Ecology as a specific aspect of environmental thinking. Arne Naess (1973) was identified as the first author to make the distinction between deep and shallow ecological thinking as contrasting ways in which people have responded to the environmental crisis. Deep ecology may be seen as centred on the idea that human beings can only come to a true self-realisation by going beyond their individual or species centred thinking towards an identification with nature as a whole. In addition, through this process they should come to understand that there is equality between all species, with no sense of the existence of an evolutionary hierarchy. By engaging in such a personal transformation we would become engaged with the rest of nature and human behaviour would become more in tune with the planet, rendering the idea of the human exploitation of nature redundant.

Shallow ecology is deemed to be inadequate as a response to the deterioration of the environment because it perceives nature from a human (or anthropocentric) standpoint in which we act as conservationists or stewards. Deep ecologists argue that such an approach is less radical when compared to theirs in that changes to our way of thinking and our approach to living are only partly modified with an emphasis on technological solutions in an attempt to reform industrial society rather than overhaul more thoroughly the way we live. As Barry (1999) has noted, the relationship with nature that is emphasised is one of direct experience rather than an approach that centres on rational thought and investigation. In this way it is believed that we can get back to a lost relationship with nature as experienced by aboriginal cultures. The Western tradition of rational, scientific thought, which emerged from the Enlightenment, is held to be a cause of our alienation in which nature is seen as 'other' and identified as an object for experimental research. The existence of other traditions of thought based on a more direct understanding of nature and our place within it brings to the centre an appreciation of the needs of other cultures that may be under threat from the continuing expansion of Western culture and global capital. For Deep Ecologists 'Re-enchantment of nature goes hand in hand with psychological reconnection and the overcoming of the self's alienated state' (Barry, 1999: 23). Consequently, it is a question of how we come to know the rest of nature and our place within it that leads to differences in our attitudes towards the use of natural resources, particularly within the industrialised world.

## History of the new environmental agenda

It is the way in which we think about industrial society that is at the heart of the development of the new environmental agenda. The concern with the depletion of natural resources and the increasing levels of pollution lead to attempts to identify the causes of these developments. The key problems were identified as the emergence of industrial society and the associated dependency on economic growth. Dryzek (1997: 12) has argued that the environmental movement has to respond to a discourse or way of thinking, which has been determined by the development of industrialism. He argued that industrialism 'may be characterised in terms of its overarching commitment to growth in the quantity of goods and services and to the material well-being which that growth brings'. However, he goes on to contend that this problem is not dependent on the associated political ideology within which a particular nation-state operates. Whether the state and the economy is organised on the basis of capitalism, socialism or Marxism the main identifying factor is the commitment of all these societies and ideologies to industrialism and the associated economic growth. This was identified by environmentalists as an important distinguishing factor whereby the political ideas developed from a so-called 'Green' perspective could be seen as part of a new politics for the twenty-first Century. The ideologies of industrialism, such as liberal capitalism or Marxism, were developed in the nineteenth century and as such were unable to cope with the emerging challenges presented by the environmental crisis.

For Green critics, the relationship between industrialism, economic growth and the development of polluting technologies is seen as an intimate relationship, which not only results in environmental crisis but also is a cause of the alienation of humanity from the rest of the natural world. A key argument is that the nature of industrial society, particularly under modern global capitalism, is one that only places value on something that can be exchanged as a commodity. Whether it be fossil fuels or endangered hardwood from the tropical rainforests industrialism does not see these as having a value in themselves, only a value that can be established through their commodification. Environmentalists contend that this leads to an exploitative position and one which sees no value on the preservation of an ecology unless it provides immediate exchange value as a commodity, and as a consequence rainforests are cut down for timber and marshland drained for agriculture.

In addition, certain parts of the environment are seen as free goods, or commons, which by their nature cannot be subject to private ownership. Instead they are seen to be held in common, but rather than being valued because of that they are exploited for the purposes of dumping the by-products of industrial activity. The atmosphere and the oceans are seen as examples of these kinds of resources. One of the most significant concepts which has emerged around this issue is that of 'The Tragedy of the Commons', first developed by Garrett Hardin (1968). This concept centred on ideas related to the use of common pasture land in the nineteenth century, where it was seen that the rational self-interest of an individual herdsman was to increase the number of cattle he grazed on the common land. They would benefit through the increase in their herds, while the damage to the common grazing land caused by the number of cattle exceeding the ability of the pasture to recover from use, or its carrying capacity, would be shared by all. The result would be overuse and permanent damage to the pasture to the detriment of future generations. Hardin and others have extrapolated this analogy to the use of other common resources, such as the oceans, to identify the potential consequences of overuse and pollution.

It is through the development of this perspective on environmental issues that we can see the key issues that have emerged onto the environmental agenda. The nature of industrialisation and economic growth has resulted in a concern that the planet's carrying capacity is being breached in certain areas. Consequently resource depletion, particularly in the area of energy and the use of fossil fuels, the reduction in biodiversity and the global problem of climate change as a result of atmospheric pollution are seen as the key areas for environmental concern. In addition, from a Green perspective it is argued that these problems are intimately linked around an ecological cycle. While increased resource use employing fossil fuels leads to a decline in biodiversity and an increase in so-called 'greenhouse gases', the decline in biodiversity particularly in the rainforests damages the ability of the atmosphere to cope with the increase in these polluting gases. As a result, the view is that we are on a collision course where the carrying capacity of the planet will be exceeded and sustainability undermined.

## Issues in environmental policy

### *Resource depletion*

One of the most significant issues, which started the concern with environmental degradation, was the idea that the earth is a finite resource. Viewed from the space missions of the 1970s the planet was seen as small and possibly unique. Consequently, the possibility that the resources of the planet could be exhausted became a central concern of environmentalists. The concept of 'limits to growth' became a defining part of environmental thought, with predictions being made about the possible exhaustion of key resources. The oil crises of the 1970s seemed more than a coincidence and the reliance of industrial society on a range of key resources led some to predict a very rapid demise. The use of oil and its various by-products as well as metals such as aluminium and copper was seen as undermining the long-term stability of industrial society. The growth in the global population, with emerging states wanting to emulate the wealthy industrialised nations, simply added to the problem. As the global population increases the demand for the resources associated with industrialism and economic growth is predicted as becoming unsustainable, with a decline in access to more basic resources, such as fresh water and timber, adding to the problem. Indeed, access to fresh water is seen by some as being one of the key areas of conflict in the future due to the demands of cities and industry for ever greater supplies.

For many in the environmental movement the need to live within the confines of ecological sustainability has become crucial to the survival of the planet. The perception is that resource use is beyond the carrying capacity of the earth, in which the ability of the planet to replenish the resources being consumed by humanity is beginning to break down. Because of this situation there is a concern that future generations will be denied the options available to us at present. This is because the exhaustion of finite resources will lead to environmental breakdown and a future in which sustainability at a high level of resource use will become impossible. The future will require a much lower level of demand on the environment to maintain a sustainable level of use.

The concern with the needs of future generations and the legacy being left to them is identified as being at odds with the demands of industrial capitalism where the immediate need to respond to market changes and a short-term aim of ensuring profitability are central to the operation of the economy. Intergenerational responsibility is at odds with the operation of the market, where it is assumed that the price mechanism will ensure that problems of resource depletion are overcome through increased prices for scarce resources forcing down demand. Equally, such changes would stimulate the development of new sustainable technologies to replace environmentally damaging fossil fuel dependent technologies. Environmentalists argue that market failure and the imminence of the crisis make dependency on the market mechanism too problematic.

In particular, the main change in the circumstances surrounding resource use is increasingly centred on the atmosphere and the oceans where the market fails to operate effectively as these are seen as free goods. Environmentalists point to pollution of the oceans and climate change as signs that we are approaching limits to the carrying capacity which go beyond the previously perceived issues associated with the exhaustion of specific minerals and other key resources.

### Energy issues

Problems associated with energy use are central to the whole of the environmental debate whether this relates to problems of resource depletion or the pollution that results from its use, notably the release of carbon dioxide and associated climate change. The identification of fossil fuels as a finite resource led to various predictions as to their exhaustion, and while new stocks have been identified the dependency of modern industrial society on fossil fuels has led to a significant area of potential conflict. Access to oil has been identified as a key factor in state policies towards various conflicts, particularly in the Middle East where threats to supply during the Gulf War and the consequences of a widening of Arab–Israeli disputes have been seen as a key issue in US foreign policy.

On a local level, the environmental movement has promoted the development of new and renewable energy sources. The prospects for wind, wave and solar energy technologies are becoming increasingly viable in the production of local electricity supplies. Critics note that the pace of development and the scale of supply are still very limited when compared to the contribution made by fossil fuels such as oil, coal and gas as well as nuclear fission. However, supporters of renewable energy sources argue that their long-term benefit will make them increasingly viable and as fossil fuels become more difficult to extract and scarcer as limits start to emerge, renewables will become more economic. In addition, supporters of small scale and more flexible energy forms argue that renewables do not entail the large-scale production methods of fossil fuels with the associated issues of ownership and control by large companies.

*Biodiversity*

For many in the environmental movement the issue of biodiversity is becoming increasingly significant with the continuing erosion of rainforests in South America and the Far East. The rain forests of the Amazon and Indonesia are seen as essential to the sustainability of the planet and are associated with problems of atmospheric pollution and the control of greenhouse gases. More particularly, these areas are seen as some of the richest areas of the globe in their numbers of species, both plant and animal life. Their decline puts at risk the whole of the range of species which is both an intergenerational loss but also a possible loss as source of new drugs and medicines.

Biodiversity is even more challenged by the increasing industrialisation of agriculture. The development of monocultures, in which a single or limited range of species are identified as profitable and productive in areas such as wheat crops and rice production, has long been seen as a risk to agricultural production. Environmentalists have noted that the development and use of such approaches to agriculture means that producers are more at risk from crop losses due to monocultures being potentially more vulnerable to destruction by pests or diseases than more diverse crops. This leads to the overuse of chemical fertilisers and pesticides as controls to protect such plants. In addition, critics also note the potential for large-scale agri-business to dominate the food producers through patents and the supply of seeds. The use of patents on crops by large multinational companies has become a particularly high profile issue within the environmental movement.

This problem has been aggravated by the development of Genetically Modified (GM) foods by Monsanto and others where fears have been expressed about both their potential impact on the environment and the way in which they may reinforce the dominance of large-scale agri-business over small-scale local producers. Environmentally the concerns relate to the development of new crops that are resistant to pesticides. Such genetically modified products may, it is argued, lead to cross-pollination with other species resulting in the development of so-called 'super-weeds', resistant to chemical and natural controls. The growth of these super-weeds could be a particular threat within the context of an agriculture that is increasingly based on monocultures.

### Global warming and ozone depletion

The emergence of global warming is perhaps the single most problematic issue on the environmental agenda. The problem is one that raises most of the questions concerning the use of resources by humanity and the impact that it is having on the planet. It is also the area where both local and international conflicts most express themselves, because of the impact of individual actions and the very unequal distribution of resource use between states and the consequent production of greenhouse gases. The issue surrounding global warming or climate change centres on the apparent increase in average temperatures that we are experiencing globally. While detailed records of global temperatures are relatively recent there is an increasing, though not complete, consensus that this is becoming a significant problem. The 1990s saw a number of years recording the highest global temperatures since detailed records began. Predictions concerning global warming vary between a 1 and 5 degree Celsius rise in temperature during the twenty-first century, the consequences of which are for some beginning to be seen in increasing levels of storm activity, changing migratory activity amongst animals and birds, and significant melting of the ice shelves in the polar regions.

While there seems to be general scientific consensus that there is evidence of climate change, the debate centres increasingly on what impact this may have on the planet and on the extent to which this change is due to the activities of humanity. The global climate has undergone very significant change throughout its existence, as the ice caps have expanded and contracted, forests have moved and geological changes have given rise to volcanic and other activity. The concern that is now being expressed is that the speed at which the climate is changing under present conditions is of such significance that we might not be able to reverse the trend unless action on a large scale is taken now.

## Role of NGOs

### National and international groups

These environmental issues have given rise to the development of major new organised pressure groups from a local through to an international level in a way that has been identified as part of a new social movement. The alienation of many people from mainstream politics is evident throughout many countries from declining membership of political parties, declining voting patterns and increased membership of pressure groups. Environmental pressure groups are among the most successful beneficiaries of this trend and can range from small local groups concerned with amenity, such as protestors against a new road or industrial plant, to large international groups with sophisti-cated web sites and professional activists, such as Greenpeace and Friends of the Earth.

A number of authors have identified ways in which such groups can be grouped into historical periods and associated with an increasingly radical approach to the environment. Initially groups emerged around the concepts of conservation and amenity, with a strong link to the development of na-tional parks and the maintenance of landscape and important aspects of the built environment. Later groups developed around a concern with environ-mental pollution, particularly associated with the use of chemical fertilisers and pesticides in agriculture where changing patterns of production were leading to the loss of a diversity of species on farmland. More radical groups developed later when ecological concepts identified a link between the de-struction of the natural world and the technological developments associated with late capitalism. These groups began to see the need for a change in lifestyles with a stance that also became associated with concepts of anti-globalisation.

In the first category, organisations such as the Royal Society for the Pre-vention of Cruelty to Animals (RSPCA) and its American equivalent (ASPCA), or the Council for the Protection of Rural England (CPRE) were founded to protect animals and the countryside. Later groups, such as the Conservation Society began to take on a more radical stance seeing the broader social and political issues surrounding environmental degradation. The 1970s saw the greatest period of new and significant groups being founded, most notably Greenpeace, Friends of the Earth (FoE) and the World Wide Fund for Nature (WWF) which emerged on an international scale. The work of these groups highlighted the problems of the environment in dramatic ways through the use of large popular demonstrations and media events in the case of Friends of the Earth, or more direct action tactics of a very dramatic kind by Greenpeace. More radical groups have emerged among those who have iden-tified Friends of the Earth for example as too conservative in their approach to change. Earth First! for example has been seen to engage in what its oppo-nents have termed 'eco-terrorism' as a radical form of direct action, while anti-roads protesters in the United Kingdom such as Reclaim the Streets have allied themselves with other radical groups in anti-capitalist and anti-globalisation protests.

Garner (1996) has noted that there is an important distinction to be made between those organisations which have a narrow remit concerned with spe-cific aspects of conservation, such as the RSPB and the CPRE, and those with a wider, ecological position such as Greenpeace and Friends of the Earth. A similar grouping of organisations can be made in other countries, including the United States, where conservationist groups such as the Audubon Society and the National Parks movement had long traditions of support for steward-ship and the protection of wilderness. This view supports that of Dobson and the distinction between environmentalism and ecologism noted above. The greater radicalism of the newer, ecologically based groups can be clearly asso-ciated with the way in which the adoption of this broader perspective makes the link between the environmental crisis and the nature of industrialisation and modern global capitalism more apparent. Indeed, the establishment of the newer, ecologically based groups was the result of individuals becoming dissatisfied with the level of progress being made by conservationist organisa-tions in the face of increasing evidence of a more severe environmental crisis. For example, Dave Brower left the Sierra Club to help found Friends of the Earth in 1969 (McCormick, 1995), and there is evidence that a continuing radicalisation has occurred as new generations have grown up and perceived the tactics employed by existing groups as having failed to meet the challenge of a growing urgency.

This generational change has led to criticism of the more established or-ganisations such as Friends of the Earth and Greenpeace, and more recent organisations have emerged in response to an ever changing agenda. Friends of the Earth, for example, is a large organisation with a substantial member-ship base. It is organised on traditional interest group lines with local mem-bers organising around a decentralised structure. However, the main headquarters of the organisation has sometimes been identified as being too conventional in their approach, such as lobbying national governments and participating in consultation events. This was identified as a problem at an early stage in the organisation's development, where Dave Brower continued on his movement towards a more radical position on direct action campaigns by leaving Friends of the Earth to establish Earth First! (Garner, 1996).

Greenpeace perceives itself as having a different role to play when com-pared with Friends of the Earth, through the use of direct action methods by a well organised and disciplined group of activists. The high-level media at-tention assured through the work of these activists and the use of the Greenpeace vessels has ensured that they have a high profile resulting in some success around issues such as whaling. As with Friends of the Earth, the organisational arrangements have enabled them to become a successful, well-financed and influential group.

The role of these organisations has been identified with providing an alter-native to mainstream politics and diplomacy. Princen and Finger (1994) have identified these groups as providing a more fragmented form of political ac-tion and an approach that provides a multiplicity of solutions to environmen-tal problems built on local community needs. In particular, they have been identified as part of a continuing disillusionment with traditional forms of political action and in the United Kingdom their growth in membership closely parallels the decline in traditional political party membership. This has presented mainstream politics with the problem of how to respond to the demands of such groups. Initially they were dismissed as single-issue organisations with mainstream politicians identifying the environment as a narrow issue purely based around specific issues of conservation or pollution. Their success in placing the environment on the agenda has resulted in large, international groups such as Friends of the Earth being consulted on various issues by Government. Equally, they have established a series of parallel conferences to shadow the work of the United Nations as it continues with its programme of international conventions on the environment and sustainable development.

### *Link between environment and anti-globalisation protests*

Partly as a result of the analysis of the causes of environmental degradation discussed above, the environmental movement has found itself linked to a range of other protest groups at various inter-governmental summits. Under the broad heading of anti-globalisation there have been frequent and often violent confrontations between protestors and security forces. The environmentalist perception that economic growth, the nature of industrialism, and the destruction of the environment are all closely interrelated has led to the development of a loose coalition of groups with Greens being only one section. Environmental degradation, resource depletion and the destruction of traditional cultures are all seen as the consequence of the continuing development and globalisation of capitalism.

This is not surprising as the emergence of the environmental movement was linked with the New Left and the Counter Culture of the 1960s. As such the development of the Green critique of industrialism is close to that of other anti-globalisation protesters. However, as noted above, the position of the environmental movement is that it is not necessarily capitalism that is the cause of the global trends but rather the consequence of the dominant perspective of industrialism, with capitalism being a particular form of industrial development. Dryzek (1997) has noted that while the Green critique is in his view the most important development of the late twentieth century, it has not developed a blueprint for a new society. In his view, Green thinking does not really know what to do with late capitalism as a whole, but instead is involved in the development of a range of decentralised social and political experiments aimed at resolving problems associated with the environment and the varied needs of local, decentralised communities. Consequently, the links with other groups such as anarchists and Marxists within the anti-globalisation movement is not surprising, but also presents potential problems as far as strategies for developing alternative futures.

## Role of states and the UN

The problems facing national governments and the United Nations in developing policies on the environment are centred on the difficulty of trying to establish international laws and agreements to tackle a perceived challenge that can rarely be contained within the boundaries of a single nation state. The variety of issues covered by the problem of the environment is obviously very significant and as such these are not covered by any single international agreement. Relationships between states can be bilateral where there are clear problems concerning the flow of resources or pollution across borders. More importantly there are clear areas where multi-lateral discussions are held between many states frequently under the auspices of the United Nations. It is through such multinational conferences that the environment has been brought to the attention of the public and these conferences have often led the way in developing of the agenda. Indeed, the 1972 UN Conference on the Human Environment held in Stockholm was in many ways the genesis of the contemporary concern with the environment.

This conference was linked with the publication of the Sierra Club's 'Limits to Growth' and in the United Kingdom the 'Blueprint for Survival', both of which set out to identify the problems surrounding resource depletion and population growth. The conference made it clear that the nature of environmental problems was such that solutions could only be arrived at through international cooperation. However, it also revealed a basic contradiction at the heart of efforts to tackle environmental problems within the context of the existence of the nation state. Principle 21 of the Conference Declaration held that states had a sovereign right over their own resources while being responsible for environmental pollution across their borders (Elliott, 1998: 12). A further principle established related to the impact of human settlements on the environment and the prospect for sustainability, while an agenda was set out for the development of institutional arrangements for further environmental diplomacy. Elliott noted that through the latter process the UN established its position at the centre of international environmental arrangements and international law.

### Rio conference and the UN

The 1992 United Nations Conference on Environment and Development held in Rio was the main successor to the Stockholm conference. The key principles established at Rio centred on efforts at resolving the problems identified at Stockholm. These included global warming through the Framework Convention on Climate Change, biodiversity and control of the exploitation of forests. Each of these areas had specific declarations and formal arrangements established to explore ways in which they might be tackled. However, the sovereign rights of individual nation states made the development of these principals into binding and enforceable laws very difficult to establish.

The Rio Declaration established twenty-seven principles aimed at pushing forward the original themes identified at Stockholm. As at Stockholm the principles were couched within terms that were acceptable to the maintenance of state sovereignty rather than a more wholly international framework. Perhaps the most significant of these principles was embodied in Agenda 21 which identified key commitments for governments and international organisations (Bryner, 1997: 16–18). Local groups and communities, as a way of encouraging a sense of participation in the wider aim of achieving sustainable development, have adopted the key elements of this Agenda. Out of this approach has come a key environmental rallying cry, to 'Think Globally, Act Locally', whereby groups and organisations promote the idea that local activity can help if perceived at part of a global perspective on environmental issues.

### Kyoto and post-Kyoto issues

While the meeting at Kyoto in 1997 continued the development of the programme identified at both Stockholm and Rio, the issue that was to be the clear symbol of this conference was global warming. The Kyoto protocol identified the emissions of greenhouse gases, particularly carbon dioxide ($CO_2$), as the cause of increasing global temperatures and adopted an initial aim of reducing emissions to the levels of 1990. Where the debate has become most critical is over the contribution made to the overall level of $CO_2$ in the atmosphere by human activity, for example through car fumes and emissions from fossil fuel power stations. While many scientists studying these issues tend to believe that the impact of human activity is very significant there is an important minority who disagree.

The views of this minority are proving to be particularly influential in US government circles where first of all the Clinton administration and more directly the Bush administration have raised doubts about the whole agenda surrounding the reduction in carbon emissions. Clinton's position was centred on the need to ensure that a reduction in carbon emissions by the US should not be at the expense of economic growth or jobs. As noted above, such an approach contrasts with those in the environmental movement who consider economic growth to be a central cause of the ecological crisis. The Bush administration is even more opposed to the implementation of the Kyoto protocols and has unilaterally refused to sign up to it, arguing that the cost of reducing carbon emissions is much too high in terms of damage to the economy and jobs, when compared to the costs of global warming itself. This attitude of the US government has come in for criticism from other states, notably members of the European Union and Japan who have responded in a variety of ways over whether proceeding towards the targets established at Kyoto is worthwhile without the participation of the United States as the largest consumer of resources and producer of greenhouse gases.

The main area of contention does not lie in the acknowledgement that climate change is happening; rather it centres on the extent to which human activity is contributing to it and therefore the potential for human actions to reverse the trend. A major critic of the Kyoto agreement on climate change, Bjørn Lomborg (2001) has argued that the cost of around $150 billion per year to reduce $CO_2$ emissions, and other greenhouse gasses, outweighs the benefits. This is particularly of concern if our aim is to protect those in the developing world who are seen as the main victims of climate change. He contends that 'UNICEF estimates that just $70–80 billion a year could give all Third World inhabitants access to the basics like health, education, water and sanitation' and that this would enable them to meet the challenges of climate change better than a concentration on reducing $CO_2$ emissions (p. 322).

## Conclusion

The emergence of the environment as a significant issue on the world political agenda has been one of rapid growth and increasing salience. Not only has it raised questions about how we perceive the importance of the environment as an issue that has to be dealt with by the traditional political structures of individual states, it has also opened up a debate around the nature of political action. The development of environmental pressure groups of varying size and political styles has transformed the landscape of local, national and international politics. There is now perceived to be a role for public participation through these groups in determining the debate on national and cross-national issues.

However, as Garner (1996) has argued, while there has been a recognition of the importance of the environmental crisis as a consequences of the activities of the environmental movement, the response of states has been comparatively sluggish. The importance of the United Nations to the development of the agenda, both at the most senior political and diplomatic levels, and at the grass roots level of local activists, should not be underestimated. But the difficulties encountered in trying to develop an international response within the context of respect for the sovereign rights of nations over their own resources appear to be largely insurmountable. The key relationship between multinational companies operating on a global scale and the nation states within which they operate can be seen as an important constraint on the development of a comprehensive response to the issues of climate change and resource depletion.

Since the Stockholm Conference on the environment progress has been made on identifying the challenges, but only limited success has been achieved in resolving the problems. Significant victories have been made in areas such as the agreement to eradicate pollutants that damage the ozone layer, but these have emerged when there are obvious alternatives and a relatively small industry involved. The challenge emerging from the dependency of the world on fossil fuels, particularly oil, is much more problematic. The conflict that is emerging is between those engaged in pressure groups and direct action on environmental issues, who see the need for rapid and radical change, and those linked to the conventional political system who see the necessity of painstaking diplomacy and international agreement, who recognise the complexity of meeting the needs of economic development within a more complex physical environment. While the former may well develop new ways of thinking about the way we live as alternatives to an industrial and technologically based capitalism, the latter group will continue to struggle to find policy responses utilising the technological creativity of industrialism to the practical problems of environmental deterioration.

## Bibliography

Barry, J. (1999), *Rethinking Green Politics*, London: Sage.

Bryner, G.C. (1997), *From Promises to Performance: Achieving Environmental Goals*, New York and London: W.W. Norton.

de-Shalit, A. (1995), *Why Posterity Matters: Environmental Policies and Future Generations*, London: Routledge.

Dickens, P. (1996), *Reconstructing Nature: Alienation, Emancipation and the Division of Labour*, London: Routledge.

Dobson, A. (1995), *Green Political Thought*, second edition, London: Routledge.

Dowie, M. (1996), *Losing Ground*, Cambridge MA: MIT Press.

Dryzek, J.S. (1997), *The Politics of the Earth: Environmental Discourses*, Oxford: Oxford University Press.

Eckersley, R. (1992), *Environmentalism and Political Theory*, London: UCL Press.

Ehrlich, A.H. and Ehrlich, P.R. (1970), *Population, Resources and Environment*, San Francisco, CA: Freeman.

Ehrlich, P.R. (1971), *The Population Bomb*, London: Pan/Ballantine.

Ehrlich, P.R. and Pirages, D.C. (1974), *Ark II*, San Francisco, CA: Freeman.

Elliott, L. (1998), *The Global Politics of the Environment*, Basingstoke: Macmillan.

Garner, R. (1996), *Environmental Politics*, London: Prentice-Hall/Harvester Wheatsheaf.

Garner, R. (2001), *Environmental Politics*, second edition, London: Palgrave Macmillan.

Hardin, G. (1968), 'The Tragedy of the Commons', *Science*, Vol. 162, pp. 243–8.

Lomborg, B. (2001), *The Skeptical Environmentalist: Measuring the Real State of the World*, Cambridge: Cambridge University Press.

McCormick, J. (1995), *The Global Environmental Movement*, London: John Wiley & Son.

Meadows, D. *et al.* (1972), *The Limits to Growth*, London: Pan/Earth Island.

Naess, A. (1973), 'The Shallow and the Deep, Long Range Ecology Movement', *Inquiry*, Vol. 16, pp. 95–100.

O'Riordan, T. and Jäger, J. (1996), *Politics of Climate Change: A European Perspective*, London: Routledge.

Princen, T. and Finger, M. (1994), *Environmental NGOs in World Politics*, London: Routledge.

Radcliffe, J. (2000), *Green Politics: Dictatorship or Democracy?* Houndmills: Macmillan.

# 12

# Health

*Calum Paton*

At the outset, it should be pointed out that, in order to analyse the politics *of* health, it is necessary to analyse politics *in* health. First, while there may be certain respects in which the politics of health is unique to health, it is generally true that the effect of general political factors upon health and the delivery of healthcare is more significant. Political economy (both national and international), political structures and political systems condition healthcare systems and the prospects for health. Secondly, although a distinction is often made between health and healthcare, the argument of this essay is that the purpose of healthcare systems is to improve health, and as equitably as possible. Then healthcare systems and healthcare providers are crucial to health.

This is not to deny that hospitals and other providers are only one contribution to the total health of individuals, classes and nations. Clearly a whole range of factors affect health status – genetic inheritance, personal behaviour, social and environmental influences and 'causes', and 'lifestyle' issues which combine different elements, for example position at work, balance of life between work and leisure and so on. Nevertheless, healthcare and healthcare systems are still crucial, not least in that some of these wider factors are difficult to change. This may be true either for scientific or technical reasons or indeed for political reasons: despite all the rhetoric about public health and 'co-production' of health in a contract between the individual and the state, changing personal and community behaviour is very difficult. As a result, healthcare systems and health care providers within them, including hospitals – although they may have a limited effect upon the prevention of ill-health and the promotion of good health – are significant for both 'rescue and repair' on the one hand, and care, on the other hand. Managed in appropriate ways, they make significant contributions to improved health and the prevention of what would otherwise be worsened health, especially for poor citizens.

Meanwhile, let us remember why the issue of health is political. Conflict over resources for both health and healthcare put health at the centre of politics. Consider also the role of the state. Moran (1999) argues that 'the healthcare state', with echoes of the welfare state, implies both that the state affects healthcare (and health) and that healthcare systems in turn affect the state and politics. The traditional concerns of political science, ranging from the nature of the good society and the role of the state to the nature, uses and consequences of power are central to the analysis of health and healthcare.

Political history is also important. In the developed world (partially excluding the United States and Japan but including the communist Bloc and some of South America), the twentieth century saw the expansion of health systems, often into 'universal' systems (i.e. open to all) but not always comprehensive (i.e. covering people for everything). This reflected the politics of the twentieth century in many Western societies as laissez-faire gave way to either social democracy or at least increased government intervention. While this seems to describe the developed world, the expansion of schemes of health insurance in the developing world, particularly South America, and the export to Africa and Asia of healthcare systems from the developed world make it a broader picture. This does not alter the fact that, in poorer countries, due both to urgent health needs and shortage of resources, concerns have been different: for example, to provide basic sanitation, to protect the community from diseases which have been eradicated from the developed world; and to provide mutual and community-based forms of health insurance where either the resources, the politics or the state capacity and logistics for national systems do not exist.

This chapter first considers the political economy of health and healthcare and then examines changing healthcare systems and health sector 'reform', raising some wider considerations about global health, in both 'developed' and 'developing' societies.

### Political economy and healthcare

In this section it is argued that the twentieth century trend to a 'universal welfare state' is now being challenged under the new political economy of global capitalism and that the implications for health and healthcare are significant.

The argument is that economic globalisation is the main influence upon national economies in the world today, and that political economy is the most significant determinant of health policy. First, it heavily influences how much money is available for public healthcare systems and how such revenue is raised, that is, the prospects for equitably-funded and adequately-financed health services. Secondly, it influences who benefits most from publicly funded services: whether they are available to everybody on the basis of need or whether access is influenced by economic considerations, such as the need for a healthy workforce, or the need to invest in particular cadres of employees.

Thirdly, in the globalised economy, health services must compete with the rest of the economy for skilled labour, which often creates budgetary problems for public health services.

Global capitalism creates uneven development, in which there are 'Third World' laagers in developed countries like the USA and highly advanced niches in the economies of developing countries like Brazil. The nation state and national economy are both less autonomous and less homogeneous in today's world. This means that inequalities in health and access to health services are better considered in an international rather than a national context.

In the West the 'boom years' from 1945 to 1975 were the archetypal years of the industrial welfare state. Economically and fiscally, mass production, mass consumption and mass welfare were the order of the day. Politically, it was the heyday of social democracy but the West's social democracy depended economically upon cheap primary products, particularly cheap oil, from developing countries. What is sometimes called 'post-Fordist capitalism' is the technological, economic and political phenomenon which has characterised the development of 'advanced capitalism' in the years since the long boom. Post-Fordism refers to the decline of mass manufacturing and of the industrial welfare state which developed to meet the demands of the working class who were predominant in the electorate.

For health policy, the political consequences of post-Fordism are the decline of the 'left-wing majority' which depended on the industrial working class being a majority within the voting public and the rise of the 'contented majority' which supported the Thatcher governments in the UK and the Reagan Presidencies in the United States. The contented majority is a phrase coined by Galbraith (1992) to describe the fact that a majority of those who vote now have an economic stake in the status quo. In the language of 'first, second and third ways', the first way was the industrial welfare state, the second way was Thatcherism and the 'third way' is the attempt to combine globalisation with economic and welfare security for national and local communities.

The argument is that, under global capitalism, the era of the contented majority has given way to the era of the insecure majority. People cannot see a way out of global capitalism, but are disquieted consciously or otherwise by its manifestations. Employment is less secure even when it is better paid, exploitation is intensified even when incomes are higher, and more 'welfare state', in particular health and education, is sought by a majority yet the means of mobilising the revenue to achieve it is problematical.

The issue for healthcare systems is three-fold. The first consideration is the generation of revenue for public healthcare systems. A National Health Service, funded from taxation as in the UK or Sweden, requires a progressive tax system to generate enough revenue to provide a health service adequate to the needs of a majority of citizens. The middle classes want a health service if it is well enough funded to minimise waiting lists and waiting times, but they may resist paying for such a service for all from general taxation.

The second consideration is access to services. Global capitalism is the era of the 'competition state' (Cerny and Evans, 1998) and it is perfectly plausible to argue that the state may invest in 'cheap health services' to provide healthy workers which increase both the profitability of enterprise and the attractiveness of the country as a location for enterprise. As the neo-classical economists point out, individual firms may be unable or unwilling to invest in the social infrastructure which both they and the capitalist system need. If carried out rationally, this investment will not be universal, but will be restricted to particular cadres of workers or particular sectors of the economy where there are shortages of skilled workers. This selective state investment would do through the public sector what private healthcare systems, as in the USA, already do privately: firms invest in their workers and in the healthcare of their workers, where it is necessary to do so. Good quality health insurance is both an investment in and a perk for skilled and scarce workers and managers and an attempt to 'lock in' such workers to the company. This, in a nutshell, is US healthcare – mostly provided by private corporations, and highly inegalitarian.

The third consideration is employment. Public health services will have to compete to attract workers. From the very beginning of the chain, medical students and other potential professionals will choose their education according to alternative options, in turn linked to alternative economic conditions. Salaries and conditions in the health service will condition the health service's ability to compete within the economy generally, both national and international. The limited public service budget can pay enough to train and recruit the scarce skilled workers such as doctors in particular specialisms or pay living wages to the poorer unskilled workers, or see limits placed upon numbers in both categories. This is what the NHS faces with its various staff shortages, ranging from one discipline to another, from one time to another, depending upon the political priorities of the day.

Putting the three considerations together (the political economy of financing public health services; priorities in access to services; and employment considerations), we can see that keeping the better off 'on board' the NHS means providing a comprehensive National Health Service which provides quality treatment in a timely manner. And yet for the worse off – those whose labour is expendable – there is a requirement to provide rescue and care through the National Health Service, if it is to be a humanitarian social institution. Paradoxically, therefore, economists' solutions, such as cost utility analysis to decide who gets healthcare and who does not, are unhelpful to the NHS as a political project, considering the views of both middle classes and the poor. Both have to get ready access without technocratic denials of care or the political constituency for the NHS is undermined. Healthcare is an exceptional service with exceptional, yet justified, expectations.

It is a paradox that, even as the UK, for example, was agonising about whether its NHS was or ought to be sustainable for the twenty-first century, continental systems such as those in France – which enjoy lots of domestic popularity – were adopting some of the planning mechanisms of Beveridge systems such as the National Health Service. These mechanisms include regional planning agencies for hospital care (both public and private), the pooling of insurance funds to ensure more global purchasing, and so on. Clearly the level of financing is crucial. In 2002 France spent more than 10 per cent of its GDP on health, while Britain spent 7 per cent. When one looks at the source of France's social insurance, one finds significant payment by employers as well as individuals towards the statutory system. Even though there is more 'private top-up' than in Britain, the statutory public system still spends substantially more than does the NHS.

Paradoxically again, a move towards to a national health service in a country like France could actually mean less progressive means of funding the system: the less progressive income tax is, the less progressive is the National Health Service option (in terms of redistributing from rich to poor) as compared to (for example) France's system of significant employer contributions to social and health insurance. In other words, a National Health Service (Beveridge model) can actually be favoured by business and perhaps government as a means of resting the burden on industry.

The British NHS – a traditional low spender – could spend half the difference between its expenditure and the levels in France and Germany and, as a result of the intrinsic efficiency and effectiveness of NHS-style spending, achieve as good results as these countries. The danger is that with an inadequate service, better-off voters will only support those elements of the NHS which they feel they can secure more cheaply and promptly through the public service. That is, the NHS will be eroded towards a core – and perhaps emergency service in the long run if we do not 'get the political economy right'. Indeed countries such as the UK and Sweden are 'bucking the trend' to the extent that they maintain universal and comprehensive public health services, as opposed to skewing the priorities to maintain the allegiance of the better-off. How sustainable such systems are in the environment of laissez-faire global capitalism is an open question. This was the broad political context within which the British 'internal market' in the NHS was developed (Paton *et al.*, 1998, 1999b).

## Health sector reform

The 'logic' of globalisation has been transmitted directly to the world of health policy. For example, a 'think tank' of leading businessmen from multinational corporations in Europe in the mid–1980s, setting out this rationale had as one of its members a certain Dekker, from the Phillips group in the Netherlands, who also chaired the Dutch health reform committee leading to the Dekker plan of 1987 which was partially implemented during the 1990s (Warner, 1994).

The Dutch model of 'managed competition' became the prototype for reform of Bismarckian social insurance schemes in Europe and South America as well as for the failed Clinton Plan in the USA (Paton, 1996). The UK model of internal markets and purchaser/provider splits in tax-funded Beveridge or government health systems became the prototype for reform of national health service and government funded systems both in developed and developing worlds. It was devised by right-wing political advisers and politicians who advocated commercialisation in the public sector. This model of reform even became the prototype, somewhat incredibly, for health system reform in the poorest countries of Asia and Africa. Later in the 1990s and early 2000s, the World Bank sought to broaden the framework by which reform ideas and criteria were assessed, but the watchwords were still competition, market forces and privatisation.

The World Health Organisation (WHO) has sought a broader basis for evaluating and therefore, implicitly, exporting health system reform. The WHO has sought to evaluate health systems around the world by a variety of criteria, including quality, cost-effectiveness, acceptability to citizens and 'good governance' (World Health Reports, 2000; 2003). The World Bank's approach, as stated, is heavily influenced by the neo-liberal economic agenda applied to health and welfare, an agenda itself influenced by public choice theory (Dunleavy, 1989; Riley, 1998) especially purchaser/provider splits between buyers and seller of health services; 'managed competition', and quasi-commercial providers.

The assumption is that publicly-funded healthcare has to be delivered more efficiently, or cheaply, and has to be more carefully targeted. In Western countries, such as the Netherlands, the latter could be done by advocating publicly-funded universal access for a restricted basket of services (i.e. universality but not comprehensiveness).

In the 'developing' world from the 1980s onwards, usually under the aegis of multilateral agencies such as the World Bank and bilateral aid departments such as Britain's Overseas Development Administration (which became the Department for International Development in 1997),'Western' policies promoting market forces in healthcare have been advocated and partially implemented. In other developing countries, the watchword has been 'decentralisation', but the political intention has frequently been both to limit the role of the state in healthcare and to make communities more responsible for their own health, which sounds culturally progressive but is likely to be fiscally regressive.

The key question for developing countries is: how is better health and healthcare to be financed? The options range from private payment by means of private insurance, through community self-help or cooperation; by public insurance to national systems financed from government revenues, whether operated from the political centre or from devolved, decentralised or field agencies. In developing countries, however, the infrastructure for 'modern' tax-based or national insurance systems does not always exist.

Moreover, the decline of 'tax and spend' in the developing as well as developed world means that 'third way' solutions (meaning neither traditional state or public services nor unregulated markets) are also sought in the 'third world', irrespective of the names and slogans used. In health, the poorest countries have focused upon 'building social capital' (as in the West): communities, with aid from bilateral and multilateral agencies as well as NGOs, have sought to create mutual or cooperative local (informed) insurance schemes.

The priorities for investment in health are often set through a mixture of 'expert-based' needs assessment and local choice by 'rapid appraisal' of local people's needs. This leads to a focus upon the primary determinants of public health such as sanitation, immunisation, reproductive and sexual health (embracing maternal and child health) and so on. Regarding access to more expensive and acute/secondary health services, key issues are: the availability of pharmaceuticals at affordable prices (with both 'state and 'market' solutions, such as parallel imports, being attempted), the provision of integrated primary and secondary care, often though actually siting primary care facilities at hospitals, and the charging policy of public hospitals (i.e. should they be free; should they implement user charges; and, if so, how can equity be protected?) Politics is important in all of these areas. For example, if the private sector in hospital provision is encouraged, it may undermine public hospitals' ability to raise revenue from user charges for better-off patients.

Considering the regions of the world, the 'Western' world (Europe, Japan, North America and Australasia) is characterised by (mostly) public healthcare systems, using either general tax or health-specific revenues. Reforms have focused upon the importance of market mechanisms, but with mixed results (Paton *et al.*, 2000).

In Central and South America, there are significant traditions of public/national health insurance and reforms therein also involve the kind of 'managed competition' which European insurance systems have partially implemented. The danger of 'copy catting' rather than more appropriate forms of policy transfer should be noted. We can also note the health successes in Cuba's fully socialised system, although of course recent events are threatening its economic viability.

In South Central Asia (e.g. India, Pakistan and Bangladesh), parsimonious public services coexist with the private sector. In the Far East, the 'economic tigers' have tended to develop insurance systems and/or 'health cards' (as in Thailand), using both public and private finances. In China, significant problems of equity and access for the poor have developed, with the collapse of the old communist system and the new reality of private payment in a private market system. In Shanghai, the largest city, there is a new insurance scheme for employees, but the unemployed and indigent remain a worry both there and nationwide.

The continent of Africa probably contains the greatest unmet health needs and the most unsure prospects for meeting them. The economic prospects for regions and countries are the most significant factor affecting investment in health (i.e. economic success allows health expenditure) although aid is and should be premised on the fact that investment in health is necessary to stimulate and facilitate economic success.

Finally, in the former communist countries there is great diversity in prospects for health, again reflecting how the former territories have or have not integrated into the world economy. Developed services exist in the likes of the Czech Republic and Hungary, while there is destitution – along with collapse in health status – in large parts of Central Asia, in Russia itself and in the poorer East European countries such as Romania.

Access to affordable care is the most recurring issue globally. Achieving access to 'appropriate' care in developing countries depends on: political stability, the siting of health policy within anti-poverty strategy, the building of capacity within government (and the state) and the health system to deliver aims and objectives, and an appropriate balance between 'centralised' policy and local delivery of care.

At the beginning of the new millennium, the greatest challenges to effective healthcare in parts of the developing world stem from war and conflict, migration, lack of political and social infrastructure (often related to conflict), inadequate finance for care (or inability to mobilise both formal and informal sources of finance) and inadequate development of human resources for health. Coupled with the challenges of AIDS and other epidemics, both national governments and global agencies need to collaborate to facilitate the provision of medicines and technology to the neediest. Community mobilisation for development (including health) requires development of 'social capital'.

### The changing capitalist state and health system reform

Paradoxically, while the *capacity* of the 'healthcare state' (Paton, *et al.*, 2000) is increasing in proportion to the complexity of social regulation, the *autonomy* of the state in relation to economic interests is diminishing. Either the 'new managerialism' i.e. business systems to replace public administration (Exworthy and Halford (eds), 1999) or direct politicisation of public sector targets (Paton, 2002) is used to tailor health services to both economic needs and economically filtered social needs. It is argued here that use of the central state to extract maximum additional 'surplus value' for private business from healthcare provision reaches its apotheosis in the NHS model. Two paradoxes therefore arise. Firstly, the NHS, the most progressive and egalitarian model for health services is also the most easily subverted as the central state can be used and abused. Secondly, where the NHS model is 'off the political agenda' (as in the USA) because of a pro-business ideology, policy for 'taming healthcare' in the interests of business is much less 'cost-effective'. To a lesser extent, this latter situation also pertains in the 'Bismarckian', or social insurance, systems of Europe.

The UK provides a good example of how central government can be used to link health concerns with a wider economic agenda. Both Conservative and New Labour health reforms have sought an amalgam of increased efficiency and quality. The quasi-market reforms in the early 1990s sought more productive efficiency from a system of competitive (or potentially competitive) contracting between hospitals and other providers for income from purchasers (health authorities or groups of 'GP fundholders'). The initial New Labour approach in the UK was to 'abolish the market' yet rely heavily on systems of 'benchmarking' to ensure that the most efficient and the highest quality became the norm. While this relied upon an inspection system as in education policy, it also relied on many of the costing systems and efficiency mechanisms established to 'run' the internal market, with the difference that it would be the Man in Whitehall rather than the local purchaser who would dominate the process. New Labour subsequently replicated the market mechanisms of the 1990s by introducing 'Foundation Trusts', franchising, and other mechanisms (Milburn, 2002) – although this system of consumer choice and funding flows meant that New Labour's market was both different and more radical than the Conservatives' version (Paton, 2003).

Overall, the details of the various UK reforms may matter less than the future for any 'NHS' in a post-Fordist political economy. Consider the hypothesis that state-funded health services (such as the NHS) are a cheap means of investment in the workforce and the economy. If social spending enables firms to derive extra profit by having healthier workers, then that extra profit can be regarded as the extra income minus the cost of the social spending, such as the corporate tax through which firms contribute to the NHS. The residual – the extra profit -is composed of two elements: first, the contribution which workers make (e.g. through tax) to their own healthcare costs, which increases their productivity and firms' profits; and secondly, the exploitation (i.e. 'surplus value') extracted from healthcare workers. This latter element, if it exists, derives from the incomes of healthcare workers being less than the value they create, the classic Marxist definition of surplus value.

It might be objected that governments do not plot this situation but socio-political pressures produce it in reality. The changing socio-economic structure of Western societies and the international class structure produced under global capitalism leads to pressures on publicly-financed health systems. This is *inter alia* because more inequality and more complex differentiation of social structures leads to different ability and willingness to pay progressive taxes and social contributions. Either private financing of healthcare will increase, or public services will have to 'please' affluent and corporate consumers, as well as 'investing in health' on behalf of the economy's needs. The latter may not be equitable, if equity means equal access to services on the basis of equal need. Put bluntly, the healthcare demands of the rich and 'investment' in the health of scarce, skilled employees will conflict with egalitarianism in health service delivery.

Greater social inequality together with the absence of a left-of-centre electoral majority thus puts pressure on egalitarian policy and on institutions such as an NHS available to all irrespective of ability to pay. Attempts to defend such a service tend to rely on economic justifications, that international competitive advantage requires a healthy workforce. But workforce is not the same as society. Nor is a 'post-Fordist' workforce (i.e. a national class structure shaped by international capitalism) an undifferentiated structure: some workers are more equal than others when it comes to prioritising health for economic reasons. It is here that arguments about 'social capital' are sometimes used – a healthy workforce requires a healthy civil society. This in turn may be a zero-sum game between regions and communities.

If, as Marxists would argue, the state is the executive board of the capitalist class, its secret minutes might say: It makes economic sense for us, the state, to fund and provide healthcare. That way, we will pay less than if we directly provide health benefits for our workforce, company by company or industry by industry. It makes sense because taxation is less progressive than it used to be (so workers pay more, we pay less); the state can force hospitals and other providers to 'do more for less' i.e. exploit the health workforce to produce additional surplus value for us; and the public services can invest in the productive, using allegedly technocratic means of rationing.

If the healthcare providers were private, for-profit concerns, however, they might object that the interests of other capitalists went against their interests – namely, to derive as much profit as possible from a generously funded health system (broadly, the US model). Equally corporate insurers in the USA resist a single-payer or statist model. Such a situation does not pertain in the UK, with the commercial sector in healthcare being less economically and therefore less politically salient and content with marginal income from the NHS, important as that is in itself. Additionally, leaving 'investment in the workforce' to individual firms means a system whereby there is a problem of collective action: firms will not do it for fear of fattening up workers who then move to another firm; or rather, they will only do it to recruit and retain the most valuable workers. Again, this is broadly the situation in the United States.

On the other hand, if the state finances and provides a 'common basket' of health services for all (the European model), mechanisms will have to be put in place to limit that basket and to increase productivity in its production. Then wider benefits will be sought privately by individuals or employers. This, very broadly, is the agenda driving European health system reform.

If the state is more than a committee of capitalists, then ironically the 'hard-nosed' longer-term agenda of competitiveness may be easier to implement. Hence the continuing viability of the British NHS on economic as opposed to ethical lines, compared to the messy and expensive American system. Thus New Labour – in defending the NHS – stresses that European social insurance taxes business directly.

The choice between state healthcare to promote 'selective investment' rather than 'equitable consumption' is glossed over in the rhetoric of the 'third way' whereby the former becomes 'social investment' and the latter is downplayed either as 'old' tax and spend or as failing to emphasise health promotion. Overall, the state in the developed world 'balances' the claims of individual firms, the overall capitalist system and particular 'labourist' or 'welfarist' interests, but in today's international capitalism, securing inward investment is the crucial imperative.

There is therefore a parallel between the role of the state in developed countries and the imperative driving international agencies which work with developing countries. While investing in the basic determinants of health (e.g. sanitation) makes economic sense for poor countries, at a higher level of development the more likely question is, in whom and for what shall we invest, including social investment and investment in health services?

A dilemma arises when increasing engagement in the world economy raises hard questions for both international agencies and developing countries. Health is generally a consequence of other social, environmental and employment factors: although a minimum level of health is necessary for employability, different sectors of the economy will require different levels of general health as well as skills, particularly as unskilled workers can be easily replaced, and employment and income inequalities in the global capitalist economy will widen health inequalities in developing countries even if the basic level is raised. And at the bottom level of the socio-economic hierarchy there may simply be a 're-shuffling of the pack' in terms of who is employable or employed, if projects and initiatives to improve education and health in particular locations and communities are not translated into a wider egalitarian policy. The same, in other words, applies as with 'third way' initiatives in countries such as the UK. 'Social capital' may be a zero-sum game. The same logic applies to the whole of the public sector: both 'social capital' and 'social expenses' (O'Connor, 1973) have to be cheaper, linked to a more productive economy (local or national) if inward investment is to be secured.

Another issue for developing countries concerns globalisation – but whereas the above concerns economic necessity, this time the issue is 'policy transfer' and 'faddism' in copycatting where trendy policies are concerned. No managerial innovation has been more exported to the 'developing' world than the purchaser/provider split in the public sector and especially health. Inspired internationally by the idea of 'steering but not rowing' (Osborne and Gaebler, 1993) the purchaser/provider split has acquired the status of orthodoxy. Thus health reform has had to invest heavily in management, and therefore incur large management costs, with increased pressure on 'frontline' service costs (primarily hospital beds in the 1980s and 1990s). Some of the latter, namely spending more on management to 'cut waste' in services, is deliberate (but see Leys, 1999). Some, however, is simply the result of the need to make savings, however haphazard, to compensate for huge increased management costs. This was one of the ironies of the internal market reforms in the NHS (Paton *et al.*,

1998) – and is a major worry for 'health sector reform' in the developing world. Ironically, as increased management costs are 'abolished' in the UK and New Zealand (where they originated), they are implemented in Zambia and Ghana!

In the NHS systems of Europe other than the UK (Sweden, Denmark, Finland, Spain, Italy, Portugal and Greece in the Western Europe and certain countries in East Europe) the only country to copy the UK's market reforms unequivocally, at least on paper, was Italy. The 1993 reforms which led to regionalisation and less central determination of service availability, however never translated the blueprint into reality while the 1999 reform led to 'less market and more regionalisation', although, if right-wing governments continue in Italy after 2004, there may be more privatisation. As in Greece and Portugal, the privately-financed sector per se has grown in Italy. This reflects limitations on public financing and the fact that the 'NHSs' never dominated overall health spending in these 'Southern' European countries, because they developed later than in the UK and Nordic countries. They developed in the 1980s, a 'colder economic climate' than the systems of their richer neighbours which developed much earlier in the twentieth centure (Paton *et al.*, 2000).

In Sweden, a range of initiatives occurred at county level which involved – on the surface – 'purchaser/provider splits' (Bergman, 1998; Harrison and Calltorp, 1999) but this was in the context of national reforms which, with patient choice of provider, went in the opposite direction to the original British market reforms, where the patient had to follow the money. In Sweden, the seemingly impossible combination of much shorter waiting times, stabilisation of spending and increased patient choice occurred – stimulated by the economic crisis of the early 1990s, when Swedish social democracy met global capitalism, resulting in a 'one off' productivity improvement in Swedish hospitals, which had hitherto led a very relaxed life by the standards of the typical British hospital with its overbooking and waiting times.

In Denmark and Finland, initiatives were more piecemeal, consisting in new 'waiting-time' and reimbursement policies, and the unification of health and social services in the latter. Certain parts of Spain used the 'purchaser/provider split', but more as a device to separate out the functions of planning and management rather than part of a wider political project (Paton *et al.*, 2000).

The social insurance or 'Bismarckian' countries of Europe, Germany and the Netherlands have seen (respectively) most action and rhetoric in 'market forces', but of a different type to that in national health service systems. In social insurance systems, with sickness funds (i.e. mostly not-for-profit insurance companies) reimbursing or purchasing healthcare, market forces (or 'managed competition') have involved sickness funds competing for citizen enrolments. This in turn may have led to new purchaser/provider relationships e.g. between sickness funds and hospitals, but as a by-product.

In 'advanced' Europe, then, market forces have not had the ideological verve that they did in the UK. The situation in formerly communist Eastern Europe is different. The desire to consign the Soviet system to the historical bonfire, especially in the Czech Republic, led to much hasty action in privatising and liberalising the provision of healthcare which soon proved to be unaffordable as well as inequitable.

As a result, 'pro-market' reforms after 1990 have been partially reversed in many East European countries. A trend all over Europe and indeed the world is the move to the 'new regulation' rather than direct provision in public systems (Saltman *et al.* (eds), 2002). This trend may be a cause for concern if it ignores the benefits of public planning and integrated regulation, and leads instead to piecemeal regulation of entrepreneurial activity.

The following tables summarise key reforms in Europe.

Table 12.1 *Key reforms in Bismarck countries*

| Country | Main (specific) types of market force/reform |
| --- | --- |
| Germany | Competing payers (sickness-funds); (limited) provider competition for contracts in future |
| Belgium | Limited change to risk adjustment for payers (sickness-funds); limited change to reimbursement of providers (partial moves towards more capitated form of payment for radiotherapy, medical imaging and lab testing) |
| Netherlands | (Some) competition by payers; some competition by providers; redefinition of 'core services' |
| Luxembourg | No change |
| Austria | Amended financing of hospitals (to per-case payments) |

Table 12.2 *Key reforms in Beveridge countries*

| Country | Main (specific) types of market force/reform |
| --- | --- |
| UK | Internal market, 1991–1997; contracting; purchaser/provider split; GP fundholding; Patient's Charter; changing primary/secondary configurations; decline in competition (post-1997); Private Finance Initiative |
| Sweden | Purchaser/provider varieties, county level; further marketisation in some countries; overall national trend to regionalisation, post-1995 |
| Denmark | Free choice of hospital by patient; reimbursement changes; waiting list initiatives |
| Finland | (Full) decentralisation of payer; new resource allocation to (municipality-based) payers; union of health and social care |
| Spain | Limited purchaser/provider distinction; self-governing providers in some autonomous regions; business-like reforms; waiting list initiatives |

Table 12.3 *Key reforms in countries of mixed group*

| Country | Main (specific) types of market force/reform |
| --- | --- |
| Italy | 'Official structures' of internal market; limited 'operationalisation'; partial reversal; increased choice of private insurer |
| Greece | Gradual decentralisation; encouragement of private paying/provision (1992), partially reversed (1997); increased role of private sector; complexity: change depends on hospital category; per-case payment; 'new public management' |
| Portugal | Some 'out sourcing'; internal contracting; increased role for private sector; (co-payments as cost-containment) |
| France | Move to cost-containment by regional planning; change from insurees' contributions based only on income to an earmarked tax based on total income |
| Ireland | Move to regionalisation; (limited) contracting/service agreements; competition in private insurance sector, following legislation of 1994; DRG funding |

## Conclusion

If global capitalism is 'causing' the decline of egalitarianism and pressures for radical 'reform' within public healthcare systems, then one may ask why the UK in particular has seen more radical 'right-wing' reform than countries such as France and the rest of 'developed' Europe. The answer probably lies in the fact that globalisation happens unevenly (Gray, 1998), and the UK, with its closeness to the USA as well as its unique access to global financial markets, may be expected to embrace the necessities of global capitalism sooner. However, there are some further observations.

A definite trend in Europe, embracing both NHS and social insurance systems, is to limit what is available from public healthcare, variously known as rationing or prioritisation of a 'common basket of services'. In countries more generously funded or equitable or both (such as Germany, France and Sweden, in their different ways), this is less likely to lead immediately to significantly larger private sectors outside the state-regulated or state-financed system than currently exist. Yet there are trends, even in Germany and France, towards cost-control and 'purchasing' rather than simply reimbursing retrospectively for whatever services are provided as a result of patient–doctor decisions. This trend is clearly of significance in the developing world, where government-financed health services are facing huge pressures. There are initiatives towards 'formal rationing' in developing countries, using analytical tools such as the DALY – the Disability-Adjusted Life Year, paralleling the concept of the QALY (Quality-Adjusted Life Year) in developed countries. In developing countries as well as developed, however, political crises and politico-social pressures are likely to continue to influence health expenditures (often quite rightly, as with AIDS and HIV-linked expenditures in Africa).

'Purchasing' indeed is the most significant continuity between Tory and Labour reforms to the British NHS. With all the talk of the 'purchaser/provider split' in 1991, it tended to go unnoticed that purchasing per se was a new development. Although used haltingly if at all at first, it is the mechanism (decisions a priori as to what to pay for) which informs New Labour's 'cash-limited global budget' to Primary Care Trusts – cash-limiting the parts (primary care and drugs) that even Margaret Thatcher did not try to reach, in the process. It is 'purchasing' – and the need to 'strengthen' it – which dominates healthcare reform agendas across Europe, and indeed the world. Nevertheless, such 'purchasing' or 'commissioning' is often swept aside when popular and political pressure demands investment in acute hospital services. France, the most significant European country to have escaped most of this agenda, topped the poll in the WHO's report on effectiveness and quality in healthcare systems, while in England 'patient choice' is undermining purchasing.

Another issue is the role of the European Union (Paton *et al.*, 2000). There are many senses in which Europe is 'at the crossroads'. To name but a few: the European Court may or may not mandate Europe-wide access to any publicly-funded health services, whether at prevailing or regulated prices. The same Court may or may not rule (in the absence of exemption for healthcare from European Single Market 'pro-competitive' rules) that social insurance funds and providers which are not actually part of the state are economic entities and so must be competitive. This would threaten (for example) the 'reformed' NHS in Britain, with its Self-Governing Trusts and Foundation Hospitals which are outside the core state. Crucially, the EU – under pressure from large or multinational companies such as VW – may seek to develop a common fiscal policy which allows tax exemptions for employer-provided (private) health coverage. This could 'Americanise' the socialised health systems of Europe – ironically, in that the EU is often concerned to promote its own 'social model' as an alternative.

Global capitalism, although it can move in mysterious ways, is likely to augment the more individualist Anglo-American role of the state and diminish the European collectivist and statist traditions.[1] In healthcare this may lead to convergence in Europe, with or without the EU as a motive force. The reason France's public (and total) healthcare system is so expensive is not just because of 'inefficiency': it is because there is both an individualist and 'corporatist' rationale and content to both consumption of, and investment in, healthcare. To put it bluntly, individuals with the flu are likely to get seven prescriptions; and *la solidarite* demands generous access for all, via their social or civic associations. In the USA, by contrast, healthcare is individually motivated but largely employer-provided on an industrial basis, with tax benefits to both employer and recipient.

In the UK, the NHS stems from a collectivist philosophy, albeit a pragmatic British rather than a Hegelian one, but, as it has been parsimoniously funded, it has been 'shaped' by the political economy within which it has to live. Thus, generous consumption as a 'social right', French-style, is off the agenda. Hence the search, more acute in Britain, for 'circle-squaring' solutions – such as the internal market in the NHS – which promised 'more product' for believers in the NHS *and* more cost-effective investment in the view of the Tory government's business and financial supporters. New Labour has abandoned the quest for the 'magic bullet' in allocating significant additional resources and that is actually progress.

Such was the 'conspiracy'. The 'cock-up' came in the forces unleashed by the 'internal market', and the political interventions which accompanied it. Much inconsistency came from the fact that the politicians were seeking to invigorate market forces with the left hand while seeking to dampen them down with the right hand (Paton, 1995a; Paton *et al*, 1998). This pattern has been repeated – in both its aspects – under New Labour. In the quest to decentralise unpopular decisions down from central government and regions, purchasing was established at too low a level and on too small a scale either to plan effective and efficient health services or to achieve the very objectives which central government sought through decentralisation. This recent history is also being repeated in the early 2000s (Paton, 2003) bringing to mind Marx's dictum that history repeats itself, first as tragedy and then as farce.

Health sector reform, in its language and even forms. is of course part fad. Trendy ideas spread, although are often misunderstood, then implemented differently in different versions, against different backgrounds and objectives. There is however convergence, in both the constraints facing public healthcare systems and the nature of the voting publics of developed and even developing 'post-Fordist' economies. Like the very different publics of 'pre-Fordist' or least developed countries, electorates may wish it differently. Yet governments cannot 'escape the logic', unless acting at a multinational level on an agenda of controlling capitalism. Whether or not the state is run by capitalists, it is they who possess the vetos and the incentives in the era of the new globalisation.

### Notes

1   The UK itself, however, is a paradox with the historical reluctance of the state to deny economic individualism except in wartime, yet with a statist tradition in healthcare since the Second World War.

## Bibliography

Altenstetter, C. and Björkman, J. (eds.) (1997), *Health Policy Reform, National Variations and Globalization*, London: Macmillan.

Bacon R. and Eltis, W. (1976), *Britain's Economic Problem: Too Few Producers*, London: Macmillan.

Bartlett, W. and Le Grand, J. (eds.) (1993), *Quasi-Markets and Social Policy*, London: Macmillan.

Bergman, S.-E. (1998), 'Swedish Models of Health Care Reform: A Review and Assessment', *International Journal of Health Planning and Management*, Vol. 13, No. 2, pp. 91–106.

Braverman, H. (1998: 25th Anniversary edition), *Labour and Monopoly Capital*, New York: Monthly Review Press[1].

Cerny, P. and Evans, M. (1998), *The Competition State*, paper presented to the Annual Conference of the Political Studies Association of the UK, Keele University, April.

Coates, D. and Hay, C. (2000), 'Home and Away? The Political Economy of New Labour', paper presented to the Annual Conference of the Political Studies Association of the UK, LSE and Birkbeck College, London, April.

Department of Health (1997), *The New NHS: Modern and Dependable*, London: The Stationery Office.

Department of Health (2000), *The NHS Plan*, London: The Stationery Office.

Downs, A. (1957), *An Economic Theory of Democracy*, New York: Harper and Row.

Dunleavy, P. (1989), *Democracy, Bureaucracy and Public Choice*, London: Harvester Wheatsheaf.

Exworthy, M. and Halford, A. (eds) (1999), *Professionals and the New Managerialism in the Public Sector*, Buckingham: Open University Press.

Galbraith, J.K. (1992), *The Culture of Contentment*, London: Sinclair-Stevenson.

Gray, J. (1998), *False Dawn: The Delusions of Global Capitalism*, London: Granta.

Greer, S. (1998), 'Why Won't Companies Reduce their Costs? Universal Health Care and the Flexible Corporation', paper to the PSA Health Politics Specialist Group Conference, Mansfield College, Oxford, January.

Harrison, M. and Calltorp, J. (1999), *The Reorientation of Market-Oriented Reform in Swedish Health Care*, paper presented to C. Paton *et al.* (2000).

Hill, M. (1997), *The Policy Process in the Modern State*, London: Harvester Wheatsheaf.

Jessop, B. (1994), in R. Burrows and B. Loader (eds), *Towards a Post-Fordist Welfare State?*, London: Routledge.

Leys, C. (1999), 'Intellectual Mercenaries and the Public Interest', *Policy and Politics*, Vol. 27, No. 4.

Marx K., *Capital*, in *Karl Marx, Frederick Engels, Collected Works*, Moscow: Progress Publishers/ New York: International Publishers Co. Inc./London: Lawrence and Wishart), See also, Marcuse, H. (1955), *Reason and Revolution*, London: Routledge and Kegan Paul, Part II, I, 6; McLellan, D. (1977), *Karl Marx: Selected Writings*, Oxford: Oxford University Press; and Wheen, F. (1999), *Karl Marx*, London: Fourth Estate.

Milburn, A. (2002), *Speech to New Health Network*, 15 January.

Moran, M. (1999), *Governing the Health Care State*, Manchester: Manchester University Press.

Navarro, V. (1978), *Class Struggle, the State and Medicine*, London: Martin Robertson.

O'Connor, J. (1973), *The Fiscal Crisis of the State*, New York: Harper and Row.

Olson, M. (1971), *The Logic of Collective Action*, Cambridge, MA: Harvard University Press.

Osborne, D. and Gaebler, T. (1993), *Reinventing Government*, New York: Plume.

Paton, C. (1992), *Competition and Planning in the NHS: The Danger of Unplanned Markets*, first edition, London: Chapman and Hall.

Paton, C. (1995a), 'Contriving Competition', *Health Service Journal*, 13 February.

Paton, C. (1995b), 'Present Dangers and Future Threats: Some Perverse Incentives in the NHS Reforms', *British Medical Journal*, 13 May.

Paton, C. (1996), 'The Clinton Plan', in Bailey *et al.* (eds), *Developments in American Politics*, London: Macmillan.

Paton, C. (1999a), Commentary on 'Intellectual Mercenaries and the Public Interest', *Policy and Politics*, Vol. 21, No. 4.

Paton, C. (1999b), 'New Labour's Health Policy: The New Healthcare State', in M. Powell (ed.), *New Labour, New Welfare State?*, Bristol: Policy Press.

Paton, C. (2000), *World, Class, Britain: Political Economy, Political Theory and Public Policy*, London: Macmillan.

Paton, C. (2002), 'Cheques and Checks', in M. Powell (ed.), *Evaluating New Labour's Welfare Reforms*, Bristol: Policy Press.

Paton, C. (2003), *The State of the Healthcare State*, Cambridge: Judge Institute.

Paton, C. *et al.* (1998), *Competition and Planning in the NHS: The Consequences of the Reforms*, second edition, Cheltenham: Stanley Thornes.

Paton, C. with Bellanger, M.-M., Berman P., Busse, R. and Hunter, D. *et al.* (2000), *The Impact of Market Forces on Health Systems: A Review of Evidence in the 15 European Union Member States*, Dublin: European Health Management Association (for European Commission).

Price, D., Pollock, A. and Shaoul, J. (1999), 'How the WTO is Shaping Domestic Policies in Healthcare', *Lancet*, No. 354, 27 November.

Poulantzas, N. (1973), *Political Power and Social Classes*, London: New Left Books.

Powell, M. (2000), 'Analysing the 'New' British National Health Service', *International Journal of Health Planning and Management*, Vol. 15, No. 2, pp. 89–102.

Riley, D. (1998), 'Providers or Enablers? ...' paper presented to PSA Politics of Health Specialist Group, Mansfield College, Oxford, January.

Robinson, R. and Steiner, A. (1998), *Managed Health Care*, Buckingham: Open University Press.

Saltman, R., Busse, R. and Mossialos, E. (eds) (2002), *Regulating Entrepreneurial Behaviour in European Health Care Systems*, Buckingham: Open University Press (for European Observatory on Health Care Systems).

Segall, M. (2000), 'From Co-operation to Competition in National Health Systems – and Back? Impact on Professional Ethics and Quality of Care', *International Journal of Health Planning and Management*, Vol. 15, No. 1.

Skocpol, T. (1997), *Boomerang: Health Care Reform and the Turn Against Government*, second edition, New York: W.W. Norton.

Warner, M. in Lee, K. (ed.) (1994), *Health Care Systems: Can They Deliver?*, Keele: Keele University Press.

World Health Organisation (2000), *The World Health Report 2000 Health Systems: Improving Performance*, Geneva: WHO.

World Health Organisation (2003), *The World Health Report 2003*, Geneva: WHO.

# 13

# Sport

*Barrie Houlihan*

There are few people today who still subscribe to the romantic notion of sport as an activity that takes place outside of normal society. Most readily acknowledge that sport is an integral aspect of the social structure and, as such, falls within the normal sphere of political activity. Most obviously sport is a frequently used resource by governments to attempt to achieve largely non-sports objectives such as urban regeneration, social control and the improvement of cardio-vascular health. Second, sport is also the recipient of substantial amounts of public money which is used, for example, to build and manage facilities, operate sports development programmes and to fund bids for major sports events such as the Olympic Games. Finally, sport is also a source of issues for governments whether it concerns the behaviour of individual sportsmen and women, for example in relation to drug use or violence, or whether it concerns the decisions of teams and their governing bodies, for example the decision by the England and Wales Cricket Board to host the Zimbabwe cricket tour in 2003. There are a number of reasons for the recent rise in the salience of sport to governments. Among the most significant is the increased commercialisation of sport which, for example, has generated demand for closer regulation of the ownership of football teams by media companies or of the access of the public to watch major sports events such as the Wimbledon tennis championships on 'free to air' television. A second reason is that the steady growth in the amount of international sport has generated opportunities for governments to use sport to promote the image of their country either through hosting events or by the success of their athletes. Third, and closely related to the previous reason, the growth of international sport provides opportunities for governments to use sport as a relatively low cost, yet high profile, diplomatic resource to demonstrate support or, more usually, opposition to governments and regimes.

The utility and adaptability of sport is easily illustrated. For example rather than follow Olympic protocol and say 'I declare open the Games of Salt Lake

City ...' President George Bush proclaimed: 'On behalf of a proud, determined and grateful nation I declare ...' Bush took ample opportunity to be photographed with members of the US team as 72 million Americans tuned in to watch and NBC, the US host broadcaster, reminded them that the two skiers from Iran were part of the 'axis of evil' identified by the President. Given the attacks on New York and Washington five months earlier, perhaps it is not surprising that the 2002 Salt Lake City Winter Olympic Games were overlain with expressions of American patriotism. Meanwhile in Afghanistan the first contact was being made between the post-Taliban sports authorities and the International Olympic Committee to discuss the future involvement of the country in the Olympic Games. At about the same time a news story in the Western press told of the revival of a local sport, involving a headless goat and teams of horsemen, previously banned by the Taliban. For both the United States and Afghanistan sport fulfilled significant symbolic political functions: it betokened resolution, normality and solidarity for the United States and international recognition and revival for Afghanistan. The capacity of sport, especially international sport, to provide a source of political symbolism and a context for political posturing is well established. Few politicians can resist using sport and national sporting success as a political metaphor or an aid to self-promotion. The number of national leaders who attend World Cup soccer matches, send well publicised messages of congratulation to victorious athletes, or host receptions for national Olympic teams all attest to the continuing attraction of sport to politicians. For students of politics, however, the important question is whether the political significance of sport extends beyond the symbolic, the metaphorical and the contextual. In other words, in contemporary politics does sport constitute a valuable resource available for use by political interests and does sport itself constitute a distinct issue in the same way that the environment, trade and migration do?

It will be argued that sport is significant in politics in four distinct ways: first, as a diplomatic resource; second, as an increasingly valuable economic resource; third as an important ingredient in the politics of identity; and fourth, as a source of problems, such as doping and corruption, that require international cooperation.

## International sport and diplomacy

A wide repertoire of resources is required to communicate the range of messages of support, solidarity, disapproval, engagement, independence etc. that comprise modern diplomacy. For many years sport has proved itself to be a highly adaptable and sensitive addition to the language of diplomacy. Perhaps the most notable diplomatic use of sport was by the former German Democratic Republic (GDR) which used sport as a tool for making the transition, in the years following the end of the Second World War, from being the Soviet controlled zone of the defeated German Reich to an independent state. In the face of staunch opposition from the United States and its allies the East German Communist Party (SED) used sport in a highly innovative and effective way. International sporting contact, initially with communist states, provided the opportunity to demonstrate the de facto existence of the East German state which in time would lead to *de jure* recognition. The nascent GDR pursued a dual strategy of hosting and participating in international sports events under its own flag and seeking membership of international sports federations and the International Olympic Committee. During the early 1950s the GDR hosted a number of sports events involving foreign teams and athletes and also accepted invitations from sympathetic states to attend events abroad, thus gradually raising the profile of the country as an independent state. In parallel, the GDR and its allies, particularly the Soviet Union, were putting sustained pressure on the IOC to recognise the Democratic Republic as a state in its own right, distinct from the Federal Republic of Germany (FRG or West Germany). Despite initially adhering to its principle of 'one country – one National Olympic Committee' and insisting that the 'two Germanies' participate as a united team, the IOC granted the GDR full membership of the Olympic movement in 1968. At the next Olympic Games in 1972, ironically held in Munich, the GDR participated as a state with the same status as the FRG.

Although GDR membership of the IOC was followed within two or three years by diplomatic recognition from most of the major Western states and also membership of the United Nations it is not possible to conclude that recognition by the IOC led directly to wider diplomatic recognition. Sports diplomacy was only one aspect, albeit an important aspect, of a broader strategy designed to achieve recognition for the GDR. Nevertheless, to ignore the significance of sport would be rash. There is ample evidence that sport had been identified by the SED leadership in the GDR as a key resource in its strategy for recognition. The East German government provided substantial public resources to support its athletes not only because they were seen as 'diplomats in tracksuits' (Strenk, 1980) but also because they were 'conscious builders of the socialist GDR', according to the sports minister Manfred Ewald (quoted in Hardman 1987). The particular success of the GDR in pursuing sports diplomacy was due partly to its powerful communist allies who were constantly lobbying on its behalf within the major international sports federations and within the IOC and partly to the consistent outstanding success of GDR athletes in sports competitions, especially the Olympic Games.

The case of the GDR is the best known of a number of examples where sport has been used to promote or challenge claims for statehood and diplomatic recognition. Taiwan took advantage of the withdrawal of the People's Republic of China (PRC) from international sport in the 1960s to consolidate its claim to recognition as an independent state. Following the end of the Cultural Revolution in the PRC in the 1970s and the country's re-engagement with the international community it made the expulsion of Taiwan a condition of its membership of international sports organisations. In the early 1980s Palestine was successful in gaining membership of the International Amateur Athletic Federation (responsible for track and field sports) at a time, the 1980s, when it controlled no independent territory. More recently still one of the first actions of the states emerging from the crumbling Soviet Union was to apply for membership of the IOC.

Apart from its use in the search for international recognition, sport has also been used extensively to make the first tentative steps in improving relations between previously hostile states. The best known use of sport in this way was in the early 1970s when attempts were being made to improve relations between the United States and the People's Republic of China. In 1971, following an invitation from the Chinese, the USA sent a table tennis team and a year later a basketball team to the PRC. The sports were well chosen as the inevitable defeat of the US table tennis team did not result in any damage to diplomatic dignity as the USA has little history of success in the sport. The success of the touring US basketball team redressed the sporting balance without any harm to Chinese prestige as the sport was not widely played in the PRC. These sporting contacts provided an important, but low risk, stepping stone towards the historic meeting between President Nixon and Mao Zedong in 1972. In the late 1990s, a visit by the Baltimore Orioles baseball team to Havana and a return visit by the Cuban national team to Baltimore were part of a subsequent, though short-lived, attempt to improve relations between Cuba and the United States during the Clinton administration.

However, sports diplomacy does not always have a benign effect as demonstrated in October 2001 by the French government's attempt to use an international soccer match with Algeria to improve relations with the Algerian government and with the large immigrant population of Algerian origin living in France. Apart from a low level match in the Mediterranean Games in the 1970s this was the first time that the two countries had played each other in the forty years since Algeria won its independence after a long and bitter war. The French sports minister, Marie-Georges Buffet and Prime Minister Lionel Jospin attended the match which Mourad Bouchemia, head of the Algerian Football Association, claimed went 'way, way beyond a simple sporting encounter' (*Guardian*, 6 October 2001, p. 21). Unfortunately, the hope that the match might be a step towards better international and community relations was dashed as the match was abandoned twelve minutes from full time when fighting broke out and riot police were called in to restore order. More recently in June 2003 the fragile diplomatic relations between Serbia and Croatia were highlighted by the attack by Serbs on the Croatian embassy in Belgrade following fighting between Serbian and Croatian fans at the final of the European water polo championship which Serbia won nine goals to eight. The problems at both these matches were a reminder that, while sporting contact can build upon already improving relations, it can also provide confirmation of just how poor existing diplomatic or community relations are.

The use of sport to indicate disapproval or press for policy change is better documented and probably more widespread (Keech and Houlihan, 1999). There are many examples of the country hosting a major sports event refusing to invite or allow entry to countries of which it disapproved. Canada in 1976 refused visas to the Taiwan team for the 1976 Olympic Games in Montreal as it had just given diplomatic recognition to the People's Republic of China, while Israel was regularly excluded from Asian sports competitions. Much more common are the instances of countries refusing to participate in events because they wish to show disapproval of the policies of either the host country or of another participating country. In 1968, as part of the campaign against apartheid, thirty-two African countries threatened to boycott the forthcoming Olympic Games in Mexico City if the South African team was permitted to participate. Although the IOC initially resisted African pressure it agreed to withdraw its invitation to the South African team when it became clear that a number of countries from the communist bloc, particularly China and the Soviet Union would support the boycott. Soviet support for the boycott was crucial, but far from unequivocal, as the Soviet authorities had to weigh up the relative diplomatic advantage of demonstrating solidarity with the opponents of apartheid against the possibility of embarrassing the Americans by winning more Olympic medals. The Soviet Union finally agreed to back the boycott (and forego the opportunity to demonstrate that communism was at least the equal, if not the superior, of capitalism) because of its concern that China might exploit its participation in the Games and challenge its leadership within the communist bloc and its prestige among the non-aligned states of the Third World. Further boycotts related to apartheid were either threatened or took place at the Olympic games of 1972 and 1976 and at the Commonwealth Games of 1978 and 1986.

While international sport, and especially Olympic competition, provided the United States and the Soviet Union for many years with an opportunity to demonstrate the success and vitality of their respective ideologies, both powers used boycotts as part of Cold War politics. In 1980 the United States, along with a number of its allies, boycotted the Moscow Olympic Games primarily to protest against the recent Soviet invasion of Afghanistan and the treatment of Soviet dissidents, but also to avoid the embarrassment of appearing to contribute to a successful 'communist Olympics'. Not surprisingly the Soviet Union and its allies (with the exception of Romania) boycotted the 1984 Olympic Games held in Los Angeles (Peppard and Riordan, 1993).

For sport to be an effective diplomatic resource a number of conditions must be met: first, the issue must be clear-cut (such as an end to apartheid or the withdrawal of troops from Afghanistan); second, there must be some expectation that a boycott will have some effect on policy (possible in relation to apartheid, but extremely doubtful in the case of the Soviet invasion of Afghanistan); thirdly, the boycott must be achieved without too much arm-twisting of one's allies (anti-apartheid boycotts were relatively easy to assemble while both the USA and the USSR generated considerable resentment among their allies in assembling the boycotts of 1980 and 1984); and finally, the event must be perceived as being diminished by the absence of the boycotting countries. This condition was a problem for African states in the 1970s as their sporting profile was low, but not so for either the United States or the Soviet Union, the two superpowers of Olympic sport (Houlihan 1994). Today it is possible that the use of boycotts has gone out of fashion, not only because both apartheid and the Cold War have come to an end, but also because the diplomatic opportunities arising from participation now clearly outweigh the value of a boycott. However, there are still occasional calls to withdraw invitations to participate in an event, as was the case recently when the British government suggested that it would be inappropriate for the England cricket team to play one of its World Cup matches in Zimbabwe's capital Harare. Although England eventually withdrew from the fixture and forfeited the points the issue was hardly clear-cut with the South African government opposing an England boycott and the symbolism of boycotting a predominantly white sport to show opposition to the repressive policies of President Mugabe was blurred.

### Sport as an economic resource

Despite claims that major sports events are self-funding, most receive substantial direct or indirect subsidy from public funds. As a result the motives for hosting the Olympics or the football World Cup are highly political and may include the promotion of a particular ideology or regime (e.g. the Olympic Games in Berlin 1936, Moscow 1980 and Los Angeles 1984), the symbolic readmission of a country to the international community (e.g. the 1964 Tokyo Olympics and the 1972 Munich Olympics), the promotion of a city/ region/ country (e.g. the Olympic Games in Montreal 1976, Seoul 1988 and Barcelona 1992). However, since the early 1980s, especially since the Los Angeles Olympic Games in 1984, there has been a recognition on the part of governments that major sports events, while still likely to require public subsidy, are capable of generating considerable direct and indirect economic benefits. For example, while the total bill for staging the 2000 Sydney Olympic Games was £2.4 billion it was estimated that the Games would reduce Australia's current account deficit by 1.25 per cent of gross domestic profit largely through the attraction of an additional 2.1 million tourists. This expectation was based on assessments of Australia's previous experience in bidding for and hosting major sports events. For example, it was estimated that the hosting of the 1987 America's Cup generated expenditure of £230m and the equivalent of 9,500 full-time jobs. Even Brisbane's failed bid for the 1992 Olympic Games provided a significant boost to the local economy as it focused 'world-wide attention on Australia, its tourism potential, its excellent sporting facilities and its professional sports administration' (Department of Sport 1987: 49). The hosting by England of the Euro 96 football competition brought similar economic benefits, with the city of Sheffield alone receiving about £5.8m income from hosting the first round matches, contributing to the estimated £1.5 billion income generated annually from sports tourism in the UK.

The rapidly increasing value of sport to national economies has been matched and stimulated by a similar rise in the commercialisation of sport. At the level of the individual athlete, the team and the sports goods company, sport is a substantial business. For example in 2000, the American basketball player, Shaquille O'Neal signed a contract with the Los Angeles Lakers worth £52 million over three years, the sportswear company Adidas-Salomon reported sales of £3 billion, the English Premier League football club Manchester United signed a £28 million deal with communications company, Vodaphone, and was valued at over £1 billion on the stock market. The value of broadcasting rights has also escalated rapidly in the last thirty years. In 1980 the US broadcasting rights for the Olympic Games were valued at £51m: twenty years later NBC paid £415m. Sport is also of increasing significance to regional, national and local economies. Sport is estimated to contribute 3 per cent of GDP to the economies of member states of the Council of Europe (Henry, 2003). The estimated income from sport and sport events amounted to 1.8 per cent of the Gross National Product of the Netherlands in 1997 (Van Puffelen *et al.*, 1988, quoted in Robinson, 2003) while estimated revenue from sport in the late 1990s amounted to nearly 5 per cent of Sheffield's gross domestic product (Davies, 2000).

Not surprisingly, the growth of sports business has attracted the interest of supranational bodies such as the European Union as well as that of individual governments. Despite having only a tenuous basis for intervention the EU has steadily increased its influence in sport largely through its remit for competition policy. From the mid-1970s the European Court of Justice (ECJ) has made a series of judgments which have gradually enhanced the regulatory capacity of the European Commission and limited the autonomy of national sports systems. The landmark case was that of the Belgian footballer Jean-Marc Bosman in 1995 who successfully challenged the right of his employing club to prevent him moving to another club even though he was out of contract. The ECJ decision not only confirmed Bosman's right to freedom of movement for employment but, more significantly, confirmed that the rules of the European football federation, UEFA, governing the number of foreign players that a team could field were illegal regarding citizens of EU members. The judgment allowed Europe's major clubs to assemble extensive squads drawn from countries within the EU and the European Economic Area and consequently field teams with few national players. More recently, in 2001, the EU modified its stance on the free movement of football players by agreeing with UEFA and FIFA that contracts would be limited to five years and that the smaller clubs who often develop young players would receive compensation for the costs of education and training of a player if that player moved on to a larger and richer club.

The EU has also been important in regulation of the sports broadcasting industry. While the 1989 EU Directive, 'Television without frontiers', represented 'a victory for the new commercial operators' (Parrish, 1998: 12) and embodied the deregulatory ethos dominant within the EU Commission, the review of the Directive in 1994 saw a shift in the regulatory stance of the EU with the new Directive more concerned to ensure an adequate level of access for the public by allowing member states to draw up lists of major sports events which must be broadcast unencrypted or 'free to air'. A number of arguments were presented in support of this revision including a recognition that action by the EU represented the most effective way for member states to protect sports broadcasts and that, given the significance of sport to the success of television companies, member states might need to ensure unencrypted broadcasting of major sporting events in order to secure the long-term survival of their national public service broadcasting. Of more significance, the revision was a recognition that 'sport is, in effect, part of a nation's cultural heritage and may be subject to protectionism' (Henry, 2003).

The rulings of the ECJ and the European Commission illustrate the ambivalent attitude of the EU towards sport. In relation to both the free movement of football players and the sale of broadcasting rights the initial liberalisation of competition was followed by a retreat which appeared to acknowledge the peculiar status of sport. The ambiguity of the EU toward sport notwithstanding, what is clear is that within Europe sport operates increasingly within a regulatory framework determined by the institutions of the European Union.

While the significance of the EU has increased it has simply complemented the increasing concern of many national governments to exercise tighter control of an increasingly commercialised sports sector. In the UK, for example, the government, through the Monopolies and Mergers Commission, acted to block the takeover of Manchester United by the broadcaster BSkyB in the UK in 1998 and has also provided funding to support football fans wishing to establish trusts to provide an alternative to the commercial ownership of clubs. It has also intervened to protect the 'free to air' broadcasting of sports events of national significance and also to promote the commercial sponsorship of local sports clubs. Similar examples may be found in most European countries as well as in Australia, Canada and the United States (Robinson, 2003; Slack, 2003).

### Sport and the politics of identity

Part of the ambiguity of the EU's attitude towards sport is that while the Union is adamant that sport, as an industry, should be subject to the same competition regulations as other businesses it also acknowledges that sport possesses a unique cultural significance. Indeed, just as many countries have used sport to demonstrate, define, or invent their sense of national identity so the European Union, since the 1980s, has been well aware of the value of sport in contributing to the development of a sense of 'European citizenship' which, for many member states, marks progress on the road to the 'ever closer union' referred to in the Treaty of Rome. In 1985, the Adonnino Report, *A People's Europe*, identified the contribution that sport might make to the development of a cultural identity for EU citizens. Although the EU has persisted with funding a number of EU-related sports events, such as the European Clubs Swimming Championship, the European Schools Games and the extension of the Tour de France into other countries such as the Netherlands, Belgium, Germany and the UK, its attempts to use sport to create a sense of common identity have generally been low key. Yet the attempts to harness the cultural potential of sport raise important issues regarding the extent to which sport has the capacity to be a vehicle for globalisation of culture. On the one hand the evidence appears compelling: the dominance of a largely Western diet of sport in the global media, the spread and acceptance of global sports events such as the football World Cup, the Olympic Games and the Athletics World Championships, and the global reach of brands such as Nike and Adidas. On the other hand there are a number of reasons to be cautious when assessing the cultural significance of sport. First, there is a need to distinguish between the cultural effects of the marketplace as reflected in the playing of non-local sports or the wearing of particular brands, and cultural change at a deeper level affecting patterns of social organisation such as gender or inter-generational relations or attitudes towards political participation and property. Most of the impact of sport globalisation is at the more superficial level and not too much significance should be read into the simple fact of playing the same sports or participating in the same events. However, there are one or two areas where sport might be contributing to social change at a deeper level, with the pressure from women's groups to achieve greater equality of participation in international sport contributing to the gradual acceptance of women's sport in Islamic countries such as Iran and Kuwait.

Second, just at the time when we are coming to terms with the impact of sport globalisation a contradictory phenomenon appears to be emerging, that of localisation. If globalisation reflects the power of universal socio-cultural flows then localisation emphasises spatial definition and socio-cultural specificity. This phenomenon is evident in politics, especially in Europe, where supranational consolidation through the enlargement of the European Union is taking place following a period of rapid increase in the number of new states. Sixteen new states have been established in Europe since 1989 and six of the ten countries that joined the European Union in 2004 were new states. Globalisation involves the reconciliation of a paradox which is the 'particularisation of universalism (the rendering of the world as a single place) and the universalisation of particularism (the globalised expectation that societies ... should have distinct identities)' (Robertson, 1987: 9). The simultaneous celebration of local sporting culture and conscious embrace of global sport is by no means unusual. Many, perhaps most, countries can provide examples of dual sporting cultures sitting comfortably alongside one another. The Irish have various Gaelic sports yet participate enthusiastically in the soccer World Cup and the Olympic Games; Australia has its own sport of Australian Rules Football, but is also active across a wide range of Western team and individual sports; Americans play their own team games, American football and baseball, but still compete in international athletics and other sports.

Third, the capacity of globalisation to reach into every community is not denied, but what is less clear is the impact of that 'reach'. For a number of writers, the impact of globalisation on culture is to lead to synchronisation, Americanisation or homogenisation and, as Sholte observes, 'Depending on one's perspective, this homogenisation entails either progressive cosmopolitanism or oppressive imperialism' (2000: 23). However, there is little evidence of a consensus on the impact of globalisation on culture generally or sports culture in particular. In contrast to those who see only cultural homogeneity and the 'end of the national project' (Brown, 1995) there is an equally strong view that globalisation is not only compatible with continuing cultural heterogeneity but may even stimulate greater heterogeneity.

Underlying much of the discussion of the impact of globalisation is an appreciation that the basis on which national identity is defined has subtly shifted. It has long been accepted that defining national/regional identity is a mutually constitutive process insofar as identity is defined in relation to contrasts with 'foreigners'. More recently, it can be argued that there is a set of globally recognised reference points which are now also important in establishing identity and against which each nation or community has to position itself. These reference points range from the relatively mundane, such as distinctive postage stamps, national flags and anthems, to the more significant such as membership of the World Trade Organisation and the United Nations, and attitudes towards global 'principles' of human rights and state sovereignty. One of these reference points is clearly participation in international sport and the Olympic Games in particular. Sport is thus an example of the paradox of utilising a standardised medium for the demonstration of difference.

On one level therefore the reach of globalisation should not be equated with homogeneity as its 'arrival' may be a welcome opportunity to demonstrate community/national distinctiveness. At another level the capacity of communities to modify and adapt global culture should not be underestimated. James (1963) argued that cricket was significant in establishing a West Indian identity while St Pierre suggests that cricket 'has been reshaped in sympathy with the cultural ethos of the West Indies [and] has been used as a tool to foster and further nationalist sentiment and racial pride' (1991: 23). As Jensen noted, in the face of cultural globalisation local culture 'shines through' (1998: 195). In his study of baseball and the relationship between the Dominican Republic and the United States Klein (1991) argues strongly that the game of baseball has been metamorphosed and that far from simply reflecting American cultural hegemony it has become a vehicle for demonstrating Dominican excellence. Baseball has been reshaped to infuse it with distinctive Dominican characteristics and qualities suggesting a clear capacity for a community to import, redefine, and re-export a sports cultural product. However, such views might be over-optimistic as US baseball clubs and European football clubs have recruited sporting talent from poorer countries in substantial numbers in a way that equates to the crude asset-stripping of nineteenth-century imperialism. Not only are the young recruits treated as a disposable commodity but their removal from their home country often undermines the viability of domestic leagues and sports systems.

### Sport as a source of international problems

Western governments have been generally reluctant to get too closely involved in sport, partly in reaction to the extensive state manipulation of sport in many former communist countries and partly due to a romantic view of sport as a private matter and deference towards sports organisations on questions of regulation. Since the 1970s that deference has declined as a series of serious problems have emerged around sport including soccer hooliganism, match-fixing in cricket, doping by athletes and corruption within the IOC, most of which have required close cooperation between governments. The responses to these issues share a number of common features, most notably the involvement of a number of governments and a requirement for cooperation between governments and international nongovernmental sports organisations.

Of the problems associated with sport, doping has proved to be one of the most persistent. Up to the late 1980s the dominant view held by individual sports federations, governments and event organising bodies such as the IOC was that doping in sport was exceptional, limited to a few sports such as weight-lifting and cycling, and could be contained through the use of in-competition testing. As a result investment in testing was minimal and international sports federations, governments and the IOC tended to operate in isolation, concerned only to protect the reputation of their particular sport, national squad or event. Governments could be located in one of three categories: activists, such as France, Norway and the UK, which attempted to establish an effective anti-doping policy in their countries; the passive – mainly countries that lacked the resources to tackle the problem but also countries such as Australia, Canada and West Germany that choose to ignore the problem, partly because of the behaviour of the third category, the subversives, which included the GDR and the Soviet Union, who systematically doped their athletes (Franke and Berendonk, 1997; Ungerleider, 2001).

By the late 1980s it was clear that far from being exceptional, doping was routine, extensive across a range of sports rather than limited, and increasingly used to aid training thus making in-competition testing largely irrelevant. The scandal of the Canadian sprinter Ben Johnson testing positive for steroids after winning the gold medal in the 100 metres sprint at the 1988 Seoul Olympics forced the Canadian government to take action on the issue. The discovery of extensive doping at the elite Australian Institute of Sport forced a similar revision of policy by the Australian government. The collapse of the Soviet Union and the subsequent re-unification of East and West Germany and the steady exposure of the extent of state-organised doping resulted in a short-lived flurry of action by both governments and international sports organisations. This subsided in the mid-1990s as the long-standing mistrust between activist governments on the one hand and the IOC and the major sports federations on the other resurfaced.

It was the near collapse of the 1998 Tour de France due to the extent of doping discovered by the French police that reinvigorated efforts to enhance the policy response to doping. The IOC convened a conference in early 1999 out of which emerged the World Anti-Doping Agency (WADA) a body which for the first time brought together both governments and sports organisations, with a substantial budget to fund research into testing methods and education and also to cover the cost of approximately 5,000 additional drug tests. As it took over thirty years to establish a global organisation to coordinate anti-doping efforts it may well be some considerable time before WADA is able to make an appreciable impact on what has proved to be a deeply intractable problem.

### Conclusion

Many aspects of sport, especially at the elite level, have long outgrown the boundaries of national political systems. Elite sporting success is increasingly seen as a valuable political asset, whether to be deployed as part of a diplomatic strategy or simply as a symbol of national identity and vitality. A number of international sports organisations, such as the IOC and the international federations for cycling, rugby union, football and athletics, have been transformed from generally poorly resourced bodies with modest ambitions to being influential international bodies, generally rich and courted by governments and major commercial sponsors and media businesses eager to host or be associated with their major competitions. Consequently, there are few industrial countries whose governments do not provide substantial public investment in elite sport (the United States being a partial exception). Yet, as should be clear from this brief review of sport as a political issue, sport tends to be valued by governments as a means to non-sporting ends whether those are diplomatic objectives such as displaying approval or disapproval to other countries, asserting ideological superiority, or fostering a sense of national identity, or stimulating economic or urban regeneration.

The undoubted attractiveness of sport to both governmental and commercial interests has to be set in the context of a series of problems, such as doping, match fixing and spectator violence, that detract from the political utility of sport and threaten the continuing capacity of sport to generate profit. The resolution, or at least management, of these problems requires increasingly close cooperation between governmental and non-governmental bodies at both domestic and international levels. A further source of pressure for cooperation comes from the scale and complexity of major sport events such as the Tour de France, Olympic Games and soccer World Cup. The planning and preparation for the Olympic Games requires the close liaison between the host government, the IOC and the various international sports federations over a six-year period prior to the Games.

However, there are a number of factors that inhibit a close relationship between governments and sports organisations. First, sports organisations are acutely aware that few governments appear to value sport for the intrinsic pleasure it gives to participants and spectators. The problem with the rather shallow instrumentalist attitude of most governments is that their commitment to sport, and particularly to the continued public funding of sport, remains precarious. Second, there is a long history of mutual suspicion between the international federations and governments especially in relation to doping in sport. While governments with a history of opposition to doping are understandably exasperated by the apparent weakness of international federations in dealing with drug-abusing athletes the international federations argue, with considerable justification, that it was governments who, whether by neglect or design, were largely responsible for stimulating drug use over the last quarter of the last century.

## Bibliography

Brown, R. (1995), 'Globalisation and the End of the National Project', in J. MacMillan and A. Linklater (eds), *Boundaries in Question: New Directions in International Relations*, London: Pinter, pp. 54–68.

Davies, L.E. (2000), 'The Economic Impact of Sport in Sheffield' thesis, Sheffield: Sheffield Hallam University.

Department of Sport [Australia] (1987), *Recreation and Tourism, Annual Report 1986–87*, Brisbane: Department of Sport.

Franke, W.W. and Berendonk, B. (1997), Hormonal Doping and Androgenization of Athletes: A Secret Program of the German Democratic Republic, *Clinical Chemistry,*

Vol. 43, No. 7, pp. 1262–79.

Hardman, K. (1987), 'Politics, Ideology and Physical Education in the German Democratic Republic', *British Journal of Physical Education*, Vol. 18, No.1, pp. 20–2.

Henry, I. (2003), 'Sport, the Role of the European Union and the Decline of the Nation-state?', in B. Houlihan (ed.), *Sport and Society*, London: Sage.

Houlihan, B. (1994), *Sport and International Politics*, Hemel Hempstead: Harvester-Wheatsheaf.

James, C.L.R. (1963), *Beyond a Boundary*, London: Stanley Paul.

Jensen, C.B. (1998), 'Conclusion', in C.B. Jensen (ed.), *News of the World*, London: Routledge.

Keech, M. and Houlihan, B. (1999), Sport and the End of Apartheid, *The Round Table: The Commonwealth Journal of International Affairs*, No. 349, Spring.

Klein, A. (1991), *Sugarball: The American Game, the Dominican Dream*, New Haven, CT: Yale University Press.

Parrish, R. (1998), 'The Broadcasting of Sport in Europe: The Television Without Frontiers Directive', *Sports Law Bulletin*, July/August, p. 7.

Peppard, V. and Riordan, J. (1993), *Playing Politics: Soviet Sports Diplomacy to 1992*, Greenwich, CT: JAI Press Inc.

Robertson, R. (1987), 'Globalization and Societal Modernization: A Note on Japan and Japanese Religion', *Sociological Analysis*, 47, (Summer), pp. 35–43.

Robertson, R. (1995), 'Glocalization: Time-Space and Homogeneity-Heterogeneity', in M. Featherstone, S. Lash and R. Robertson (eds), *Global Modernities*, London: Sage.

Robinson, L. (2003), 'The Business of Sport', in B. Houlihan (ed.), *Sport and Society: A Student Introduction*, London: Sage.

Scholte, J.A. (2000), *Globalisation: A Critical Introduction*, Basingstoke: Palgrave.

Slack, T. (ed.) (2003), *The Commercialisation of Sport*, London: Frank Cass.

St Pierre, M. (1991), 'West Indian Cricket: A Cultural Contradiction?', *Arena Review*, Vol. 14, No. 1, pp. 13–24.

Strenk, A. (1980), 'Diplomats in Tracksuits: The Role of Sports in the German Democratic Republic', *Journal of Sport and Social Issues*, Vol. 4, No. 1, pp. 34–45.

Ungerleider, S. (2001), *Faust's Gold: Inside the East German Doping Machine*, New York: Thomas Dunn.

Van Puffelen, F., Reijnen, J. and Velthuisjsen, J.W. (1988), *De Macro Economische Betekenis Van Sport* Stichting voor Economisch Onderzoek der Universiteint Van Amsterdam, Netherlands.

# 14

# Technology

*Alan Russell*

## Thinking about technology

Technology is a political issue for no other reason than the fact that the modern world cannot function without it – in all walks of life. This means ownership or control of technological processes confers power and influence. Vested interests come into conflict over the direction technology takes, its impact on our lives and the economic dependency associated with it. The application of technology all but defines what we mean by modernisation.

Technology pervades our everyday lives and is so widespread that identifying its political aspects demands a sharp focus. The fruits of technological progress are everywhere to be seen from the ubiquitous digital watch to world threatening nuclear arsenals. The latter is surely political but what of the former? If the digital watch is too mundane to have any political context then where do we draw the line in identifying specific technologies as having political significance? Pulp science fiction of the 1950s described laser beams as highly destructive weapons – 'political', no doubt. But who would have thought that the laser could become a means to play recorded music or movies – this time hardly a politically sensitive development? No wonder then that much of the literature of political science has been content to take technology as an external 'given'. That is, the prevailing level of technology in a particular historical era, or global location, is identified as merely part of the environment within which other political issues unfold.

Politics is not the only discipline to take levels of technology as given. Mainstream economics too tended until the late 1980s to see technology as external to the study of market dynamics. There has been a tendency to give up on finding ways to 'internalise' technology into our analysis of the political and economic workings of society. More recently, however, some economists have attempted to bring technology in – to open the 'black box', so to speak, of the relationship between technology and the productive process

226

(Archibugi and Michie, 1997: 1; Rosenberg, 1982, 1994). The work of *innovation* economists has helped in drawing technology in from the cold. For the innovation economist technology is the driving force of innovation and is necessarily included in their vision of how markets work. Their work touches on political concerns and offers a useful terminology. Some political scientists have begun to make up lost ground as well and have seen the need to locate technology more centrally in their concerns. One reason for this has been the explosion of interest in globalisation. Technology is at the heart of claims surrounding 'the death of distance', the communications revolution, the diffusion of technology from North to South, the globalisation of culture (in part through media developments), networking the world, leading-edge technologies, the information technology revolution and the biotechnology revolution.

Much more fundamentally, we cannot ignore technology, as a phenomenon, when it has from time to time changed the world with wide-ranging political consequence. The eighteenth-century Enlightenment and the mobilisation of political ideologies gained huge momentum from the earlier invention of the printing press, dating from the mid-fifteenth century – which enabled the rapid spread of ideas and new ways of thinking. Technology brought us total war, courtesy of the machine gun that delivered the slaughter in the trenches during the First World War, and the strategic bombing campaigns of the Second World War. The globalisation of culture, in part brought about by the global awareness produced by complex media technologies, is altering our contemporary world. Individual technologies have often been singled out – the transistor, television, the automobile, the aeroplane, automated bottling and canning, orbital satellites, coaxial cable, telecommunications, the micro-chip, fibre optics, digital technologies and biotechnology. Between them they have led to massive transformations in the food industry, transportation, communications systems, information manipulation and storage, financial transactions, computing, automated production, and the means to wage war (Scholte, 2000: 99–101; Held, *et al.*, 1999: 108). Moreover, technology is driving the erosion of national borders allowing greater levels of inter-penetration of societies the world over.

This chapter will initially identify key practical and theoretical questions about technology as a political issue. It will consider a range of perspectives and viewpoints. Then the effects of technologies on political actors will be considered along with attendant problems generated within political systems. A comparative appraisal of responses to the issues at the national, transnational and international levels will follow. Of necessity this will be selective and certain technology developments will be chosen to highlight particularly significant responses, for example in relation to biotechnology, pharmaceuticals, IT and communications and the process of production. The chapter will conclude with a return to how we might conceptualise the progression of technologies.

The approach adopted will draw on insight from a field of study noted for bringing together the national and international levels and for bridging political and economic perspectives – an approach that adopts the description 'international political economy' (Balaam and Veseth, 1996; Strange, 1994). This approach is suited to a diverse issue like technology and has been striving to include technology more centrally in its general concerns (Talalay, Farrands and Tooze (eds), 1997).

### Theoretical and practical questions

Technology is more than simply technological artefacts – such as the automobile, the television set or the genetically modified crop. It also includes the knowledge base and the research and development processes that lead to such artefacts, and may also be taken to include the management and organisational structures, within a society, that encourage technological progress.

Three approaches have come to dominate efforts to understand the global political economy and consequently the place of technology. They each provide the intellectual basis for analysis of issues but are also associated with distinct ideologies. The *liberal* approach is most commonly associated with a view that the decisions of autonomous individuals acting in markets are the drivers of wealth creation and that technology is an important part of the production process. The liberal approach also recognises that technology artefacts themselves may be products that are then sold – the personal stereo, the state-of-the-art personal computer, or complex machines and components sold on to become part of the production process for other products. In this approach the general level of technological progress is 'neutral' and external to the understanding of the dynamics of markets. Yet, the liberal approach encourages technological progress and the global interdependence that may follow from ever higher levels of technological achievement. Comparative advantage is seen by the liberal perspective to be the bedrock of trade, and technology resources are an essential component of a nation's comparative advantage, along with resources, the skills of the population and other factors. Each nation has identifiable trading strengths leading to specialisation in what it produces and trades with others. As competition drives the market technology will almost inevitably diffuse across borders, between economies and between firms, thus transferring a key aspect of comparative advantage and adding to the overall increase in levels of wealth.

The second approach is really quite old – going back at least to seventeenth-century Europe – and used to be known as mercantilism. Today, the term *'economic nationalism'* may suffice (Gilpin, 1987). This approach associates technological prowess with the overall importance of a nation and its economy in the global political economy. This view encourages the state to work with its technological leaders to ensure a continued place at the 'leading edge' of technological developments – and this may also be taken to mean at the leading edge of military technologies, associated with the defence of the nation. In particular the governments of individual states might identify 'strategic' technologies that are to be acquired, nurtured, protected and exploited – such as semi-conductors, telecommunications, machine-tool industries, and more recently biotechnology. With high-technology sectors dominated by big multi-national corporations, governments may be drawn into promoting the interests of their national champions in this respect.

The third approach is Marxism and variants that adopt a more international orientation, such as neo-Gramscian theory, dependency theory and world system theory. In general, the perspective locates technology development within the control of capital and the means of production. It becomes part of the dynamics of the social relations of production and can be identified 'as being shaped by social forces at least as much as it shapes these forces' (Cox, 1987: 21). The economics of the global economy are seen to shape political processes and generally to lead to exploitation of the economies of developing countries. The large multi-national corporations are identified in terms of technological dominance and their ability to control the process of technology transfer to developing countries. The latter are seen to be weak – indeed 'dependent' – in terms of their options to acquire technologies to assist in their economic development. The neo-Gramscian variant of the approach borrows from the work of Antonio Gramsci who described his native Italy in the 1930s as being subjected to a hegemony of social forces, including common religion, shared history and sense of destiny, and capitalism. In the contemporary world a similar hegemony can be identified with respect to a transnational business elite, sharing a common set of ideas based on a (liberal) view of the world (Cox, 1987). In general Marxist approaches reject the liberal view that modernisation – including technological modernisation – will result from a trickle down effect as technology automatically transfers along with other aspects of comparative advantage. Instead, they see the liberal ideology embedded within powerful states, corporations and international organisations so that developing countries remain in a weak and dependent position.

These approaches shape our interpretation of the importance of technology within economic systems and underpin political activity given their ideological context. For example, the Marxist approach could support a strong case that claims that big companies are seeking to control the biodiversity resources of the Third World in order to develop biotechnology products. In turn these products could then be sold back to the developing countries, leaving the Third World farmer powerless to resist the restructuring of the agricultural industry that would follow. The signs are already evident in the genetic manipulation of seeds in order to change the characteristics of crops to enhance yields and perhaps to confer resistance to proprietary herbicides. Seeds could then be sold to farmers in the Third World, weakening their traditional relationship with indigenous crops. This development has led to considerable protest in India for example. From a liberal perspective this is simply a feature of the market and the farmers from all countries could benefit from the increased yields, even if they have to buy the seeds each year. The economic nationalist perspective can help explain the response of the United States government to lobbying by US biotechnology firms during the negotiations of the Uruguay Trade Round. The collective US position was to bring patent protection to bear on developing countries, so that technological developments like the new seeds could be patented, to ensure that the firms could maximise the return on their investment. Signed in December 1993 the Uruguay Trade agreement is today at the heart of the global trade regime itself centred on the World Trade Organisation.[1]

A very contentious issue is the availability of pharmaceuticals in the developing world. The patent issue has gained prominence as certain developing countries simply allowed their firms to create generic copies of proprietary drugs developed by Western firms, usually at great expense. The treatment of HIV infection is a case in point. Many HIV infected individuals in the developed world have lived with the infection for more than a decade courtesy of expensive cocktails of drugs that hold the virus at bay. African countries simply cannot afford to treat their infected people. As they would not buy the expensive drugs in the first place it could be argued that there would be no loss of sales for the Western firms if the drugs were copied and distributed in the Third World at much lower cost and indeed some agreement has emerged for this to happen on a limited scale. This example illustrates both the dominance of the West in developing technology, controlling its distribution and its significant influence in determining what technologies will develop and for whom. Of the many forms of the HIV virus the research effort has tended to focus on the strains infecting people in developed countries.

The three perspectives offer differing interpretations of politically sensitive technology issues. However, distinct clusters of actors hold the individual perspectives, reflecting particular interests. The liberal perspective is fundamental to 'Western' interests shared by banks, companies, governments and key global economic institutions such as the WTO, the IMF and the World Bank – indeed the neo-Gramscian argument is precisely this. The economic nationalist perspective has a history of association with modernisation from the early days of industrialisation so it is somewhat ironic that Western interests generally criticise developing Third World countries for undue protectionism and conveniently forget their own recent past (including high protection measures against cheap Third World manufactures). Indeed, in some strategically important technology sectors Western interests remain nationalistic and protectionist against each other (such as government support for defence and aerospace sectors). The third perspective, with its Marxist origins, is today most likely to be held by critical movements including the anti-globalists, radical environmentalists and intellectual groups attempting to challenge conventional thinking.

Whichever perspective individuals adopt there are some useful concepts provided by innovation economists (Archibugi and Michie, 1997; Foray and Freeman, 1993). The term *technological trajectory* helps identify a broad technological pathway of innovation, such as medical biotechnology, agricultural biotechnology or pharmaceutical biotechnology, within a more general *technological paradigm* that in this case would be biotechnology itself.[2] Similarly, within the broad technological paradigm of information technology, there are pathways such as the development of ever faster computer central processors, or software development such as operating systems. These two concepts let us distinguish the broad *enabling* technology that may be at the heart of a variety of specialist application pathways. The terms are useful in investigating the politics behind technological progress in the sense that we can focus attention on who gains and who loses when particular technological paradigms come to dominate over others. Political activity may revolve around challenges to established technological paradigms, such as the advocates of alternative energy challenging the established technological paradigm based on fossil fuels. Alternatively, we may witness resistance to new technological paradigms, such as biotechnology, or resistance to particular trajectories, such as GM crops or human cloning (if it becomes possible). Scale is important here and sometimes we can get technological developments that link many sectors or branches of the economy, and these developments we can describe as *technological systems*. This term applies when the technology is seen as pervasive throughout the whole economy. Yet even more pervasive technologies exist whereby the world economy would be unable to function without them. Such pervasiveness would apply to the electricity industry, micro-electronics or the oil industry. The term *techno-economic paradigm* has been coined for this category.[3] In this respect information technology has progressed beyond simply being a technological paradigm as its impact has been truly extensive, affecting most aspects of economic activity. It has certainly passed through the stage of technological system and may better be described as a techno-economic paradigm (Dicken, 1998: 165). How could the world adapt if IT were suddenly 'removed'? In effect this set of concepts, taken from the work of the innovation economists, lets us conceptualise progressive stages of pervasiveness of a technology as it diffuses through the global economy. Along the way we can focus on power relations between actors at the heart of the respective levels – especially in terms of control of the direction technological pervasiveness follows. Of course conceptual judgements have to be made in terms of when a technology passes from one stage to another.

Archibugie and Michie, in the foreword to a collection of essays identify a variety of viewpoints addressing the broad question 'where do technological capabilities reside?' (1997: xv–xvi). They suggest that economists and science and technology policy makers locate technological capabilities within the nation-state as a whole, while business school scholars and business historians suggest the focus should be on firms, and increasingly large transnational firms. Another viewpoint suggests technological capabilities lie at a level less than the nation-state but higher than the firm – including technology regions such as Silicon Valley and networks of firms. In many respects this becomes a technical debate about the deployment of technological capabilities, the means of technological innovation and subsequent dissemination through economies. However, the assessment of technological impact and the control of capabilities is not complete without a political and social context.

## The effects on political actors

Technology has, through history, invited clashes of viewpoints about its impact on society. In the early nineteenth century, Luddites smashed the machines that they feared were displacing them in their jobs, while today protest groups around the world object to the sowing of genetically engineered seeds. Standing against such groups are the modern 'captains of industry' – the leaders of the large, often multinational, firms that generate the big technological leaps, often with the support of the governments of the developed countries.[4] The twentieth century saw technological transformations unlike any previous century. The achievements of commercial air travel, computers and pharmaceuticals have literally changed the world. But the pathways or technological trajectories that technology has followed have not always been smooth. The nuclear industry, once seen as heralding an abundance of cheap, clean and efficient energy has witnessed extensive decline the world over. This has been due to the realisation that there are huge problems of disposing of nuclear waste, potential risks of nuclear disaster – made tangible at Windscale, Three Mile Island and Chernobyl – and the immense difficulty involved in decommissioning radioactive reactors. Factoring such costs into the equation has altered the economics.

Since the 1970s biotechnology has never been far from controversy. The late 1970s and early 1980s saw protests, notably in the United States, over the safety of undertaking genetic engineering work in public and industrial research laboratories. Now generally regarded as unrealised concerns, their fears at the time focused on possible new cancer causing viruses, or escaped genetically modified bacteria passing inserted genes to similar bacteria that reside in the human digestive tract. As the technology has developed and diversified concerns have arisen over various specific trajectories within the technological paradigm such as the release of genetically modified organisms into the wild, ethical questions about potentially cloning humans and experimenting on tissue taken from human embryos.

Actors in these and other areas of technological controversy often include governments, small and large firms, environmental pressure groups, the media (who can influence the perceptions of all the others) and international agencies. It is not uncommon to see directly opposing views between those who will directly gain from the exploitation of a new technology and those who may suffer some consequence without gain. In the middle may be groups who both gain and suffer some consequence. For example: building a high speed rail link from London to the Channel tunnel has drawn opposition from people who live on the planned route; air travellers may live well away from the airports, whereas aircraft noise levels may disturb those who live near them; the sowing of genetically modified seed by some farmers may contaminate the crops of organic farmers if they are too near; replacing analogue television transmissions by digital broadcasting could leave many people with televisions and video recorders that can no longer function fully (even if their main living room television is connected to a digital provider); and using broadband internet to transfer movies between continents may deny firms their rightful copyright protection in certain markets.

In other words many technological developments have the ability to create disputes centred on who gains and who loses. Many protest groups have sought alliances with concerned scientists, who understand the technology but do not share the view of their optimistic colleagues. Greenpeace and Friends of the Earth have, for example, developed impressive scientific and technological credentials in their own right – knowledge is power in a game that can be played both ways. However, technological progress often requires societies to balance these viewpoints and governments and regulators must sometimes resolve the differences in a legitimate fashion. This can involve public enquiries, the establishment of regulative bodies and the passing of legislation. Nevertheless we must not forget that governments themselves may have an agenda when it comes to new technology, including the protection of national economic interests as they see it. Nowhere is this three-way relationship more evident than in respect to the question of risk and safety associated with some technologies.

Perceptions about 'acceptable risk' differ in relation to direct gains and exposure to any risks. Local communities may be divided about proposals to build a nuclear reactor or chemical plant. All in the vicinity face the same actual risk, but perceptions of its acceptability may differ between those who may hope to obtain a well-paid job in the plant and those not seeking employment. Risk analysers – including professionals who may be called to evaluate complex technological systems or investigate the causes of actual disasters – often consider risk simply in terms of the *probability* of specified untoward events occurring. Adding the consequences of those events into the mix allows us to address various possibilities including 'low probability/high consequence' risk (such as nuclear reactor meltdowns) or 'high probability/low consequence' risk (such as minor collisions between motor vehicles). Most uncertainty exists where both the probability of the risk event and its consequences are very difficult to estimate or are unknown – as with laboratory-based genetic manipulation in the mid-1970s. Complexity is extended yet further when perceptions of risk are set against perceptions of potential benefit.

This last category opens up much greater socio-political divergence in perception of whether risks associated with technologies are acceptable after measures are taken to reduce them. Consequently 'risk management' 'usually denotes a procedure for keeping risks within acceptable limits, while balancing risks with benefits' (Levidow, 1994: 273). Questions then arise over the resources to be deployed (and their cost) in achieving a given level of reduction of risk, assuming the given level is acceptable to society (Adams, 1995; Douglas, 1986). Much of this culminates in the regulatory process.

Regulatory authorities therefore often face the task of reconciling divergent viewpoints regarding risks associated with many technologies. Those who clearly benefit from the exploitation of a technology may be willing to accept a higher level of risk than those who face the same risks but perceive themselves to gain little. Sometimes the gain is identified at a societal level and the regulatory authority must set this gain against a level of risk estimated to be acceptable – perhaps in consultation with representative interest groups. Moreover, regulatory authorities may also be charged with monitoring adherence to safety procedures in the exploitation of the technology concerned perhaps through inspection supported by legal sanctions. Yet regulatory bodies can themselves become politicised, or at least subject to enormous lobbying pressures from powerful interests. This charge has often been made in terms of aviation safety (Golich, 1989).

Many of the debates about technological progress, and associated issues such as risk, involve transnational and international actors as well as actors in a domestic context. Transnational firms, transnational pressure groups, international organisations and governments are all involved, as are consumer groups, scientific communities and the military. Sometimes there are considerable differences between individual countries with respect to controversies over technology and this can consequently cause sluggish responses in international regulatory regimes – a notable example being the slow international response to concerns over the safety of roll-on, roll-off ferries. In the UK and in other European countries, and some developing countries such as India, there are vociferous debates between groups with differing perspectives over genetically modified crops – with some activists attempting to destroy fields of modified crops. In contrast the issue is very low key in the United States and genetically modified crops are quite widespread. Yet, in the United States, following the nuclear disaster at Three Mile Island in Pennsylvania, there was a cessation of the construction of new reactors, while in other countries the nuclear industry has fared much better.

A long-standing question relates to whether military requirements drive a process of technology development, in turn creating a spin-off effect into other markets; or whether technological progress is something more general and the defence industries are opportunist in adapting technology for their purpose. Examples of each direction of flow are possible. There is no doubt that advancements in military aircraft have influenced the design of modern commercial jets – for example in the use of 'fly-by-wire' techniques. In contrast, the military were slow to see the potential of nuclear weapons and scientists involved in the early work on nuclear physics had to convince a sceptical military establishment of the weapons potential (notably Leo Szilard and Enrico Fermi, who lobbied the British and American governments). On a broader scale some have argued that the technology requirements of war have actually contributed to 'human progress' (Nef, 1968).

Technology and weapons development bring together actors such as the individual armed services, governments, a defence industry, and in a world of globalisation, a myriad of components suppliers often from many countries, in an industry that often seems on the surface to be intensely nationalistic. Indeed, defence is one industrial activity often described as at the heart of the economic nationalist perspective. Whole trajectories of technological development have become associated with the military imperative. These include the understanding and application of ballistics, the development of armour through history – from chain mail to modern tank armour – and the development of radar (although the civil use has also grown immeasurably). Unfortunately, trajectories of development of weapons of mass destruction have emerged in the realms of nuclear, chemical and biological weapons.

The term 'big' science or technology has sometimes been used to describe technological endeavours that can only succeed with the direct involvement of government. Such technologies are noted by their sheer scale and have included electricity-generating nuclear reactors, space exploration technologies and large-scale military developments such as nuclear weapons. This, in the past, has created a close relationship between the governments (or specialised agencies within government) and large industrial actors – and economic nationalists identify such technologies as particularly significant. Once established and commonplace the relationship between such technology sectors and government can change. Nuclear industries have been privatised, space exploration has become much more commercialised – most notably in the design, construction and use of satellites.

## Global political responses to technological issues

When judging the responses of political actors in a global context there is a contrast between 'big' and clearly focused technologies and more diffused and intensive technology. The former includes nuclear technology and large-scale energy technologies that have brought together governments, international agencies and big businesses. The key point is that governments have a central role in shaping the development of big technologies. At the other extreme highly diverse and diffused technologies involve numerous actors of many sorts in very complex networks of relations – so complex it is not easy to unpick them. Small and large firms, research institutions, universities, private investors, financial institutions and, in general, markets, are all involved. This latter type of technology would include information technology and biotechnology. Moreover, this second category is at the heart of globalisation and some developments are bringing about a momentous transformation in the method of industrial production, in turn transforming our traditional working relations. This has become known as post-Fordism.

The political context of technology is also shifting in emphasis from a concern with the international political economy of big technology towards highly diffused technology. The post-war era, clouded by the Cold War, saw governments and international agencies concerned with those technologies that could underpin the proliferation of weapons of mass destruction. The International Atomic Energy Agency was, for example at the centre of a nuclear non-proliferation regime established in the late 1960s. It would be followed by regimes to try to restrict chemical weapons and biological weapons. High stakes in the Cold War saw the use of correspondingly high level diplomatic efforts associated with arms control negotiations, as the superpowers tried to limit the runaway nuclear arms race – leading to a coining of the term 'nuclear diplomacy'. Governments often protected and nurtured national technology champions, especially if there was a military dimension to the technological prowess – for example in aerospace technologies and civil nuclear technology. For the United States, in the 1980s this culminated in a massive technological programme, embracing many interlinked technologies, under the rubric of the Strategic Defence Initiative – more commonly known as 'Star Wars'. Today, there are still powerful elements of this national competition. The United States is at the forefront of many of the bigger technological developments. This is especially the case with regard to military technologies including the use of information technologies on the battlefield and the dependence of NATO on the United States providing aircraft capable of heavy lift capacity – the only competitor with such aircraft being Russia. Yet despite all this US technological dominance is perhaps most impressive in highly diffuse and intensive endeavours.

The United States spends more on Research and Development (R&D) than any other country in the world. This gives it a clear technological edge. The United States dominates the 'knowledge structure' of the global political economy, itself changing rapidly as new technologies facilitate the control of information and create a whole new class of information workers (Strange, 1994). Nowhere are these changes more evident than in the technological dominance of production. Strange observes:

> There are implications for the international political system of the impact which these technological changes in the knowledge structure have had on the production structure. They have centralised power in the big transnational corporations. Not only are these corporations predominantly headquartered in the United States, but the importance of selling on a global market means that even those corporations based in other places – Europe, Japan, Korea – cannot

afford *not* to sell on the US market. It is still the largest, richest market under one national bureaucracy. In short, the technological changes have led to a greater concentration of power in one state (Strange, 1994: 133).

Thus technological power resides primarily with large transnational corporations, and especially US ones. Other analysts, adopting the neo-Gramscian perspective, agree that the corporations have the power, but that the US and its firms together constitute simply one element in a larger transnational business elite characterised by a shared liberal ideology (Cox, 1987; Gill and Law, 1988: 63–8).

Technology, however, is transforming the nature of global production in a way that is commonly described as a shift from Fordism to post-Fordism. Henry Ford obtained his place in history by maximising the potential of the production line. Mass production came at the expense of uniformity and a shift from skilled workers – who in this instance assembled entire cars from the chassis up – to unskilled workers given very mundane and repetitive tasks to do, as the endless stream of semi-completed cars passed their workstation. Unions were effectively bought off by the much higher wages that resulted. From the early twentieth century the production line has been the mainstay of mass production – a technique that creates economies of scale and results in lower unit costs.

Post-Fordism has emerged in part from the massive technological changes that have taken place in the last few decades. Again the motor industry is at the forefront. The trend is encapsulated in the idea of 'just in time' production. Instead of every car coming off the production line being identical to those before and after it – as in Henry Ford's day – the customer may in the future walk into a car showroom, browse through a catalogue (probably online), select from a wide range of colours, engine specifications, interior fittings, wheels, sun-roof, quality of hi-fi system, and other features like navigation systems and car phones. The helpful assistant (probably not a robot) will complete the order and the car is then built that afternoon and delivered the next day!

For this to happen all the component suppliers must be able to respond very rapidly indeed to changes in consumer fashion and taste as well as dealing with the unusual combination of features required. Moreover all the component suppliers and contributors to the production process must be networked through very sophisticated IT systems that coordinate everything that is required in the flexible production system. A key thing to avoid is the need to maintain inventories of components sitting on shelves in case they are needed. They should only be manufactured when it is clear they are needed. 'Just in time' is effectively taking the place of 'just in case' production with its reliance on inventories (Dicken, 1998: 169). Where Fordism saw the de-skilling of the workforce, as they were allocated boring and repetitive tasks on the line, post-Fordism involves re-skilling. In addition close links develop with the consumer as the firm strives to respond to changes in consumer demand.

Flexible and adaptable production processes have led to the technological achievement of producing *small* batches cheaply – thus bypassing the need for 'economies of scale' and the mass production of identical products. It has also created a marketplace where the consumer faces many competing products differentiated less by price than by a confusion of incomparable features. You can buy any number of hi-fi systems at key price points but try comparing them! Moreover, such is the rate of change in the global market that products rarely stay in the stores for more than a few months before a newer upgraded replacement model appears, often with little more than cosmetic difference and launched across the world at the same time. But the technology of flexible, and transnational, production facilitates this.

Individuals, groups, firms, organisations and nations all in some fashion *interact* with technology. Choices of technological pathway are made; national technological policy is shaped; firms back particular new technologies in place of alternatives; pressure groups object to some technologies; children run rings around adults in playing computer games; and advertisements spell out the merits of embracing the digital future. In each case *interaction* with technology is evident and when there are a variety of actors in interaction it is sometimes appropriate to describe this in terms of networks.

The consequences of post-Fordism with its complex transnational network of technology based production, may best be described through the IPE perspectives developed by neo-Gramscians like Robert Cox (1987) or global structural analysts such as Susan Strange (1994). If the concept of a transnational business hegemony – forged around a common set of ideals, institutions and material capabilities – is accepted then the business networks locked into post-Fordist production can be seen to link many players who share a vested interest in maintaining a stable and open global economy, based around liberal economic principles with little government interference other than to support the general liberal requirements. The modern technology networks embedded in global production are at the forefront of the drive towards stability in global economic relations. For Susan Strange knowledge and production structures share the strong transnational features identified by Cox, and also involve the actions of firms and technology drivers in complex network relations. Her approach is less class oriented but nevertheless recognises important consequences in terms of the power of key actors (often states) to shape how global production and technology will develop. The United States, with its firms at the very centre of important production and technology networks, reflects a collective position of structural power – collective in the sense that the power is not solely with the US government but more broadly with the US political economy as a whole.

While the power to shape technologically sophisticated production processes may reside with powerful Western groups, there are very significant impacts on the Third World. In seeking to reduce production costs the big companies have moved production to parts of Asia and elsewhere, including the giant that is China. IT skills are plentiful in these economies where labour in general is also cheap. The global patterns of manufacturing are therefore changing but in all this the poorest countries, often in Africa, are left behind.

## Conclusion

Perhaps as we begin the twenty-first century it is acceptable to indulge in a little speculation on the future of technology and consequent political issues.

Biotechnology has been flagged, by many, as *the* technology for the twenty-first century, and it is one that will undoubtedly remain controversial. The manipulation of the foundation blocks of all life will bring incredible advances in agriculture, energy production, medicine, treatment of diseases and ailments, and the production of fine chemicals. It will also remain politically controversial because of its potential to alter the processes of evolution, risks associated with the release of modified organisms into the eco-system and the possible production of 'designer' biological weapons alongside designer drugs.

The information revolution embedded in information technologies will also advance with ever more sophistication. The replacement for the Internet is already on the cards based on the networking of computers not just to share information and communicate but to share processing capacity effectively creating supercomputing networks that we all can patch into – even from wireless devices. The political dimension will no doubt centre on who controls and benefits from such developments.

New materials will go on being developed, including materials that aid the performance and durability of machines, the functioning of IT devices and the manufacturing process. Some developments will enable increasing combinations of the biological and non-biological, in effect bringing biotechnology and IT closer together. This will include biological materials being used in computing technologies. Associated with such developments will be the controversial use of nano-technology, potentially involving incredibly small self-replicating machines. Aviation, space exploration, energy solutions – such as fuel cells, biomass, microwave transmission of solar energy from orbit – will all no doubt figure. Again political and economic dominance is likely to reside within the Western developed world and its ever more sophisticated production networks.

Technology and weaponry will also continue to change rapidly, perhaps even more rapidly than in the twentieth century. Money will continue to be poured into developing high-tech war fighting capacity, ironically particularly useful against poorer and weaker enemies! These 'enemies' in a post 9/11 context are all too often claimed to be in the Third World. The United States is particularly keen to develop the electronic battlefield alongside other technological developments designed to limit US casualties in any conflict. Overall, configurations of power in the global political economy are likely to harden around the control of production and knowledge structures, leaving the weaker players in the world ever more behind. The transnational networks of Western business and political elites look secure for the foreseeable future.

## Notes

1  The Uruguay Round is the name given to the last completed set of global trade negotiations. The name derives from the place where the round began. The latest round now underway is called the Doha Round. In order to join the WTO a state must accept the Uruguay Trade Round agreement in its entirety.
2  The term 'paradigm' refers essentially to a common view of things shared by those working within the technology activity. Technological paradigm is a specific reconceptualisation of the more common term paradigm, applied to shared perspectives within scientific communities.
3  In a sense this represents a 'super' technological paradigm.
4  Many technological innovations are often the result of the work of small firms or research institutions, including universities. However, development to large-scale deployment usually requires the funding resources of big firms, who may provide development contracts to the smaller firm or research institution. This has been very common in biotechnology.

## Bibliography

Adams, J. (1995), *Risk*, London: UCL Press.
Archibugi, D. and Michie, J. (eds) (1997), *Technology, Globalisation and Economic Performance*, Cambridge: Cambridge University Press.
Archibugi, D. and Michie, J. (1997), 'Foreword', in Archibugie and Michie (eds) (1997), pp. xv–xvi.
Balaam, D.N. and Veseth, M. (1996), *Introduction to International Political* Economy, Upper Saddle River, NJ: Prentice-Hall.
Cardwell, D. (1994), *The Fontana History of Technology*, London: Fontana Press.
Cox, R. (1987), *Production, Power and World Order*, New York: Columbia University Press.
Dicken, P. (1998) *Global Shift*, third edition, London: Paul Chapman.
Douglas, M. (1986), *Risk Acceptability According to the Social Sciences*, London: Routledge and Kegan Paul.
Foray, D. and Freeman, C. (eds) (1993), *Technology and the Wealth of Nations*, London and New York: Pinter.
Gill, S. and Law, D. (1988), *The Global Political Economy*, London: Harvester Wheatsheaf.
Gilpin, R. (1987), *The Political Economy of International Relations*, Princeton NJ: Princeton University Press.
Golich, V. (1989), *The Political Economy of International Air Safety: Design for Disaster?* New York: St. Martin's Press.
Held, D., McGrew, A., Goldblatt, D. and Perraton, J. (1999), *Global Transformations*,

Cambridge: Polity Press.

Levidow, L. (1994), 'Biotechnology Regulation as Symbolic Normalization', *Technology Policy & Strategic Management*, Vol. 6, No.3, pp. 173–288.

Nef, J. (1968), *War and Human Progress*, New York: W.W. Norton & Co.

Rosenberg, N. (1982), *Inside the Black Box*, Cambridge: Cambridge University Press.

Rosenberg, N. (1994), *Exploring the Black Box*: Cambridge: Cambridge University Press.

Scholte, J.A. (2000), *Globalization: A Critical Introduction*, London: Macmillan.

Strange, S. (1994), *States and Markets*, second edition, London: Pinter.

Talalay, M., Farrands, C. and Tooze, R. (eds) (1997), *Technology, Culture and Competitiveness*, London: Routledge.

## Note on bibliography

An excellent and accessible overview of the history of technology has been produced by Donald Cardwell (1994), while the international political economy of technology has been addressed in the edited volume by Talalay, Farrands and Tooze (1997). Archibugi and Michie provide a comprehensive collection from the perspectives of innovation economists. Finally, Peter Dicken (1998) locates technology against the changing patterns of global production.

# 15

# Trade

*Chris Farrands*

The world trade system is a crucial part of the contemporary global political system just as much as it is a key factor in economic welfare and well-being. It is about power, competition and cooperation as well as about the allocation of resources. It is also one of the main fields of political conflict where domestic politics and international politics intersect. The domestic arena, usually characterised by clear, authoritative government powers, a settled framework of justice, the lobbying activities of diverse special interests, and competition between specific parts of national bureaucracies, intersects and overlaps with the international arena, where there is less certain authority and an often more brutal kind of power struggle. But in global politics too there is a great deal of cooperation between both governments and non-governmental organisations in which law is of central importance. Cooperation and legal procedures are particularly important in trade politics, but one has also to remember that they make sense only within the distinctive context of global politics, in which major states, large firms and key institutions exercise different kinds of power and authority. If we ask how trade politics matter in more detail, we find that world trade is central to the working of at least three related but distinctive systems of power, each of which links global and sub-national politics.

Firstly production – created mainly by firms rather than governments – needs markets, raw materials, labour and components. When production exceeds domestic needs, exchange is necessary. As Adam Smith, the founder of liberal economics, suggested in *The Wealth of Nations* in 1776, a division of labour between different workers and different production centres creates conditions for trade. Smith and other classical liberal economists, notably David Ricardo, argued for the rationality of trade where one economy had a *comparative advantage* in the production of a particular good which might lead to specialisation and improved efficiency in the system as a whole, even if the gains from trade were not evenly distributed. There is no reason to think that this trade is equal or brings equal benefits, as Smith himself recognised, and over time the accumulation of wealth by the more powerful or more effective trading partners may create powerful political structures. Thus the world trade system has depended on the simultaneous growth of firms and empires and of the production of goods and services. The interests of firms and governments are not always the same but firms and governments work closely together to promote the interests they do share.

Secondly, governments see trade as important to national power and prosperity and it has always been a source of tax or customs revenue. Trade is also a key focus of foreign policy in richer and poorer states alike and it matters even more today in an era of 'globalisation'.

Thirdly, behind both firms and governments, and closely shaping their behaviour, are the broader power structures of the global economy or 'world system'. This is above all an advanced capitalist system, driven by competition for profits, markets and capital accumulation. This capitalist system has a dynamic capacity to produce both growth and impoverishment that underpins the behaviour and relationships of firms and governments and their outcomes. The world system is dominated by particular countries and power blocs which are themselves centres of trade, capital accumulation and financial power. An account of this system needs to pay particular attention to the ways in which that power is articulated.

World trade also matters directly to people: workers depend for employment on global trade; much of the apparatus of international financial services, which is now a much larger employer than manufacturing, is concerned with the finance and insurance of trade; and while we can justly label the system as exploitative, many very poor and rich people across the world depend for their livelihood on activities which depend in turn on world trade. The origins of food on the ordinary supermarket shelf in richer societies shows how much consumer choice is created and constrained by patterns of world trade. Many other kinds of employment and economic activity, including transport, smuggling, marketing, advertising, distribution, money laundering, and of course customs regulation depend on a flourishing of world trade.

In the past fifty years, world trade has grown more rapidly than overall economic product (world GNP). This implies a steadily increasing dependence on trade, and a simultaneous growth of world economic integration. Trade dependence as a percentage of global product is one way of measuring economic integration. The expectation of growth has encouraged investment which in turn encourages markets both for equities (shares) and for goods and services. It is not necessary for trade to decline for serious economic consequences to follow: it is sufficient for the rate of growth of world trade to slow down to produce a decline in expectations and so to induce a sharp setback in any trading market. Actual falls in the volume of world trade are rare, although one has occurred at the start of the 2000s.

The pattern of trade interdependence is very uneven, however,and general statistics do not necessarily reveal this.

While some groups of states may increase trade and growth together, as happened among the developed economies between 1947 and 1973, trade may increase without overall growth, and in some groups of countries it may actually decline, as it did in many of the poorest in the period from 1979 to 1996). Some countries may disengage from the world economy, a phenomenon mostly associated with failing poor economies dependent on raw material exports whose price falls. In the later 1990s, the US economy grew more rapidly internally than its external trade, partly because its trading partners, including the continental part of the EU, Japan, and much of Asia, excluding China, all had sluggish economies. US trade continued to increase in volume but because the internal economy grew so much more rapidly in those years, trade as a proportion of GNP actually fell. Thus the USA became less trade dependent between 1993 and 2001. One cannot think about the global politics of trade without recognising that the USA is significantly less trade dependent (because of the strength and diversity of its internal economy) than most other countries; but it is vulnerable to changes in trade patterns and increasingly dependent on stable trade relations to generate surpluses in other countries which can then be lent to the USA, which is the world's largest debtor and highly dependent on imports of capital. By contrast, in the late 1990s, when there was much justified concern about the future of African economies, the fastest growing economies in the world included some African ones, such as Mozambique, a heavily indebted recent victim of civil war but a newly dynamic and effective trader. To understand the global trade system, therefore, it is important to take account not only of the global aggregate figures but also of their range and diversity.

It is clear, therefore, that a purely economic approach is inadequate to explain world trade. Economics tells us important things about human behaviour in markets. To understand world trade we also need a political economy approach that recognises the importance of both economic behaviour and of the political and social framework within which economic activity takes place. If one took a broadly Marxist approach, this might well read that the economic system 'determines' behaviour; if it was a broadly liberal or neo-liberal approach, it might concentrate on economics and markets alone; or if it was a liberal institutional approach, it would emphasise the politics and behaviour of specific institutions. This is a political economy analysis that is neither orthodox Marxist nor orthodox liberal. First of all, it will make a descriptive account of the world trade system and its growth. Then it will look at the role of specific characteristics and sectors within the world trade system, including the 'knowledge based economy'. Finally it will return to the theoretical question of how best to understand the working of world trade.

## The world trade system

### *The scale of world trade*

World trade (exports and imports taken together) in goods and services accounts for around one half of total world production. Total world income is roughly $32 trillion, of which developing countries (with 85 per cent of world population) account for $6 trillion, the US for just under $10 trillion, and Japan just under $5 trillion (World Bank, 2003). The pattern of trade was, and has remained, most intensive between the most developed economies. Today, the most traded goods and services are industrial goods (manufactures, including components as well as finished products) and financial services. This is intra-industry trade, where comparative advantage works rather differently from the obvious cases considered by Smith and Ricardo. Moreover, from the mid-eighteenth century, through Marx in the mid-nineteenth century and Joan Robinson in the mid-twentieth century through most recently to writers such as Robert Cox, there have always been critics who argued that world trade was about the creation and protection of monopoly power rather than about an attempt to make economic relations as efficient as possible.

Table 15.1 *World trade, production and GDP 1990–2001 (all annual % change)*

|  | 1990–91 | 1998 | 1999 | 2000 | 2001 |
|---|---|---|---|---|---|
| World merchandise exports | 5.5 | 4.5 | 4.5 | 11.0 | −1.5 |
| World merchandise production | 2.0 | 2.0 | 3.0 | 4.5 | −1.0 |
| World GDP | 2.0 | 2.5 | 3.0 | 4.0 | 1.5 |

*Source: World Trade Organisation Annual Report 2003 at www.wto.org.*

Table 15.1 shows the growth in world trade from 1990–2001. As suggested earlier, world GDP has grown at a steady rate, but slower than trade and significantly slower than merchandise production (as greater emphasis has shifted towards trade in financial services and in things such as intellectual property or knowledge based services). There was a significant slow-down in 2001 associated with a fall off in demand and a crisis of confidence connected at least in part to the collapse of the 'dot com' boom, but also to the constraints of debt and of a continuing decline in domestic economic activity in countries such as Japan. This was seen by many world economic elites as a signal to accelerate change in the institutional management of world trade; this means that they used the decline as an argument to further liberalise the world trade system, although as writers such as Stiglitz point out, the problems may be at least in part due to liberalisation in the first place.

## The growth of world trade

Briefly, we can say that world trade and global politics have always shaped each other. Historians explain the growth of the state in its ability to wage war, raise taxes and control trade. Trade has been an important feature of human societies since human settlement began. Some of the earliest archaeological evidence indicates that precious items, such as metals, narcotics, jewellery or religious artefacts, travelled long distances as part of trading networks. The Roman Empire was probably more dependent on trade than on the army for its economic cohesion. The spice trade was one of the major engines of European commercial expansion and the search for a faster route to the spices of the Indies was the motive for the accidental European discovery of the Americas. Governments of the time sought to develop, manage and tax trade, often with contradictory policies. Thus concepts that we now see as very contemporary, including trade interdependence, the impact of technology change on trade, the importance of trade credit and the level of taxation (i.e. tariffs) on the volume of trade, are in fact very old issues.

Yet the contemporary world trade system has been produced to a major extent from a particular disaster and the failure at the time to deal with it. The world trade system of the nineteenth century evolved largely without state intervention and through a series of changes culminating in British domination of maritime transport, trade insurance, maritime law and international finance by the mid-nineteenth century. This system produced important benefits in terms of wealth and growth. Those benefits accrued to investors, to large firms and to governments in the British Empire. One could imagine that this system would have had to change as larger industrial economies, including Germany and the United States, came to out-produce the United Kingdom. As others came to hold larger market shares, they would have insisted on larger shares of decision making in the regulation of the system. But before this could happen, the system was smashed by effects of the First World War, which destroyed the established system of international trade.

After 1919, no one country had either the power or the knowledge to restore the system. The UK's ability to influence the system was reduced even before 1914, and although the USA replaced the UK as the world's greatest exporter of capital after the war, no economy had the capacity or the political will to take over responsibility for system regulation. By the 1929 Wall Street Crash, the world trade system had become extremely vulnerable to instability. The significance of the crash could have been limited mainly to the New York Stock Exchange, but financial mismanagement and an uncoordinated banking system allowed it to become an event of international importance. Even though there was a higher rate of growth in the late 1920s, the consequence of the crash and the attendant collapse of credit and banking institutions was that world trade fell by one half. This was a disaster on an unimaginable scale, which produced mass unemployment and encouraged the growth of a new economic nationalism and protectionism. It created the 'Great Depression', and played a major role in events leading to the outbreak of the Second World War in 1939. It is hardly surprising that the architects of the post–1945 international economic system, including John Maynard Keynes himself, meeting at Bretton Woods in 1944, aimed above all to prevent the experience of the 1930s being repeated. For many politicians and economic planners this remains, even in today, the most important goal of global economic policy.

Encouraged by the growth of demand and production after the war, the return of monetary stability and the sense that trade risks were less rather than greater, world trade grew at unparalleled rates between 1949 and 1972. While global income rose at roughly 3 per cent p.a. over this period (an unparalleled rate over so long a period), trade in manufactured goods rose at 4 to 5 per cent p.a. across the board, with much higher rates of growth in some sectors and states. Trade in non-manufactures, including oil and foodstuffs, grew even faster and trade dependence in the world system as a whole increased steadily. Some countries, such as Japan, the Netherlands and the UK, had higher levels of dependence on trade related income, but in all countries the level of dependence on trade for jobs, income and investment increased. Even in the USA, which (as noted above) has always had an economic structure characterised by high volumes of trade between the very diverse regions of the country and a lower dependence on international trade, dependence on external trade increased from around 11 per cent of national income in 1950 to 18 per cent in 1973.

After the slow-down of the world economy which followed the dollar crisis of 1971 and the oil crisis of 1973, there was a marked reduction in spending which led to the stagnation of the mid-1970s. The growth of world trade fell, but levels of world trade held up. There was no sudden collapse (although it was widely feared), as there had been in 1931–32, partly because the institutional and financial frameworks were more robust and partly because government policy was less harmful than it had been in the early 1930s. The global economy adapted to slower growth rates and to more uneven patterns of trade growth. It also adapted to the relative instability of the international monetary system after the stable era of the Bretton Woods system, during which the value of key national currencies was fixed against gold. This greater monetary instability, however, was undoubtedly a cause of slower trade flows than would otherwise have been the case.

World trade continued to outgrow production after the series of economic shocks of the 1970s, but at a slower rate. The main growth was in telecommunications, computing equipment, software, domestic electronic products and financial and other services. Japan became a leading exporter of certain key goods, but Japanese car production relocated (notably in the USA) to avoid protectionism, and lower value products (steel, shipbuilding, basic electronic components) went first to Japan and then to lower cost economies in Asia, such as South Korea, Taiwan and Malaysia.

Since the mid-1980s, there has been more diversity in world trade, more conflicts between the USA and the EU, and a reorganisation of the institutions of global trade. This process has been driven by three main forces. Firstly, the USA, and to a lesser extent other countries, including the UK, Australia and Canada, pressed for greater openness in the world trade system. Secondly, the major institutions took up the demand for liberalisation across a wider agenda. Thirdly, some developing economies feared that they would be disadvantaged unless they could get a more equitable trade system, which, they argued, would be a more liberal one. Against this background, the USA proposed to scrap the old system managed under the General Agreement of Tariffs and Trade (GATT) since 1947, and to replace GATT with a radically new body, the World Trade Organisation. After lengthy and hard negotiations, the new WTO was in some respects closer to the GATT than the USA had sought. There was, however, a new impetus to globalisation and liberalisation of world trade, a new agenda of trade talks, and a more 'automatic' or rule-based system of dispute settlement.

### The new agenda of the WTO

The WTO covers a wide range of economic activity with the intention of promoting the rule-bound management of trade and trade disputes, greater liberalisation and the extension of international law and legal procedures into areas which were previously subject to diplomacy and negotiation. Each of these is in turn characterised by a liberal belief that institutional stability can produce growth, and that free trade is compatible with democracy and may even help to promote democratisation. The contrast between the new and old agendas is summarised in Table 15.2:

Table 15.2 *The new WTO agenda*

|  | GATT | WTO |
|---|---|---|
| Content | Tariff reductions ontrol growth of non-tariff barriers. Special regimes for agriculture, textiles and clothing. | Enlarged agenda includes intellectual property, services, investment, with agriculture, textiles and clothing in core agreement. |
| Membership | 23 originally, growing to 89 (101 in final stages of last negotiating round). | Currently 136. |
| Dispute procedure | Discussion and arbitration; a quasi-legal system rather than a formally judicial one. | A negotiated pre-hearing stage followed by formal judicial decision making with as much 'automaticity' as possible. |

There is an important relationship between trade and investment. Trade activity has to be financed, and the capital needed for trade has to be earned or borrowed. In the years after both the First and the Second World Wars a shortage of dollars was the main constraint on international trade. In the years after the collapse of the Bretton Woods system in 1971, trade finance was more risky, and so more expensive, having a significant impact in slowing the growth of trade. Furthermore, where trade does not balance, the deficit has to be financed. In 2001, the USA had a trade deficit of $450bn on merchandise trade, an imbalance which was financed largely by debt and capital imports. If the rest of the world stopped exporting capital surpluses to the USA, trade would collapse and the world system would pass into as difficult a crisis as any experienced between 1918 and 1939.

### The governance and regulation of world trade

The global trade system is regulated through a complex system of institutions in which governments have formal control. However governments in all countries are subject to influence from companies and special interest groups such as trade associations, farmers or labour organisations. Together, they compete for influence. Lobbying power is absolutely critical to understanding the outcomes. There is no limit to the capacity of the international trade system to absorb and reflect the power of special interests. In corrupt national systems, this may be characterised by overtly corrupt behaviour, but even in better regulated systems, overt corruption is unnecessary, not because policy making is open and transparent, but because public relations companies and specialist lobbying firms intervene on behalf of key interests. Nowhere is this more evident than the US Congress, and the interests represented there, has completely dominated US trade policy making for decades, although the President retains a lot of influence over specific issues if he is prepared to work hard for it. In turn, US trade policy has shaped many bilateral deals while negotiations between the USA and Japan or the USA and EU have shaped the global regulation of trade in products as diverse as computer chips, textiles, steel and bananas. The explanation of global trade patterns often lies in the dynamics of specific bilateral relationships.

Negotiations in GATT were based on 'rounds' of tariff reductions where all the negotiating partners agreed to reduce tariffs by given amounts (usually measured in percentages). In the Tokyo and Uruguay Rounds, GATT also tried to control non-tariff barriers which many countries evolved to replace tariff cuts. Since it began in 1994, the WTO has embarked on the Doha Round, intent on further trade liberalisation. One important question hanging over the Doha Round is whether it can deliver real benefits to developing countries, or whether it will only benefit large corporations. It is difficult at the time of writing in mid-2004 to see how the developed economies can reach substantive agreement on key issues while there are sharp divisions between them and the European Union is deeply divided over the Iraq war.

The disputes procedure is central to the politics of the WTO system. Dissatisfaction with the disputes procedure in the GATT was most acutely felt in the USA, and it was US leadership which determined the disputes procedures in the WTO.

## Key features of the global trade system

The global trade system today is characterised by a complexity which owes much to factors other than government policy, and it is worth remembering that governments do not control economic activity even though they may regulate it. Factors such as the division of labour, the size and strategies of key firms, the rise and effectiveness of trade blocs and the weight of the knowledge based economy all matter in understanding the politics of global trade.

### The new international division of labour

By the mid-1970s, and following from the collapse of the Bretton Woods system, new patterns of trade emerged which came to dominate the academic and policy literature. Firms were exporting capacity rather than exporting manufactured goods. They invested in markets where capital is productive and labour cheap. They sent high value production to markets where skilled labour and design or research capacity was plentiful. They pulled investment out of less productive regions. New technologies for controlling a business (accounting techniques as well as information technology) helped firms do this. Firms producing large quantities of an item (car, computer, television, clothing or whatever) produced different components in different countries. German or French clothing firms designed articles in-house but produced them in eastern Europe as the USA did in Mexico or South East Asia. This seemed to mark a fundamental shift in the character of industrial capitalism, although many of the basic characteristics of the world economy remained the same. The new international division of labour marked a shift in production from the concentrated factory of the Ford model to a more diverse process (often called 'post-Fordist') organised across the world, and finding its investment, design, components and skilled labour, as well as its suppliers and customers, across a world market.

### Firm behaviour: large–smaller–larger?

On the whole, as world trade has grown it has been characterised by two features at the level of the firm. One is the growth of ever larger corporations with increasing market share. Thus a small number of firms dominate key markets for goods which are traded on world markets. While this kind of behaviour, often called 'monopolistic', but more strictly 'oligopoly', is not new, it accelerated during the late twentieth century as more and more products and services were traded internationally and some producers tried to protect their markets. The second feature of the system follows from this first point: as oligopoly emerges, firms move from profit seeking competitive strategies to forms of collaboration either with each other or with governments. This is often referred to as 'rent seeking' (where a rent is technically defined as excessive profit above that which firms would gain in a market of 'normal' competitiveness). Rent seeking behaviour takes many forms, but often includes lobbying government to demand that they rig markets or safety or compatibility regulations to suit their particular product (something which all large firms do worldwide). It also includes the formation of 'strategic alliances' where firms divide markets, support each other or agree not to compete in particular areas. Some of this behaviour is illegitimate, and possibility illegal, although enforcing anti-cartel legislation at the international level is extremely difficult. These kinds of activity are legitimate in the sense that they are generally not illegal, but they undermine competition and work against the proclaimed idea of a liberal economy. And the larger the firm, the better resourced it is and the more incentive it has for these kinds of activity. Developed country multinationals have both the skills and the incentives to pursue non-market solutions to market problems in ways which, whatever their technical legality or illegality, serve to substantially widen the gap between rich and poor societies (to the disadvantage of the latter). On the whole, regulators allow, or even encourage, inter-firm collaboration for research and development, but the grey area of where this becomes market rigging is an arena of continuing political and juridical conflict which is reflected in both domestic and international arguments.

### Trade blocs

International economic relations have been increasingly shaped by alliances between states. Trade blocs have emerged, some of which, such as the European Union and the North American Free Trade Area, have formal existence. Another group of countries, the 'Cairns Group', led by Australia, New Zealand, Canada and Argentina seeks freer trade in agriculture and food products. The East European applicant countries for membership of the EU formed a bloc in the 1990s. The developing world group, constituted as the Group of 77, although it has long possessed over one hundred members, provides a loose alliance for common action in trade talks. Within the Group of 77, some regional groupings have more capacity for common action, including the southern African members of the SADC (Southern Africa Development Consortium). There are other regional groups which are less effective in trade negotiations or captured by other issues, often connected to security. The impact of developing countries on world trade talks is weak, not only because of the undoubted power of the developed blocs; it is also weak because they find it difficult to build and sustain effective blocs. Some blocs combine countries who have different political and ideological interests but share some common economic and environmental concerns, such as the Gulf Cooperation Council and ASEAN (Association of South East Asian Nations). Most blocs owe something to the example of EU, and at least claim to be aiming at internal free trade.

While debates about trade issues are conducted through these multilateral institutions, it remains the case that the most important trade talks are bilateral, conducted around the fringe of multilateral talks. Blocs such as the EU will take part in multilateral negotiations on trade rounds in the GATT or WTO to the extent that the framework allows them to settle bilateral deals on the side. Powerful negotiators are able to insist that weak players agree to bilateral talks separate from the formal multilateral discussions and often outside public scrutiny. This is a common condition of the acceptance of broader principles in multilateral talks. This can have results which are simply perverse. Governments may accept the principle of freer trade in multilateral talks while imposing conditions which give more power and oligopoly control to their multinational companies to dictate the terms of trade in bilateral talks, agreement on which may determine whether the main treaty is possible. Thus, developed countries impose liberalisation on developing economies while keeping their own high levels of protection in agriculture or software or other special interests.

*The knowledge based economy*

The emergence of knowledge based economies has had at least three main effects on the world trade system. The first and most obvious is the rise to prominence of intellectual property issues (Trade Related Intellectual Property issues, or TRIPS). This includes issues relating to pharmaceutical products and patents for AIDS or HIV, software piracy and control of copyright in print, films and music. Thus US copyright lawyers intervened on behalf of the music industry in the matter of internet based software which facilitated copying and exchange of music over the net through 'Napster'. In recognising the value of knowledge, patent disputes have become key elements in trade conflict. The growing dispute between the USA and EU over the reluctance of Europeans to accept genetically modified food products is a comparable example. On the EU side, there are issues of consumer choice and protection (whether or not the new bioproducts are scientifically seen as 'safe'). On the US side, there is an argument about the rationality of scientific knowledge which to date has not shown the GM crops are unsafe (although many Europeans will say they have not demonstrated that they are certainly safe), and there is a question of the rights of multinationals to deal directly with customers and to ask customers what they want. European decision makers (especially the EU Parliament) have insisted on the right of consumers to have clear labelling of GM foods. American negotiators have claimed this is in effect a restraint on trade since it encourages an unwarranted discrimination between GM and non-GM products. This argument will continue because it is symptomatic of a difference in cultural attitudes towards firms and towards science, and because it has become a focus for anti-US feeling in European countries that has little to do with the nature of scientific evidence.

Secondly, the importance of knowledge also affects the movement of labour, and especially skilled labour, around the world. There has been a large increase in migration since the 1970s, and although some emigrants may be poorly skilled, many have initiative, entrepreneurship and significant skills. Most governments have tried to control immigration, but they have at the same time sought to attract skilled labour and to train foreign workers in the hope that they would stay and contribute to the economy. This has created a 'brain drain', a shortage of key workers in developing countries, but it has also created a competitive market between key multinational companies for researchers and specialists, including specialist high grade managers, which affects the development of global service industries even more than manufacturing.

Thirdly, the growth of the knowledge economy has shaped the growth of international law. New forms of regulation to change patterns of knowledge management have become important in the conflict over what rules apply and how they apply. This is important in itself but, once again, developing countries are at a disadvantage in getting help in these highly technical debates. If, as is often said, there are more intellectual property lawyers in Manhattan than in the rest of the world together, this has some effects. Even though some countries, such as India, may be able to afford to hire some of these lawyers to work against the others, there are many occasions when the interests of developing countries are excluded because of a shortage of affordable expertise in face of rich states and corporations.

### Conclusion: the dynamism of the global trade system

Negotiations in world trade are long drawn out, very technical talks. Mostly, these involve blocs of countries, but individual governments have a central role, and lobbying groups and large firms are never very far from the action. Theories which emphasise the politics of coalition formation, the instability of alliances and the problems of operating in a very unequal negotiating framework seem to offer more convincing ways of explaining this kind of politics than theories which assume that the process is rational and controlled by a guiding rationality.

To understand the global trade system in actual practice, one needs to look at the specific conditions of particular industries or sectors. Sectoral studies often explain how patterns of governance or patterns of conflict arise differently in the world system. There is a global system of capitalism, and it conditions everything that happens in world trade. But it cannot be said to 'cause' world trade, not least because if the 'logic of capitalism' worked as effectively or as rationally as either its advocates or its critics appear to think, the system would probably perform more effectively than it does.

The world trade system is a system of political power. It reflects power, but it also creates power. To describe it simply in terms of a market or series of markets is wholly inadequate. But one misses the point if one does not recognise that what is going on is production, exchange, employment and investment, all of which underpin a process of accumulation by large interests, which may relate closely to states, but which are not states. The politics of the world trade system evolve around the conflicts that have emerged on the scope and character of international regulation and the parallel conflicts between groups or blocs of states. It is not helpful to regret these conflicts: they arise, and the WTO and its related systems should be seen as ways of managing conflicts in particular ways rather than as a structure of failed consensus. The rule making process inevitably favours the larger powers within the system, but it does not leave the smaller or poorer actors without resources. The failure of (some) developing countries – and some smaller developed ones – to use the system or to form coalitions in which they can find greater scope for effective political action has been one of the features of the system since 1994, but this does not need to be the case, and other developing countries (India in particular) and smaller developed countries (most notably Australia) have been able to exploit the margins for action they have in the system more effectively. Nonetheless, it remains the case not only that the EU and the USA dominate much of the rule making, but also that their companies, supported by vociferous and aggressively active trade associations, are able to use the system more effectively than others, and that many of the legal specialists involved come from small areas of Manhattan or the City of London even if they are paid to represent developed country interests.

## Bibliography

Arup, C. (2000), *The New World Trade Organization Agreements: Globalizing Law through Services and Intellectual Property*, Cambridge: Cambridge University Press.
Brinham, R. (1999), *US Trade Policy: History, Theory and the WTO*, London: M.E. Sharpe.
Cutler, A.C., Haufler, V. and Porter, T. (eds), *Private Authority and Public Affairs*, Albany, NY: State University of New York Press, 1999.
Farrands, C. (1996), 'The Globalization of Knowledge and the Politics of Global Intellectual Property: Power, Governance and Technology', in E. Kofman and G. Youngs (eds), *Globalization: Theory and Practice*, London: Pinter, pp. 175–90.
Farrands, C. (2002), 'Being Critical About "being critical" in Global Political Economy',

in J. Abbott and O. Worth (eds), *Critical Perspectives on International Political Economy*, Basingstoke: Palgrave, pp. 14–33.

Farrands C. (2003), 'Power, Knowledge and Governance: Globalizing Intellectual Property Management, Reproducing Inequalities', in E. Kofman and G. Youngs (eds), *Globalization: Theory and Practice*, pp. 249–61.

Grimwade, N. (2001), *International Trade: New Patterns of Trade, Production and Investment*, London: Routledge.

Hoekma, B. and Kostecki, M. (2001), *The Political Economy of the World Trade System: from GATT to WTO*, second edition, Oxford: Oxford University Press.

Jawara, F. and Kwa, A. (2003), *Behind the Scenes at the WTO: The Real World of International Trade Negotiations*, London: Zed Books.

Krueger, A.O. (ed.) (2000), *The WTO as an International Organization*, Chicago, IL: University of Chicago Press.

Lal Das, B. (2003), *WTO: The Doha Agenda – the New Negotiations in World Trade*, London: Zed Books.

May, C. (2000), *A Global Political Economy of Intellectual Property Rights: The New Enclosures?*, London: Routledge.

Michalopoulos, M. (2000), *Developing Countries in the WTO*, Basingstoke: Palgrave.

Odell, J.S. and Willett, T.D. (eds) (1993), *International Trade Policies: Gains From Exchange between Economics and Political Science*, Ann Arbor, MI: Michigan University Press.

Petersmann, E.-U. and Pollack, M. (eds) (2003), *Transatlantic Trade Disputes: The EU, the US and the WTO*, Oxford: Oxford University Press.

Ricardo, David (1817), *Principles of Political Economy and Taxation*, London.

Robles, A.C. (1994), *French Theories of Regulations and Conceptions of the International Division of Labour*, Basingstoke: Macmillan.

Ruigbruck, W. and Van Tulder, R. (1995), *The Logic of International Restructuring*, London: Routledge.

Schott, J.J. (ed.) (2000), *The WTO After Seattle*, Washington DC: Institute for International Economics.

Sinclair, S. and Grieshaber-Otto, J. (2002), *Facing the Facts: A Guide to the GATS Debate*, Toronto: Canadian Centre for Policy Studies.

Smith, A. [1776] (1987), *The Wealth of Nations*, Harmondsworth: Penguin.

Stewart, T.P. (2002), *After Doha: The Changing Attitudes and Ideas of the New WTO Round*, New York: Transnational Publishers.

Stiglitz, J. (2002), *Globalization and its Discontents*, New York: W.W. Norton.

Stubbs, R. and Underhill, G. (eds) (2000), *Political Economy and the Changing Global Order*, second edition, Oxford: Oxford University Press.

World Bank (2003), *World Bank Development Statistics*, at www.devdata.worldbankorg.

World Trade Organization (2002), *The WTO Dispute Settlement Procedures: A Collection of the Relevant Legal Texts*, Cambridge: Cambridge University Press.

World Trade Organization (2003), World Trade Organisation documentation including *Annual Report 2003* and documentation on the Doha Round at www.wto.org.

## Note on bibliography

Readers who have a knowledge of economics but little of political economy will find Stubbs and Underhill (2000) the most useful of a very wide range of political economy texts, while those with a knowledge of international relations but little idea of international economics will find Nigel Grimwade (2001) the most useful and at the same time sophisticated treatment of a much covered field.

# Index

Note: page numbers in **bold** refer to main entries.